CW00348777

# Power in Concert

# Power in Concert

*The Nineteenth-Century Origins
of Global Governance*

JENNIFER MITZEN

THE UNIVERSITY OF CHICAGO PRESS    CHICAGO AND LONDON

JENNIFER MITZEN is assistant professor of political science at Ohio State University.

The University of Chicago Press, Chicago 60637
The University of Chicago Press, Ltd., London
© 2013 by The University of Chicago
All rights reserved. Published 2013.
Printed in the United States of America
22 21 20 19 18 17 16 15 14 13     1 2 3 4 5

ISBN-13: 978-0-226-06008-8 (cloth)
ISBN-13: 978-0-226-06011-8 (paper)
ISBN-13: 978-0-226-06025-5 (e-book)
DOI: 10.7208/chicago/9780226060255.001.0001

Library of Congress Cataloging-in-Publication Data
Mitzen, Jennifer, author.
    Power in concert : the nineteenth-century origins of global governance / Jennifer
Mitzen.
        pages : cm
    Includes bibliographical references and index.
    ISBN 978-0-226-06008-8 (cloth : alkaline paper) — ISBN 978-0-226-06011-8 (paperback :
alkaline paper) — ISBN 978-0-226-06025-5 (e-book) 1. International cooperation—
History—19th century. 2. International relations—History—19th century. 3. World
politics—19th century. 4. Public relations and politics—History—19th century. 5. Concert
of Europe. I. Title.
JZ1318.M59 2013
327.1'709034—dc23
                                                                    2013000529

♾ This paper meets the requirements of ANSI/NISO Z39.48-1992 (Permanence of Paper).

# Contents

# Acknowledgments

I have been with this project for a number of years and over that time I have incurred many debts, intellectual and otherwise. I am profoundly grateful for all of the contributions to it of my colleagues and friends.

The foundations for the argument were laid during my years at the University of Chicago, and I owe an enormous debt of gratitude to James Fearon, Patchen Markell, and Duncan Snidal for their support of and engagement with the ideas in that time.

I feel fortunate to have been at Ohio State for the bulk of the writing of this book. Ted Hopf and Randy Schweller each read the entire manuscript and gave detailed comments that improved the book tremendously. Alex Thompson, first in graduate school and now as a colleague at OSU, has provided excellent, helpful feedback on many iterations of the argument. A reading group with Mike Neblo, Eric MacGilvray, and Sonja Amadae was a challenging and supportive environment for testing out theoretical ideas. As research assistants, Emilie Becault, Zoltan Buzas, Tim Luecke, Meri Ellen Lynott, John Oates, and Srdjan Vucetic each brought sharp critical eyes and expert research skills to several of the chapters, for which I am grateful. I also am fortunate to have had the opportunity to engage with Abe Roth, whose own philosophical work on collective intentionality has been inspiring.

Many generous interlocutors throughout the years have commented on conference papers, read draft chapters, served as a discussant for these ideas, and/or engaged with me in conversations about the issues. Some of these debts go back several years, and I hope my records are complete since I benefited greatly from all of their feedback. Many thanks to Michael Barnett, Burcu Bayram, Janice Bially Mattern, Corneliu Bjola, Bear Braumoeller, Jason Castillo, Neta Crawford, Alex Downes, George

Gavrilis, Margaret Gilbert, Todd Hall, Rick Herrmann, Marcus Holmes, Anne Holthoefer, Patrick Jackson, Hans Martin Jaeger, Marcus Korn-probst, Vlad Kravstsov, Ron Krebs, Charles Lipson, Tim Luecke, Chris McIntosh, Richard Mansbach, John Mueller, Michelle Murray, Dan Nexon, Fernando Nunez, John Oates, Rodger Payne, MJ Peterson, Vincent Pouliot, Matthew Rendall, Jacob Schiff, Hans Peter Schmitz, John Schuessler, Duncan Snidal, Jack Snyder, Jens Steffek, Cliff van der Linden, Daniel Verdier, Lisa Wedeen, Bob Wolfe, and Rafi Youatt. Presentations at the University of Chicago, Syracuse University, George Washington University, and the University of Toronto also helped me sharpen the ideas.

I am especially grateful to Anne Holthoefer and Burcu Bayram, who each gave the penultimate draft of the manuscript an extremely careful reading on short notice and saved me from several errors.

As a first-time author I feel lucky to have worked with David Pervin at the University of Chicago Press. The four anonymous reviewers he selected each provided extensive guidance on the first draft of the manuscript. It is a much better book because of their critiques and David's help in navigating their feedback. I also want to thank Shenyun Wu and the production team, and especially Dawn Hall for copyediting and Bonny McLaughlin for compiling the index.

I owe an incalculable debt, professional and personal, to Alex Wendt. Over the years Alex has endured countless conversations about the ideas of the book as they evolved through time and has edited and commented on many drafts of many chapters. Equally important, his own intellectual fearlessness is a model and continuing inspiration. This book would eventually have gotten finished without Alex's input, but the book and my life would not have been the same. He deserves an award. But for now what I can give is my deepest thanks and a promise that I will do my best to return his boundless generosity.

Emma and Otto, each born during the writing of this book, have been a source of great joy and happy diversion. I never managed to pull off a "work-life balance" and am convinced that it only exists in some mythic universe. Each has its own demands and timetables; each pulls whiplash-like when a need must be met. Life always comes first. But in the times when work forced life temporarily to the wings, the help of family and friends made all the difference. I am particularly grateful to Hannah Pechan, Bailey Schucker, Kathryn Connors, and Kendra Wiechart, accomplished women in their own right, who have loved the kids and brought cheerfulness and order to our home. On a personal level, for support in managing the work-life trade-off I relied all too often on Janice Bially Mattern, George Gavrilis, and Leanna Murphey Haye. Finally, I thank and Steve and Kathi Gaffney and also Jill Grabowski and Rich Murphy, who at key moments when solitude was necessary provided a writing retreat.

It is with tremendous pleasure that I dedicate this book to my parents, Phyllis and Michael Mitzen, who taught me to think, to care, and to persevere in everything important.

# CHAPTER ONE

# Public Power and Purpose in Global Governance

In antitrust law there is a distinction between rational adaptation and concerted action.[1] It is reasonable to expect that firms in market economies will take one another into account and adjust their behavior in anticipation of what others may do. In doing so, each firm is acting alone, for its own self-interested purposes. Concerted action is different. When firms concert they are doing something together, not alone but with a common purpose. From a legal standpoint their concerting is considered problematic. Rather than allowing the invisible hand of the market to operate, firms are manipulating it for private ends. Since an economy guided by the invisible hand is considered desirable, concerting undermines society's interest. If firms are found to be concerting they can be held responsible. In short, there are meaningful differences, both explanatory and normative, between these two ways of acting, rationally adapting and concerting.

Antitrust law is about firms in a market and this book is about states in anarchy, but the distinction is instructive. In this book I argue that states govern world politics by concerting their power. In doing so, they make the hand steering the international social order more visible. But because states are public powers with the responsibility to provide for society's basic needs, the hand they bring into view by concerting is one that for the most part we should be happy to see. It could be called the hand of international public power.

I make the argument by developing a conceptual framework for understanding concerting as a particular type of joint action and then

1. Del Mar 2011.

applying that framework to states in anarchy. The framework relies on the concept of collective intentionality.[2] Collective intentions to do something together are constituted by joint commitments, which give rise to obligations that can shape behavior when they are fully out in the open. I propose that among states, commitments can shape behavior when they are accompanied by forums. Forums enable states in anarchy to do what concerting firms do in a market: they can manipulate the balance of power toward shared ends. International relations (IR) scholarship already takes note of states making commitments and talking together in forums, but such a thin layer of institutionalization generally is not seen as capable of affecting outcomes separate from state interests and relative power. This book discerns those effects theoretically and links them to a system-level argument about how states inject social purpose to the international political order. I illustrate the framework in the "hard case" of security politics.

This argument intervenes in a debate on global governance. Scholars coined the term *global governance* in the early 1990s to point to a phenomenon in world politics that seemed distinct from international cooperation as IR had been studying it. At any level, to govern is to steer or self-consciously aim a society toward the pursuit of some specified ends or social purpose. In the early post–Cold War period, many saw new political potential of this kind on a global scale. In James Rosenau's seminal formulation, global governance was defined as "order plus intentionality."[3] But while the language of global governance caught on, Rosenau's analytic insight about intentionality was largely overlooked. Instead, the discourse of global governance linked up with a discourse on globalization, especially economic globalization, which had emerged in the 1980s with the rise of neoliberalism. Neoliberalism is a market-centered liberalism in which concepts central to classical liberal thought, such as freedom and liberty, are understood narrowly and in economic terms, as market free-

---

2. The literature on collective intentionality is extensive. Contributions include Bratman 1999; Gilbert 1992; Searle 1995; Schmid 2008; Tollefson 2002; Tuomela 2005; and Velleman 1997. This literature distinguishes between collective intentionality in general and joint action as a particular form. For ease of exposition I shall use the terms interchangeably. That is, when I use the term *collective intention* throughout the book I am referring to this subset and not to all forms of collective intentionality.

3. Rosenau 1992. Rosenau located the relevant intentionality "at all levels of human activity—from the family to the international organization—in which the pursuit of goals through the exercise of control has transnational repercussions." But the intentionality that most captured his attention was that of individuals, not states. See Rosenau 1995, 13.

dom and market liberty.[4] As a result of this linkage, what has come to be known as global governance in IR has been, largely, neoliberal global governance, that is, the institutional preconditions for the invisible hand of the market to operate beyond the state.

The neoliberal backdrop has had two effects on the way global governance is studied in IR. First, it has crowded out the intentional or agentic aspect of governing. If governing is mostly about setting the rules to facilitate the smooth operation of the globalizing market, it is easy to see how once that is accomplished, academics and practitioners would come to treat global governance as a set of ongoing, functional responses to imperatives of economic globalization, as if problems present themselves to a system that anonymously generates solution mechanisms.[5] As Deborah Avant, Martha Finnemore, and Susan Sell put it in their critique, we tend to see "global governance [as] something that happens; no one, apparently, actually does it."[6]

Second, the wariness of public power that characterizes neoliberalism carries over, and it is difficult to advance a positive role for the state and state-like power in global governance.[7] In neoliberalism, political freedom is the freedom to be left alone; we are the best guarantors of our own freedom. This translates to an implicit assumption in much global governance scholarship that the power to manage economic globalization and to realize new values does not reside with states. Indeed, states often are treated as sources of disorder and violence, not order and integration. To the extent there is positive agency in global governance, it is not the agency of the state's public power but that of private, particularistic interests.[8]

Pushing back against the dominance of neoliberal thinking is a key aim of this book. But neoliberalism is not the only reason why intentionality and especially the state's intentionality have been relatively neglected in global governance scholarship. The neglect also has to do with the way we think about group agency[9] and the difficulty of applying that model

4. See MacGilvray 2011. Also Baldwin 1993, 4.

5. Scholte 2000; Bjola and Kornprobst 2011.

6. Avant, Finnemore, and Sell 2010a, 1.

7. Büthe 2004 makes a similar argument.

8. Or state agency is disaggregated and treated in functionally specific transnational or intergovernmental networks, as in Slaughter 2004.

9. Agency is a contested and multidimensional concept that I will not try to address in its entirety. But any concept of agency includes intentionality, the ability to engage in goal-directed action. For a discussion of the dimensions of agency see, e.g., Ortner 2006, chapter six.

in anarchy. Quite naturally, the starting point for thinking about agency is human or anthropomorphic agency. Because humans speak and act with one locus of final authority, we tend to think of all things that have agency as being structured to act with a single locus of final authority. Groups with agency are those that are organized hierarchically or centralized to act in a unitary fashion. This move of analogizing all agents to humans is not always explicitly justified in the work that relies on it, and it certainly has critics.[10] But the assumption nonetheless dominates the way we think about agency in world politics, with the paradigmatic example being state agency. Intentional action without a unitary agent engaging in it is difficult to picture.

An anthropomorphic model of group agency is not itself problematic. Indeed, like many IR scholars, in this book I treat the state as a unitary actor. But the anthropomorphic model becomes problematic in thinking about global governance because the context for group agency in world politics is fundamentally decentralized. If purposive action requires centralization and unitary actorhood, the possibilities for agency beyond the state are limited. States either can merge their sovereignty or they can create new bodies with supranational authority. Only if group agency is possible without centralization and through concerting does it become possible to envision collective, purposive action, and its corollary of collective responsibility, among states in anarchy.

To illustrate this intentionalist, public power approach to global governance, I reach back to its origins and tell the story of the first international public power, the Concert of Europe, which came about after the defeat of Napoleon in 1815 when the five most powerful European states committed to maintain continental stability together. Their idea was that when European stability was affected, *European* power must respond. Before 1815, international order had been produced essentially behind the backs of states by the invisible hand of the balance of power. What marks the post-Napoleonic period as the first case of states concerting their power for public interests is the combination of their commitment to keep the peace together and their institutional innovation of states meeting in forums to manage crises. Because of these, the great powers were able to keep Europe at peace until the Crimean War in 1854. In the international context, among states that had maintained a long, hot rivalry, this was quite an accomplishment.

To say that nineteenth-century European great powers constituted

10. Jackson 2004.

a new and greater power by acting together can seem at once obvious and hardly worth celebrating. After all, these were "great powers," which means they already dominated the continent. But I want to separate out their individual or even their aggregate capacity to dominate from the capacity to act in concert. To be sure, action in concert can be used for domination, but that does not mean it is the same thing.[11] In its time, from a European perspective at least, great powers working together to keep the peace was a normative improvement over how they had acted in the centuries before.

## International Public Power

This book argues that by acting in concert states can create international public power, a locus of authoritative decision on matters in their common, public interest. To lay the theoretical groundwork for the framework I will develop in chapter two, it is helpful to begin by looking more closely at two central concepts: collective intentionality and public.

### Collective Intentionality

Because international governing is something states do *together,* it is a case of collective intentionality. The idea behind collective intentionality is that some group actions are neither reducible to the intentions of individual members nor necessarily collected into a unitary corporate agent. Actions are not reducible in that, in John Searle's words, "the crucial element in collective intentionality is a sense of doing . . . something together, and the individual intentionality that each person has is derived *from* the collective intentionality that they share."[12] At the same time, this top-down agency does not subsume the agency of individual participants. It is a larger, "macro" purposiveness that does not necessarily coalesce into unitary actorhood.

---

11. The notion of power as action in concert and therefore as irreducibly collective often is associated with the political thought of Hannah Arendt. Arendt did not systematically develop her thoughts about world politics, but some recent scholarship extends her thought to the international realm. E.g., Lang and Williams 2005; Owens 2007. J. Williams (2005, 206–7) discusses why Arendt did not think politics, understood as action in concert, was possible among states.

12. Searle 1995, 24–25. Italics in original.

This purposiveness is found not only when firms concert in a market, it also is common in everyday life and something we all know how to do. As a more prosaic example of team play,[13] consider the purposiveness of a basketball team. Here the players share the goal of winning the game, but accomplishing that goal requires many individual choices, often made in the spur of the moment. Each choice—passing the ball, going for a three point shot, substituting one player for another—is certainly comprehensible in individualistic terms as a discrete choice by a single person aiming for a particular goal. But the choices are perhaps better understood in the context of the game and of the overall collective goal of winning the game, which is something they all desire and intend but none can accomplish alone. Scholars of collective intentionality argue that the fact that there is a single commitment to act creates a single locus of agency. But because more than one agent is necessary to produce the actions that achieve the goal, they must act together, hand in hand so to speak.

Forming a collective intention creates what Margaret Gilbert calls a "plural subject."[14] The term *subject* conveys that a collective intention creates an agency separate from the agency of the actors participating in it; the term *plural* suggests that the intentionality of those actors is not thereby erased or subsumed. A useful way to think about plural subjecthood is as an emergent phenomenon, one that arises from interaction among a set of actors but is not reducible to them.[15] Plural subjecthood implies a normative relationship among the participants, which Gilbert calls a "relationship of owing."[16] Because the agency of each (for a particular goal) depends on the others following through, they owe one another explanations if they deviate from actions implied by their commitment. To be part of a plural subject is to take a first person plural, or "we," perspective for the purpose of pursuing some specific goal or project. "We" is an identity term, and there is a sense in which plural subjects share a collective identity. However, the "we"ness of collective intentions is circumscribed by the explicit intention toward which action is directed, and as such it can be relatively thin and potentially quite transient.

13. Sugden 1993. Among scholars of collective intentionality, team reasoning is considered a thin form, but for the purpose of illustrating the concept, the philosophical distinctions in the literature can be bracketed.

14. Gilbert 1992; 2003a.

15. On the concept of social emergence, see Sawyer 2005. On collective intentions as emergent phenomena, see Jansen 2005; Gibbs 2001.

16. Gilbert 2003a.

In short, from a collective intentionality standpoint, when actors jointly commit to do something together, they are not merely signaling cooperative intentions and the result is not merely cooperation as IR scholarship has understood it. They also are creating a new agency in which authority and responsibility over action is shared. From here, if, for example, a basketball player chooses to take a risky shot rather than pass to an open teammate in an effort to boost his individual statistics, his teammates have the standing to criticize him for undermining their agency, and he owes them an explanation. Intentions can be shared purely behaviorally or in silence. But in many cases collective intentions are produced and maintained by talking together. The crucial role of talking together generally is recognized in antitrust law as noted above, where face-to-face meetings are considered evidence of concerting.[17] Needless to say, talking together is crucial for governing together.

## Public Power

Collective intentions to do something together come in many forms. Part of what makes the case of states acting together distinctive is that states have a special status as public powers. But while that term is widely used, the meaning of *public* that stands behind it is not well theorized. For example, public can simply mean intersubjective or visible.[18] But it often is used more narrowly, as a synonym for political. Even where public means political however, usage of the term varies widely, from the thin economistic notion in public choice theory and the theory of public goods[19] to the thicker more republican-inflected notion that informs conceptualizations of the public sphere.[20] This book relies especially on two political meanings.

First, the term *public* is used to convey a type of social solidarity. When we refer to the public we tend to be talking about the people who reside in a given state but who are not in government. The public is not a random collection of people, but a group with a particular bond. Members of a public are interdependent and see themselves as sharing some common interests and as subject to the same set of rules and institutions. Generally

17. Del Mar 2011, 111–12.

18. Jeff Weintraub points out that for many theorists the political is just one among many public activities, and public means something more along the lines of visible, social, or intersubjective. Weintraub 1997, 6–7, 16ff.

19. Mueller 2003.

20. Habermas 1996; Arendt 1956.

speaking, members of a public prefer coordination to going it alone, and they expect their coordination to continue into the foreseeable future. In other words, publics rest on and require society.[21]

To clarify the solidarity a public relationship implies, it is useful to situate it relative to two other ways of understanding social solidarity that are more common in IR discourse: society and community. Hedley Bull[22] developed the concept of an international society, contrasting it to a thinner relationship where there is no social solidarity, that is, a system, and to a thicker relationship of social solidarity, a community. For Bull, a system exists "where [units] are in regular contact with one another, and where in addition there are interactions between them sufficient to make the behavior of each a necessary element in the calculations of the other."[23] In contrast, a society exists when members are "conscious of certain common interests and common values" and "conceive themselves to be bound by a common set of rules in their relations with one another, and share in the working of common institutions."[24] A key difference between society and system is that the glue of a society is not only its institutions but also an underlying norm of toleration or pluralism. At the other end of the solidarity spectrum is the thick bond that characterizes a community.[25] Community generally refers to a group whose members are tied together by an internalized, shared moral code or vision of the "good life." Whereas society is premised on pluralism, community is premised on homogeneity.[26] Some set of values and ideas beyond politics, such as god's will or universal human rights, limits what constitutes the realm of the political and sets the standards for normative judgment.[27]

---

21. This tends to be taken for granted in domestic public sphere literature, which treats the Westphalian state as an implicit baseline. See Fraser 2007.

22. Bull is helpful for distinguishing among three types of social solidarity—society, community, and public. However, my broad use of "solidarity" differs from the narrower English School usage. There, solidarism identifies one pole—cosmopolitanism or what Bull calls Kantian morality—in a debate over the potential for moral action in world politics. Solidarism is juxtaposed to the more state-centered approach to moral action, pluralism, or what Bull calls Grotian morality. See Bull 1966; Reus-Smit (2002, 496–97, 502–5) discusses this debate.

23. Bull 1977, 10.

24. Bull 1977, 13.

25. Reus-Smit 2002, 497 contrasts Wheeler's 2000 solidarism to Jackson's 2000 pluralism.

26. Bull 1966. Also see Buzan 2004; Wheeler 1992.

27. Waters 2009; Zerilli 2012.

The solidarity of a public is not one that Bull developed at the inter-state level, and it differs from that of both society and community. Publics rest on society but they are not synonymous with it. Society refers to a relationship created through sharing a social order. Members may or may not consciously desire their society's particular institutions, but they participate in them. Societies are maintained relatively habitually. Public, in contrast, refers to a more self-conscious relationship. Members of a public do not merely participate in and reproduce but also seek to steer or guide their common life. In other words, the move from society to public adds an action oriented and political sensibility. The bond among members of a public is the capacity to see themselves as a political "we" for the purpose of solving shared problems. That is, they can take a first person plural perspective and judge whether particular policies are in the general interest.[28] By itself being a public together is not a thick form of solidarity. It refers to only one aspect of the social ties that bind people to a society, and to a relationship that is not found in every society.

Like the purpose of societies, the purpose of publics is to facilitate common life. Unlike the purpose of communities, the purpose is not to discipline members at the level of extrapolitical moral codes. As such, and importantly, members of a public need not share a vision of the good life. In Jürgen Habermas's words, publics are comprised of strangers, who "concede one another the right to remain strangers."[29] Strangers maintain the right to disagree about values and need not convert to one another's value systems in order to live together. Bernard Yack speaks similarly of the political relationship when he calls it a "friendship of mutual advantage" where "members ... have little reason to expect or display especially deep and genuine concern for each other's well-being."[30] And Craig Calhoun notes that "what makes a public is not agreement among interlocutors but a discussion in which each party gives reasons for and attempts to understand views that may be quite divergent."[31]

The solidarity of a public seems a particularly apt starting point for thinking about the kind of bond necessary for states to govern together. It accommodates the fact that politics is a realm of conflict rather than

28. Habermas 1996, 91–92, 498.
29. Habermas 1996, 308.
30. Yack 2006, 430.
31. Calhoun 1998, 23.

harmony, where working together can be difficult. Yet it captures the notion that solving problems together creates a form of solidarity.[32] Some publics may very well be constituted by communities. But being able to solve problems together does not presuppose prior community (nor does political problem solving necessarily create community).

The second way the term *public* is used in this book is to point to a structure of political accountability, as in *public sphere* and *public reason*, which links publics to action capacity or *public power*. These three are related to one another in the following way. A public sphere is a communication structure containing and enabling critical conversations on the use of power. The idea is that members of a society form opinions about the use of power by talking with one another, and they demand that power be used in their general interest. These activities forge the solidarity of the public. Public discussion about common problems gives rise to public reason, which is a set of publicly acceptable considerations and rationales for action, acknowledged to apply to all members of the group. The conceptual antonym of public reason is idiosyncratic or private reason, rationales that apply only to some restricted audience and not the group as a whole.[33] A public reason is not merely one among several types of reasons but is sufficient reason to justify action. Public reasons have presumptive legitimacy over private or idiosyncratic ones in governing. Ideally, public reason shapes and constrains the use of state power.

Public spheres are desirable from a democratic standpoint because conceptually their existence implies that the authority of the people as a whole can stand behind the use and control of power. Where there is a functioning public sphere, society can be less wary or suspicious of public power—such power even has potentially a positive role as the vehicle for its public's self-determination. To reach the normative potential of public spheres, however, it is not enough for those affected by structures of power to be able to talk together about it. It must also be the case that their public reason can actually make a difference by guiding authoritative decisions. Public reason must correspond to some public power, that is, a locus of responsibility and capacity to act on the public's interests. As Nancy Fraser has emphasized, a systematic link to public power makes it possible for public opinion to be efficacious as a political force.[34] Domesti-

---

32. Calhoun 1998. This idea of public also can be linked to political realism at the domestic level. Galston 2010, 391.

33. Bohman 1997, 184.

34. Fraser 1992; 2007.

cally this public power is the state, and its capacity to act on public interests is a grounding assumption.

Turning to international politics, however, the need for a systematic link between public reason and public power poses an obvious difficulty. Without a world state, much less a global parliament or congress, as Fraser points out, it is not clear who constitutes the relevant public and it is not clear precisely which of the many powers that affect them—states, international organizations, multinational corporations, and so on—such a public would address. Recently scholars have begun to pay attention to these issues—specifying the addressee of transnational publics and the relationship between transnational civil society actors and structures of transnational and international power.[35]

The framework I develop in this book helps bring into focus a distinct and relatively neglected public beyond the state: the public power constituted by states acting together, sharing authority and responsibility for their actions. The reason I highlight this "public of publics" begins with the observation of what could be called a domestic bias in political thought about public power and democratic accountability. Democratic thought generally has treated states as if each existed in its own universe, without any need for others and without any fear of others. The salient fear is of the arbitrary power of the sovereign, and so the focus is on vertical accountability. But states do not exist in isolation; they exist with other states, in anarchy. Anarchy makes a second fear—interstate violence and war—relevant to political life. The implications of this second fear are not well appreciated in public sphere scholarship. Even states with accountable sovereigns and thriving public spheres can become overwhelmed by the problem of violence, with pernicious effects on democratic self-determination. It is fair to say that states can only fulfill their function of providing basic needs to their own people if they are not themselves engulfed in violence and war. In order to succeed as providers of basic needs to their people, states must be mindful of their security situation. Here, horizontal accountability matters. My argument is that one way states manage their security situation in a given issue is by forming collective intentions, that is, by committing to address the issue together. From here, the dynamics of sharing authority constitute those states as an international public power.

35. E.g., Nanz and Steffek 2004.

## Intentionalities in Global Governance

This book is concerned with patterns of interstate cooperation in world politics and argues that there is an element of intentionality at the system level that other approaches have overlooked. Collective intentions are macro- not microlevel phenomena, which means that the pull they exert on behavior is from the "top down" more than the "bottom up." This type of intentionality among states has not been thematized in IR scholarship.

How does my intentionalist approach relate to other approaches to international cooperation in IR scholarship? Existing scholarship can be organized according to two questions. First, where is agency in the international system? Is it located in the units themselves or at the level of the system? Answers fall along a continuum from the claim that the order producers are the individual units at the microlevel who exert agency from the bottom up, to the claim the order producer(s) is or are phenomena at the macrolevel that exert(s) agency from the top down.[36] Second, to what extent does agency, wherever it is located, account for the trajectory of the international social order over time? Answers to this question fall along a continuum from the claim that social order evolves behind the backs of agents to the claim that social order is intentionally designed.[37] Combining these two questions to form a 2 × 2 descriptive table organizes existing theories of international cooperation and global governance into four types:[38] the invisible hand; no hands; many hands; and a visible hand (short of a world state).

### The Invisible Hand

One way to think about intentionality in global governance is in evolutionary terms, where a social analogue to Darwinian natural selection operates at the level of the system, selecting functional institutions for international society. Here, the production of global social order is a causal process. Each actor chooses what to do based on local incentives and constraints, coordinating where necessary through institutions,

36. See Wendt's 1999, chapter four discussion of the distinction between microlevel and macrolevel social structures.

37. Wendt 2001, 1036–37 usefully juxtaposes intentional design to evolutionary approaches to global governance. See also Barnett 2009; Young 1983.

38. On descriptive versus explanatory tables, see Bennett and Elman 2007, 181.

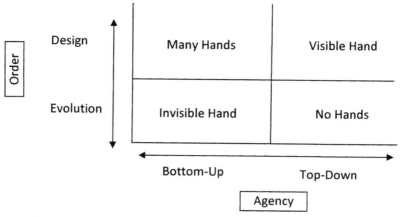

FIGURE I.I. Intentionality in global governance

and adapting their behavior incrementally, in a trial-and-error fashion.[39] The resulting system might seem well designed, but that is only because existing institutions are functional. When the institutions are no longer functional they will, eventually, decline. This is the "hand" at work at the macrolevel: it seems as if someone is in charge, designing the best institutions for society, but there are only individuals acting on their narrow interests.[40] In invisible hand accounts the units are typically conceived of as purposive, goal-directed actors. But their intentionality is at the microlevel, and, as Alexander Wendt puts it, "intentionality at the micro level is fully compatible with no intentionality at the global or macro level."[41] When agency is located only in the units of the international system, then systemic outcomes are unintended. No larger intentionality or social purpose pulls actors toward particular, chosen outcomes. The system constrains, shapes, and shoves, but it is the locale of structure, not agency.[42]

Whatever its merits more generally, such a perspective seems particularly apposite in a context like international anarchy, where there is no centralized agency but yet there can be quite a bit of order. At least two influential strands of IR theory take an invisible hand approach to the

39. Calvert 1995, 80; Elster 1983.
40. Ullmann-Margalit 1978.
41. Wendt 2001, 1037; Elster 1983.
42. Checkel 1998.

problem of order. In realist balance of power theory, order is maintained by the micromechanism of state balancing in response to internal and external threats. This process, driven by selfish interests and myopic thinking at the unit level, maintains equilibrium at the system level, keeping the system in balance between chaos and empire.[43] In its extreme, "mechanical" version, individual states need not even be aware that they are part of a balance of power system for its invisible hand to steer their interactions. States that fail to balance power are eventually selected out of the system. The eighteenth-century European balance of power system can be interpreted as somewhat mechanical. Its members were conscious that they were part of the same society, but the individualistic norms of their interaction arguably made it function like an invisible hand system.

While in many ways critical of realism, the neoliberal institutionalist scholarship of the 1980s[44] can also be interpreted in invisible hand terms. Here, as in realism, states are assumed to be driven by their self-interest and microlevel incentives. But neoliberal institutionalists argue that states need not merely balance. If they have overlapping interests states can respond to market failures by constructing institutions or regimes. Regimes then persist as long as they are functionally useful; when they are no longer useful they decline. With some exceptions, scholarship on regimes assumed that states in a competitive anarchy cannot learn in any deep or enduring sense, they cannot build on knowledge from experience and use that to steer the system toward the future.[45] Rather, institutions reflect local, microlevel incentives, and unsuccessful institutions are selected out of the system. For neoliberal institutionalists as for realists, the macrolevel mechanism—the selection of adaptive institutions—is evolutionary not human-made.[46]

## No Hands

A second way to think about the role of intentionality in global governance is to abjure the premise of intentional action altogether. Scholars

---

43. For criticism of Waltz's appropriation of evolutionary theory, see Florini 1996; Setear 2005.

44. Paradigmatic statements include Keohane 1984; Krasner 1983; Oye 1985.

45. But see Haas 1990; Nye 1987. Snidal 1997 discusses limits of regime theory along these lines.

46. Ullmann-Margalit 1978, 282.

who take this approach would not see self-conscious steering by units or human design at the system level. Instead, they would argue that what looks like intentionality at any level is actually driven by structural formations. Like with invisible hand accounts, here the social order is not freely chosen. But unlike with invisible hand accounts, here unit actions are not meaningfully chosen either because the model of agency is produced at the structural level.

For some, social structural configurations have a telos, logic, or direction that is unknown to and/or out of the control of the participants. The paradigmatic example is Hegel's cunning of history. Examples in the IR literature would be Wendt's argument for a world state that emerges over time through the playing out of a struggle for recognition;[47] and the Foucauldian idea that the forms of nonintentional social control (governmentality) associated with neoliberalism produce the modern subject essentially behind our backs.[48] A third example is the sociological institutionalism of the Stanford school, where world culture is a macrolevel configuration with causal power. Here, society is not comprised of a collection of pregiven actors who created it to serve their functional needs. Society, which is analytically prior to the actors, produces the dominant notions of actorhood and agency in the first place.[49] In all of these approaches, intentionality is beside the point.

When the hands producing social order are either nonexistent or invisible, the most that would-be international governors can do is act on their own interests and hope for the best: international order. They cannot inject social purpose or design their cooperation in a way that steers the international order over time. A corollary is that they are not responsible for the order that obtains over time, since it is produced by systemic logics and not intentional ones.

## Many Hands

A third approach to the role of intentionality in international governance is an extension of the rationalist neoliberal institutionalist approach. The

47. Wendt 2003.

48. E.g., Dean 2010; Larner and Walters 2004; Merlingen 2003; Jaeger 2010.

49. Jepperson 2001, 3; Meyer, Boli, and Thomas 1997. See Finnemore 1996 for a review of the literature. See Jackson and Nexon 1999 and Krebs and Jackson 2007 for IR extensions.

Rational Design (RD) project, developed in a special issue of *International Organization* in 2001, could be called a many hands approach. This scholarship continues the focus on unit-level intentionality but carves out a larger role for system-level design. In the framework chapter of that issue, Barbara Koremenos, Charles Lipson, and Duncan Snidal argue that institutions are "self-conscious creations of states" and other actors, and therefore design differences "are not random.... [They] are the result of rational, purposive interactions among states and other international actors to solve specific problems."[50] Like evolutionary approaches, RD is functionalist in the sense that actors will choose institutions for functions they expect those institutions will serve. But unlike evolutionary accounts, which rely on anonymous mechanisms of adaptation and selection to account for persistence over time, RD focuses on intentionality in the moment of institutional choice. RD thus differs from its invisible hand predecessor in that it has more confidence in the actors' abilities to shape their environment, even into the uncertain future.

But in RD all of this unit-level intentionality does not imply or produce intentionality at the system level. The choice of particular institutional features derives from participant preferences and is determined through bargaining. There is no sense in which RD scholarship proposes that outcomes are purposefully intended at the macrolevel. Indeed, the focus is explicitly on microfoundations and the agency of (corporate) unitary agents. This is fine, but there are empirical and normative reasons to explore the possibility of macrolevel intentionality in global governance. Empirically, what if there are processes or mechanisms that exert a top-down pull on state actions? If states can act with a collective purposiveness, we certainly would want to see it, and the RD approach is ill suited for exploring this possibility. Normatively, from a many hands perspective, at the end of the day states easily can renege on commitments, and it is harder to understand why they would keep them. The RD perspective is well suited for thinking through commitment problems, but as I will argue it is not well suited for thinking about the nature of international commitment itself—what it means for states to enter into obligations, how those obligations are constituted and how they produce effects separately from actors' dispositions toward them. With an understanding of collective intentionality among states, on the other hand, it will be easier to see how

50. Koremenos, Lipson, and Snidal 2001, 762.

states can keep commitments and why reneging might actually be difficult or even, under some conditions, less likely than we might expect.

## Visible Hand

The fourth way to think about intentionality in global governance is the one developed in this book, which is in terms of a visible hand short of a world state. Like with the many hands approach, the idea is that the international social order is to some extent designed, but here it is designed at the macro- not the microlevel.

When thinking about top-down intentionality in world politics, the first thing to come into mind is hegemony, where a state with preponderant power creates a system of rules in its image, to keep the system stable. The institutions reflect the hegemon's values and preferences, but hegemony requires the consent of the weaker states.[51] John Ruggie has analyzed US hegemony from a collective intentionality perspective.[52] He points out that when states sat down at Bretton Woods they committed to manage the global economy together by making it capitalist and linking that vision to particular institutions (IMF, World Bank, GATT). What followed was not the unfolding of a liberal order behind the backs of states with "no hands" or even by an "invisible hand." Ruggie argues that this was a purposive steering of the global economy by a group of states that had committed together, underwritten by the United States.

A hegemonic order is a relatively easy case of collective intentionality,[53] because the hegemon underwrites the international institutions and has special responsibility for their maintenance. The continued consent of weaker states is crucial and if they withdraw it then the order falls apart. But weak states are subordinate to the hegemon and the hegemon's power to enforce its institutional vision makes withdrawal relatively unlikely. The case of hegemonic order shows that the international social order can be steered. The framework I develop shows how steering is possible even without a hegemon. The steering process will look more like

---

51. Gilpin 1981.

52. Ruggie 1998.

53. Schmid 2008, 46–47. Schmid discusses three types of collective intentions. Some result in unitary action, where one person gives orders and everyone follows. But not all of them do. Wendt 2004 develops the state as a collective intention; Roth 2004 discusses how an individual can act on another individual's intentions, which is a form of sharing it.

a horizontal concert than a vertical imposition, however, which suggests that it will be more difficult to sustain. A key concern of this book is to show how states can overcome the difficulties and govern together.

## Visualizing International Public Power: The Concert of Europe

My intention in this book is to say something new about contemporary global governance, yet I illustrate the empirical purchase of my approach with the Concert of Europe. This may seem quixotic, since the Concert was neither global nor liberal, two of the main characteristics of global governance today. Moreover, allowing "Europe" to stand in for the international or global can be problematic in itself.[54] But I shall show that beginning in 1815 the five European great powers functioned for several decades as an international public power. Their power was *public* to one another because they relied on forums and gave themselves the mandate to preserve the peace together. This was a public *power* in that together they constituted a capacity to define and pursue that public interest. There is already a substantial literature on the Concert.[55] The main purpose of the Concert case study for this book is to illustrate the theoretical framework developed in chapter two and, in so doing, provide an account of the origins of global governance. But it also speaks to contemporary debates about the causes of the Concert's long peace.

### Why the Concert?

While world politics has changed considerably since the early nineteenth century, there are many reasons, both explanatory and normative, to take a closer look at the Concert. Focusing on the Concert makes sense, first of all, simply because the Concert is widely acknowledged as the first modern international security institution and thus a precursor to international governance as we know it today. Its innovation of regular consultation among the great powers survives and forms the basis of the UN Secu-

---

54. For criticisms of IR scholarship along these lines, see Keene 2002.

55. Paul Schroeder's work in particular has inspired a generation of IR scholars. His *Transformation of European Politics* (1994) marked somewhat of a transformation, fueling what Enno Kraehe (2002, 163) calls a "neo-concert challenge" to the balance of power interpretation of the concert that had dominated in the Cold War.

rity Council, the G8, the contact-group approach to crisis diplomacy, and many other institutions. Moreover, IR scholars treat the Concert as if it is relevant to contemporary institutions. After the Cold War and again after 9/11 it has been invoked in policy debates over the form that great power management should take.[56]

A second reason to turn to the Concert is methodological and has to do with the causal mechanism for producing a governed international order that I want to draw out: public, forum talk. These days, international co-operation and governance are overdetermined, by democracy, capitalism, communications technology, and international institutions. Reaching back to the nineteenth century helps control for many of these rival explanations. The Concert powers varied substantially in regime type, with only Britain resembling what we would today call a stable democracy, so self-restraint cannot be attributed to a convergence of regime type, much less a democratic one. Mercantilist rather than liberal thinking dominated this nascent capitalism. Advances in print technology had widened the audience of state action, but news still traveled relatively slowly until the telegraph was invented in the mid-1830s. The Concert was the sole international institution for managing crises (other than the balance of power understood in individualistic terms), making it easier to see the effects of forum talk distinct from effects of other institutions. In other words, the Concert is a hard or "least likely" case. It is not a case where we would expect states to talk together, much less for their talk to have constraining or steering effects on behavior. If their talk had effects in this case, then, this should give us some confidence in the analytic framework.[57]

It also is the case that the Concert helps denaturalize a practice—states talking together in public forums in order to address common problems—that today we take for granted. Prior to 1815, these European states had only ever cooperated to help defeat one another, and the idea of forum discussions on how to sustain peace among them was novel, untested, and in some ways quite threatening. It was not common sense at all and it is quite surprising that they did it, much less that it was successful. The Concert case highlights how important this practice can be for governing in a diverse international system.

Finally, and perhaps paradoxically, there are normative reasons to focus on the Concert. Reaching back to the Concert as a way of talking

---

56. E.g., Kupchan and Kupchan 1991; Daalder and Lindsay 2007.

57. Bennett and Elman 2007, 173; Levy 2008.

about something that generally is treated as a relatively new phenomenon is a way to keep in mind that despite all of the changes we have witnessed in the international system, there are significant continuities. It is difficult to assess the magnitude of any change without a clear sense of continuity.[58] A second normative reason to examine the Concert is to counter the commonsense notion today that global governance requires thick ties of (democratic or liberal) community rather than the thinner solidarities of society and public. The Concert is a case of a long peace that was not a democratic peace. These autocrats did not share ideas regarding how to rule their own populations internally. They were not governing together because they formed a community of values and sought to pursue their values on the world stage. They were governing together because despite their different values they recognized that they faced a common problem in avoiding another great power war and decided that working together was better than fighting. This suggests the political collective identity of a public. They acknowledged and acted on their shared commitment to the common interest while maintaining permission to be strangers. The process of governing together itself served as a solidarity making practice.

Notwithstanding these reasons to focus on the Concert, there clearly are limits to the insights that can transfer across two centuries. The leaders of the Concert powers were mainly autocrats who did not need to listen to publics at home, and the media environment made it easier to keep secrets. Power was less visible than it is today and less systematically accountable to public opinion. Paul Schroeder suggests that the nineteenth-century Concert worked in large part because of these differences, and so it would not work as well today. For Schroeder, the spread of liberalism and democracy and the participation of the masses in politics make it more difficult for leaders to think in international systemic terms. When leaders legitimate themselves through elections, the temptation is to engage in narrow, self-interested thinking because it is rewarded at the ballot box. Electorates do not tend to think in terms of the public good over time, because that sort of thinking is abstract and the benefits felt only in the long run.[59]

This is a serious challenge, and the limits of the Concert case in these respects need to be probed more fully. Still there is reason to believe that

58. Wight 2001; Waters 2009.
59. Schroeder 1993, 68.

these changes do not render the dynamics of governing in the Concert irrelevant to global governing today. Foreign policy—especially security—is perhaps the sphere of greatest executive freedom and insulation from public demands, and perhaps relatedly, publics in general are less attentive to foreign policy than domestic.[60] It also might be the case, contra Schroeder, that systemic thinking is more possible in an era in which so many problems seem to have global dimensions: environment, terrorism, nuclear weapons, to name just a few. In other words, there is no reason to dismiss the idea that states talking together exerts an independent pull on their behavior. It is possible that the forum effects of talking together are stronger rather than weaker today because of the extent to which publics are aware of global problems and leaders' commitments. The more public the forum, the more "the public" has a potential stake in maintaining the commitment. Nevertheless, and in sum, while there are solid reasons to focus on the Concert as a window to this dynamic of global governance, there will inevitably be limits to the lessons we can draw.

## The Concert Literature

In IR scholarship the debate on the Concert has evolved in largely paradigmatic terms, with three principle accounts corresponding to the explanatory variables associated with the three main IR paradigms: a realist, balance of power approach; a liberal, institutionalist approach; and a constructivist, collective identity approach. These often are pitched as competing explanations, but each captures important aspects of what was going on. My account includes elements of all three, but particularly supports interpretations of the Concert such as that of Schroeder, who stresses its systemic aspect and the centrality of forums. The framework developed in chapter 2 provides social theoretic underpinnings that allow us to better articulate the mechanisms that made the Concert work. These, in turn, suggest political and normative implications of states governing together that other approaches fail to see.

The materialist or balance of power approach interprets the Concert as merely a fancy name given to conventional great power politics. A methodologically sophisticated statement of this position comes from Branislav Slantchev,[61] who argues that the lack of war after 1815 can be explained

60. Dahl 1999.
61. Slantchev 2005.

by the terms of the Vienna Settlement alone: powerful states were satisfied and weaker states were deterred. The Concert, then, did not require "explicit and self-conscious management"; it simply needed "a specific structure of incentives to ensure satisfaction and credible deterrence."[62] On this view, great power meetings did no causal work. They were acrimonious not cooperative, and "what alleviated suspicions, when they were alleviated, was relative material power."[63] Stability prevailed simply because each great power, following its narrow self-interest, had nothing to gain from war. The balance of power continued to function essentially as it had in the eighteenth century. After 1815, which put power in balance, invisible hand equilibrium dynamics held that balance in place. Rules and norms to act on collective, European interests, much less collective identity, played no role.

John Mearsheimer and Korina Kagan each have offered accounts of the Concert in a similar vein. According to these scholars, what we call the Concert of Europe and laud as the first security institution was more of a flash in the pan, if not a complete "myth."[64] Matthew Rendall's interpretation of the Concert's management of the Greek revolt can be read similarly—for Rendall the status quo orientation of the strongest powers, especially Russia, kept the peace.[65] Sheldon Anderson even claims that "Metternich's Concert and the balance of power were not responsible for the short peace that followed Vienna ... [there was merely a] natural lull in great power rivalry after 1815 [because] Europe was psychologically and materially exhausted from the twenty years of war."[66]

The balance of power story is undoubtedly an important part of what was going on in the Concert, but it does not capture everything, and it leaves some important things out. Phenomenologically, it overlooks the fact that the leaders themselves intended to manage Europe together. They did not think that their redrawing of the map of Europe and redistribution of territory and political control—this "elaborate exercise in cartography"—had the force to keep the peace.[67] That is precisely why

---

62. Slantchev 2005, 580.

63. Slantchev 2005, 576.

64. Kagan 1997/98; Mearsheimer 1994/95. For other balance of power interpretations, see Gulick 1965, 1955; and Medlicott 1956. Lipson 1994, 119–20 summarizes this approach.

65. Matthew Rendall has developed this line of argument in several articles. Rendall 2000; 2002; 2006; 2007; 2009.

66. Anderson 2007, 304.

67. Craig and George 1995, 27.

they chose to renew the alliance in November 1815 and insert an article in that treaty that called for consultation. As Gordon Craig and Alexander George put it, they wanted "some executive body" to help deal with any threat to the treaty. With the commitment to consult on affairs relevant to European stability, "the new order was in a sense given both a constitution and a constitutional watchdog—a balance of power (as defined by the final act) and a concert of powers to watch over it."[68] Similarly, the balance of power interpretation discounts the prevalence of references to Europe, law, cooperation, and so on by Concert leaders as they confronted crises.[69] There was nothing "natural" about these powers' restraint. It resulted from hard-fought political battles with one another. Finally, a balance of power approach ignores the great powers' ability to find novel solutions to problems—namely, to create the sovereign states of Greece and Belgium. This simply had never been done. In sum, the process of Concert consultation drops out of a balance of power approach, and arguably as a result, important aspects of the political outcomes slip through the cracks.

Some of what is left out of the balance of power story is picked up in a second, institutionalist approach to the Concert. While not all of these accounts are paradigm conscious,[70] there is a strand of research that reads the Concert through the lens of rationalist regime theory, where the Concert functioned, in Louise Richardson's words, as a "proto-institution,"[71] a set of rules and norms established by a group of states with overlapping interests but mixed motives, to help them better pursue those interests. The Concert's importance, like that of any institution, lay in its ability to change incentives and constrain state behavior. It reduced uncertainty and tamed the security dilemma, intervening between the powers' preferences and the goal of regional stability. In these accounts, the role of forum consultation was to increase transparency or facilitate information exchange.[72] Robert Jervis notes that "higher levels of communication and more frequent meetings among national leaders increased transparency,

---

68. Craig and George 1995, 27–28.
69. Schroeder 1994 makes this point.
70. E.g., Elrod 1976; Daugherty 1993.
71. Richardson 1999.
72. In IR scholarship, Robert Jervis 1983 was among the first to interpret the Concert through the lens of rationalist regime theory. With the end of the Cold War, there was renewed interest in the Concert among rational choice institutionalists. E.g., Lipson 1994; Richardson 1999.

lowered the level of debilitating suspicions that plague many attempts at cooperation, and made it less likely that any statesman could think that he could successfully cheat in understandings with others."[73] Daniel Lindley similarly stresses the transparency-enhancing role of forums, albeit with a less benign view. For Lindley, suspicion, doubt, or mistrust were made transparent in many instances in these years,[74] and so consultation helps account for the Concert's breakdown.

In a particularly influential institutionalist account that brings in power more explicitly, John Ikenberry argues that the success of the Concert was not so much because of institutions, but because Britain's hegemonic power backed this institution.[75] After the Napoleonic wars the strongest power chose to bind itself to the lesser great powers, that is, to engage in strategic restraint, in order to lock in its preeminent role. Thus British hegemony made possible this extraordinary period of continental stability. Ikenberry further argues that Britain's liberalism played a key role since liberal regimes are particularly good at keeping commitments and at restraining power. Insofar as the Concert worked, then, it relied on *British* hegemony as much as British *hegemony* (to paraphrase John Ruggie's argument about American hegemony and embedded liberalism in the post–World War II order).[76] Ikenberry treats the Vienna Settlement as the first in a trajectory toward increasingly binding postwar orders and deepening international institutions; and he links the increasing success of this strategy to the spread of democracy.

All institutionalist approaches respond to weaknesses of the realist interpretation, and capture some of the novelty of the Concert. They show that this self-consciously constructed institution helped produce social order. But at least when it comes to Ikenberry's specific argument, the Concert case also points to a limitation of the theory. Ikenberry's argument relies on states' ability to make binding commitments, and he argues that democracies are better able to do this than autocracies.[77] But a key reason the Concert worked was restraint by the non-democracies. The Russian czar, whose power was the least constrained domestically of all of the European monarchs, repeatedly restrained Russia in the name of

---

73. Jervis 1983, 721. See also Dakin 1979; Daugherty 1993; Richardson 1999.
74. Lindley 2007.
75. Ikenberry 2001.
76. Ruggie 1982.
77. Ikenberry 2001; cf. Alvarez 2001.

Concert ideas. His commitment to the idea of Europe is especially note-worthy because Russia ended the Napoleonic wars in as strong a position as Britain. Schroeder treats post-Napoleon Europe as a bipolar system materially and multipolar only by choice.[78] Austria and Prussia similarly were committed to the Concert, and they were hardly democratic either, while democratic Britain was the first state to step back from Concert co-operation when Canning replaced Castlereagh as foreign minister in 1822 (although Canning also initiated the turn back to the Concert in 1826). Finally, while Britain is responsible for formally putting forward the idea of consultation, it is impossible to analyze the Concert's design or success without noting Austria's crucial role. In other words, to the extent that the Concert was an experiment in international cooperation, it was a joint project and not a British imposition; and to the extent that its norms were binding it was not because of unit level properties of its participants. Brit-ain's important role notwithstanding, the Concert was very much a multi-lateral institution.

A third approach to the Concert reads it through a constructivist lens that highlights the role of collective identity. Charles Kupchan and Clif-ford Kupchan made this argument in the early 1990s,[79] and most recently, Charles Kupchan linked the Concert to his larger argument about how enemies in the international system can become friends.[80] Kupchan does not cast his argument in paradigm conscious terms, but he argues that in the Concert case, these former enemies developed a sense of friendship that lasted until 1848. "The norms and practices of the Concert enabled solidarity to endure amid strategic differences that otherwise would have likely led to armed conflict."[81] War never became unthinkable, as it does in the thickest form of security community, but Kupchan argues that force was not seen as a legitimate tool among the great powers for resolving their own quarrels.[82] The Concert is one of several cases that he uses to flesh out his model.[83] Kupchan recognizes that the Concert does not fit his model very well: social orders and cultures among the powers were very diverse, and only Britain had meaningful restraints on executive power

78. Schroeder 1994.
79. Kupchan and Kupchan 1995.
80. Kupchan 2010.
81. Kupchan 2010, 196.
82. Kupchan 2010, 189.
83. Kupchan 2010, 6–7.

domestically. Nevertheless, the Concert worked in his view because Britain played a leading role, elites constituted a transnational cosmopolitan community with their own cultural bonds, and the "new discovery" of consultation gave the Concert a "high level of transparency."[84] Kupchan seems to suggest that face-to-face consultation among sovereigns stood in for domestic institutional restraints on power. The cultural commonality among diplomats made it possible for talking to one another to have restraining effects. Once nationalism took hold midcentury, however, "social divergence" among great powers strained their relationship and the glue of the Concert weakened.

Kupchan here echoes Bruce Cronin's argument that transnational identities among elites shape state preferences and therefore help account for the choice of security institution.[85] Cronin argues that the great power identity entailed a "high level of commitment, sacrifice, and trust." These states saw themselves as "constituting a unique and exclusive group with special rights and responsibilities for system management."[86] This identity gave rise to the specific institutional arrangement of vetting actions diplomatically through the group.

Kupchan and Cronin both stress the role of cultural commonality in making Concert governing last. Particularly because contemporary global governance also seems to rest on cultural ties (here, democracy and liberalism) it is important to know how such ties could produce governing, and whether they are right about the mechanism. What must governors share in order to sustain a relationship of political problem solving? Are internalized bonds of "friendship" and high levels of trust the essential criteria for political relationships? Do those ties, more than commitments and forums, account for their ability to govern together?

The questions are important both empirically, for getting the Concert right, and normatively, for translating its insights to today. It is not clear that there was ever the depth of friendship Kupchan's model assumes, or the levels of trust implied by Cronin, even at the height of Concert cooperation in the early 1820s. While diplomatic relationships certainly mat-

---

84. Kupchan 2010, 198–99.

85. Cronin 1999. Schroeder seems to agree, pointing out that "systemic thinking and practice requires a level of mutual trust and cooperation hard to achieve and harder still to maintain over the long run and inevitably leads to powerful temptations to cheat." Schroeder 1993, 67–68.

86. Cronin 1999, 10.

tered—giving participants shared norms, language, and symbols for con-
ducting their conversations—their causal role in the Concert needs to be
further fleshed out and cannot simply be assumed. After all, these relationships precede the Concert by many years yet nothing like the Concert
had emerged before. On the other hand, the relationship of being great
powers was new with the Vienna Settlement and was from the start linked
to the practice of meeting on issues of common concern.

Still, what I take from Kupchan—and from Cronin—is that some degree of shared background was necessary for talking in the forum to have
a restraining effect. I will flesh out the level of commonality that was necessary for Concert governing by looking at the Concert's historical preconditions and then examining the mechanism of restraint and its eventual breakdown in the Crimean War.

For this argument, Paul Schroeder's work is particularly helpful. First,
he argues that the Vienna Settlement succeeded not primarily because of
cultural ties felt by participants but because defeating Napoleon had required a long and messy process of learning how to think systemically.[87]
A "network of ideas" at the collective level developed and was able to
break through the more atomistic eighteenth-century ideas about the balance of power. Systemic understandings and practices then became possible.[88] Second, his argument does not rely on motives or dispositions of
the leaders. Schroeder stresses that he is not arguing that particular leaders internalized collective norms and then acted on them. He is not, in
other words, proposing a bottom-up argument or pitching his argument
in methodological individualist terms. As he puts it, the challenge was not
to teach individuals to "think systemically" but rather to "bring[] about
overall conditions under which systemic thinking and action can become
a rational choice, effective in practical terms."[89]

While Schroeder does not ground his argument in social theory, clearly
he is interested in more systemic or top-down rather than motivated or
bottom-up accounts of Concert outcomes. Kal Holsti also develops a top-
down explanation of the Concert. He conceives of the Concert as a mix

---

87. Schroeder 1993, 61. Schroeder does not argue that Concert diplomacy alone caused
the long nineteenth-century peace. He stresses two additional factors: the status quo orientation of the great powers and the Vienna Settlement's creation of Germany and Italy as an "independent center for Europe under Austrian hegemony." Schroeder 1972, 406.

88. Schroeder 1993, 48.

89. Schroeder 1993, 49.

of anarchy and hierarchy, where the "pentarchy" gave itself the right and responsibility to protect Europe from war. Holsti uses the language of governing and authority, arguing that the tasks the great powers outlined, the decision rules they followed, and the ability to steer power toward the common goal of stability meant that they functioned as a political authority in Europe.[90] Both Holsti and Schroeder imply that what made the Concert successful was top down rather than bottom up. But neither provides social theoretic underpinnings to the argument and so the systemic logic of the governing process is not clear.

Pulling together the literature on the Concert, between the two extremes of balance of power and friendship is an institutionalist account of the Concert that leaves room for the possibility that the Concert acted as a European political authority. Several accounts of the period place stress on the role of systemic thinking and of forums. But no one has yet made the argument in terms of a systemic phenomenon, governing together, that exerted a causal power from the top down to help the great powers produce their long peace.

## Plan of the Book

Chapter two develops the framework for thinking about states governing together, which treats concerting as joint action, a form of collective intentionality. The argument is that states govern by jointly committing to do something together and linking their commitment to a forum. When they do this, talking in the forum helps produce collective self-restraint and commitment-consistent behavior. The mechanism is what I call the forum effects, speech acts and norms of speech that tend to emerge when actors meet in forums.

Chapter three establishes the historical preconditions for states to govern in anarchy. I show that a context that could support joint action among states developed with the growth of international society in the eighteenth century, but that the 1815 Vienna Settlement was a key turning point. Chapters four and five trace the process through which the Concert powers avoided fighting one another in the 1820s. In 1815 they jointly committed to keep the peace; the result was no great power war in the early 1820s. In 1826, the great powers, recognizing that they faced a new problem, the Eastern Question, committed to the Treaty of London and

90. Holsti 1992, esp. 32–33. See also Dakin 1979, 32.

linked it to the London Conference on Grecian Affairs, and there was no great power war. Chapter six then traces the Concert's demise. In 1853, faced with a Russo-Turkish dispute, the great powers did not commit to defensive aims, and while they met several times between 1853 and 1885, they could not avoid great power war. Each of these three chapters examines the diplomacy to show how commitments and forums helped produce these effects at the microlevel and how those interactions sustained the macrolevel collective intention. Each of these chapters also compares my explanation to other accounts of the same outcomes.

The concluding chapter considers possible implications for today's current period of great power peace and joint management of the balance of power. Despite the breakdown of the Concert, its key innovation, face-to-face diplomacy in public, lived on and became standard practice for great power management—and of course it is the taken-for-granted mode of cooperation and global governance today.

# Governing in the Shadow of Violence

This book develops a framework for thinking about how states concert their power toward public interests and argues that when they do so, they can constitute an international public power, a locus of agency and responsibility for public interests beyond the state. As I suggested in chapter one, the idea of international public power can be difficult to grasp for two reasons. The first is conceptual. When states govern together they do not organize themselves hierarchically to act in a unitary fashion, that is, they do not merge into a world state. Because we tend to think about group agency in anthropomorphic terms, it is at first difficult to imagine their concerted action as "agentic." The analytic problem of imagining agency without a unitary agent motivates this chapter, and I address it through the concept of joint action, which is a form of collective intentionality.

The second difficulty is empirical. Even once we can envision a type of group agency that is not anthropomorphic, anarchy presents a particularly challenging context for applying it. In all governing, on any scale, violence is a live possibility.[1] Members of a political group may disagree emphatically about what is right for the group, and when disagreement cannot be contained in the political process it easily can devolve into violence, shutting down politics altogether. The problem is heightened when the group acting together is comprised of states, because each state is itself a corporate group, in which the primary loyalties and formal obligations flow downward to constituents and not laterally to other states. Add to this that each state has a local monopoly on violence and that there is a se-

---

1. This paragraph draws on Mitzen 2005. See Galston 2010 for discussion of the domestic case.

curity dilemma between them, and group agency hardly seems possible. These days the problem of violence can be difficult to see, since interstate war is rare and cooperation seems only to deepen. But the relative calm of contemporary international relations should not blind us to this fundamental political problem. The very first task of politics is how to get people and groups not to kill each other. This problem can be pushed to the background, but it never disappears. Part of the task of successful governors is to reproduce habits of thought and action that keep violence at bay and prevent political life from unraveling. At the global scale this task is accomplished by the institutions of international society.

With these conceptual and empirical difficulties in mind, this chapter conceptualizes global governance as a case of collective intentionality among states. The core of the framework is the idea of "intention," which has a meaning very different from the one used in IR scholarship. Focusing on intentions draws our attention to forms of normativity and obligation in social and political life that can be otherwise obscured. Anarchy cautions us against assuming that these forms of normativity can be salient among states. But in the second section of the chapter I propose that they can, highlighting the role of international society in making that possible. I also hypothesize that the problem of violence can be further mitigated as states act together, when forums accompany their commitments. The speech acts and norms of speech produced in a forum can produce behavioral self-restraint and commitment-consistent behavior. Because of the forum effects, states can sustain their collective intentions into the future. The chapter concludes with an outline of the claims that follow from this proposition and structure the empirical chapters.

## Collective Intentions

The few applications of the concept of collective intentionality to international politics to date, most notably by John Ruggie[2] and Alexander Wendt,[3] have focused on the collectiveness of intending rather than the intending itself. Collectiveness is certainly important, but the stakes of a collective intentionality approach come through most clearly by recognizing that collective intentions are in the first instance intentions. In IR

2. Ruggie 1998.
3. Wendt 2004.

scholarship, intentions tend to be treated as relatively synonymous with motives or preferences. The question, what are that leader's intentions? means, what is that leader planning to do?, which we discern by asking, what does he want to do—what are his preferences or desires? But to intend something is not the same as to want or desire it. Even intuitively, intending feels closer to action—we can want many things without intending to do anything about them.

With this intuition in mind, this section begins by discussing what it means to intend. The discussion is philosophical, and as such somewhat removed from IR. But the philosophical groundwork is warranted. Actors take on a specific kind of obligation when they intend to *do* something rather than merely *want* something, and when they intend to do something *together* rather than merely want or intend the same thing *individually*. These obligations are thin and content free, but they are obligations nonetheless. IR discussions of commitment have not yet considered the specific normativity of committing together to a goal. What follows is not a comprehensive treatment of the extensive literature on collective intentionality. But I flag where there are philosophical debates about the concept or where a move in my conceptualization involves taking a position in one of those debates.

### Intentions

An intentional idiom dominates discussions about world politics, in that we assume that states and other actors make purposive choices. This assumption helps justify the whole endeavor of IR scholarship, of speaking truth to power, since our truths can make a difference only if states can have a say in their destiny. But IR scholarship tends to rely on a commonsense or folk understanding of intentionality, which reduces an individual's intentions to the product of her desires and beliefs. The default theoretical assumption in contemporary IR scholarship for capturing purposive action is probably the rational actor model, where actions are understood to arise from the conjunction of desires/preferences and beliefs/knowledge (often represented by probability estimates): $D + B \rightarrow A$. Actors are further assumed to be optimizers, with already formed transitive preferences. This makes the logic of choice usually straightforward: act on the strongest desire you are most likely to be able to realize. More formally, actors choose the course of action with the greatest expected utility.

This simple but powerful model is often criticized from what seem to be opposite directions: for some the problem is its indeterminacy while for others the problem is its determinism. First, game theorists have discovered that in many situations expected utility theory does not predict a unique solution; there often are multiple equilibria.[4] The model in this sense suffers from a surfeit of possibilities, offering actors no criteria for knowing which to choose. At the same time, and second, others argue that on a deeper level the model seems to leave no room for the phenomenon of choice. A "choice" amounts to mechanically implementing our desires under the constraints of the world as we know it. To the extent that expected utility yields an action, it is produced as if by a machine. It is more of an output than a choice, and so not purposive.[5]

To be sure, not all of our actions result from genuine choices. We often act habitually or rely on rules of thumb rather than consciously weigh alternatives. For some, this suggests that the default model for action should not be the rational actor but the sociological one, who spends most of her time simply enacting norms of the social environment.[6] But for those who seek a notion of agency where choices are not mechanical, the rational model does not fully capture that phenomenon. It gives us two poles: too many options or none at all. Strangely enough, then, the model stops at the moment we most need it, leaving actors standing on the brink. By not being able to account for choice, what the model actually shows is how un-model-able or inaccessible the activity of choosing really is, at least from this perspective.

But choice is a distinct and important phenomenon. To say "I choose $X$" is a way to assert sovereignty over our indeterminate desires and beliefs and aim us toward the future. In the words of Alfred Schutz, when faced with the question of what to do, alternatives always "stand to choice," and then the actor commits to one of them and in so doing projects her will into the world.[7] This capacity to commit gives us a feeling of control over our choices, and when we feel we can control our choices we feel more in control of our lives, as if we are leading our lives rather than being swept up by events or by anonymous logics beyond our control. The

---

4. Stein 1999, 218–19; Snidal 2002; Bratman 1999.

5. Wendt 1999, 125–30; Bratman 1999.

6. March and Olsen 1998. For discussion in IR context, see Fearon and Wendt 2002; Sending 2002.

7. Schutz 1951, 161.

fact that we control our choices implies we are responsible for them. We are not slaves to our desires; we could have acted otherwise. Because it allows us to project ourselves into the future, the ability to assert sovereignty over our preferences is as crucial to our sense of self as our ability to know our desires and preferences. The rational model does not capture this capacity to assert sovereignty.

Responding to this lack, some philosophers of action have advocated the concept of intention as a crucial element of agency that cannot be reduced to desires or beliefs. Intentions are commitments, that is, action-oriented resolutions of issues that usually result from a weighing or consideration of alternatives.[8] The commitment of an intention has both external and internal dimensions. Externally actors commit to an outcome. More precisely, they commit to act in a way that tries to produce that outcome. Internally actors commit to themselves to follow through on the intention. Taken as a whole, to intend is to take a stand on how one's desires and beliefs will become manifest in the world.

More formally, intentions alter the rational actor model by forming a wedge separating desires and beliefs from action, in the following way: Desire + Belief → Intention → Action.

I shall consider each side—the relationship of desires and beliefs to intentions, and of intentions to action—in turn.

Intentions are not divorced from our desires (preferences). Both involve what philosophers call "pro attitudes," motivational states that "in concert with our beliefs ... can move us to act."[9] When we intend, just as when we desire, we are trying to mold the world to our mind (more technically, both have a "world to mind" direction of fit). This makes both desires and intentions different from beliefs, which generally aim to accurately represent the world (beliefs have a "mind to world" direction of fit). But intentions are a more restricted set of motivational states than desires. We can only intend things that we can reasonably expect to be able to do. Desires, in contrast, are relatively unconstrained on both dimensions. They can range from realistic to purely fantastical, and from specific to broad. We might desire, for example, world peace or the universalization of human rights. Those desires might have action content for us, but they might not, and even if they have action content it is not necessary to act on them in order for them to be personally meaningful.

8. Bratman 1999; Velleman 1997, 32–33; Holton 1999; Roth 2004, 375.
9. Bratman 1999, 16.

To be sure, our intentions cannot be wholly separated conceptually from either our desires or beliefs—it is irrational to commit to a goal we do not want or that we feel we have no chance of accomplishing.[10] Nonetheless, intentions are not reducible to our desires, our beliefs, or to their sum. The moment of committing is distinct and necessary; without it we cannot act. Intending to do something tomorrow, to realize one possibility among others or to accomplish some larger project, projects forward our commitment to our plans and goals. As such, intentions help us execute long-term projects—creating further commitments enables us to stitch together the smaller steps to achieve them.[11] The intention, the settling of the matter, is our way of taming or stabilizing the deep uncertainty of the future. The capacity to act on our projects and plans therefore is not just a pragmatic need (although it also is that). It is an identity need, since if we cannot act then we cannot be ourselves.[12]

The link to identity lends a normative aspect to intentions: asserting sovereignty over our desires is a good thing to do. We may have many conflicting preferences and our preferences might not yield a clear message about what to do, and so we commit. There is something to be said for being a "decider."

This raises the question on the other side of the wedge, of exactly how close to action intentions bring us? When we intend something, from that point on we tend to consider the question of what to do to be closed. Keeping our intentions is the default option, and as such the expectation is that we will follow through rather than reconsider our options. An intention is more than a mere consideration, or just another reason for or against doing something. It is a sufficient reason: simply because we have committed we ought to follow through.[13] The gap between commitment and action thus creates a second normative moment. When we intend we create a relationship between our commitment and our future action. Part of the meaning of the word commitment entails an obligation to follow through—we owe it to ourselves. This obligation is thin and content free, that is, it is independent of the normative value of the action itself. The idea is that we have decided therefore we ought to follow through. The

---

10. Bratman 1999; Schmid 2008, 28; Schutz 1951, 165–69. Intentions can meet all constraints and still not govern our actions, since we can misjudge our abilities.

11. Bratman 1999, 17.

12. Mitzen 2006, 344.

13. Malle and Knobe 2001, 47; Schutz 1951, 162.

commitment to rob a bank obligates in the same way as the commitment to keep the peace.

Follow-through is normatively important for ourselves, in that if we do not we do not fully realize a sense of agency. Our follow-through also is good for society. Social stability is necessary for all individual agency, and it rests on the assumption that people will follow through on their intentions. While it might seem problematic to grant such a thin normativity, consider the alternative, where each of us is Hamlet, endlessly considering whether to be or not. If we fail to make commitments, or if we make commitments but fail to follow through, then no matter how noble those commitments might be, we are not linking world to mind. We are not really acting at all, but living in a fantasy.

However, while following through is normatively valuable, it is not automatic. Settling a matter in our mind is different from acting in the world, and—default options notwithstanding—nothing mechanistically links the one to the other. There are several reasons why an individual might not follow through on an intention, from pragmatic to moral or values-based. Or, an actor might simply be weak-willed and unable to follow through. It also is possible that the world might change in ways that make following through unnecessary or impossible. This nondeterministic relationship between intention and action highlights that we do not blindly enact our intentions any more than we do our desires. We choose (or not) to execute our intentions; we have agency.[14] Insofar as intentions have causal power over our behavior, then, it will not be through any deterministic relationship but through a probabilistic one, and it is in virtue of their obligatory force.

In sum, intending is a concept that allows us to solve some problems in our understanding of action. Adding this third element to the baseline desire and belief model draws attention to an aspect of action that can be overlooked or obscured—its intrinsic future orientation and its normativity. A gap of indeterminacy still remains, as it should, since this is the gap of genuine choice or free will. But the gap is smaller from intentions to action than it is from desires to action. Intentions thus enable us to better "mind the gap" between desiring and acting, that is, to make better sense of the leap into the unknown that constitutes choice. It is only because we have this ability to commit ourselves and steer our actions that most of the time we are not stuck on the brink of choice but able to direct our lives.

14. Roth 2004, 386.

## Collective Intentions

The concept of intentions captures aspects of individual agency that elude the standard "desire plus belief" model, particularly the capacity to commit to a course of action we have selected for ourselves, with both the freedom and the normative obligations that this entails. Scaling up, collective intentionality is helpful for imagining what steering action together would look like in a context where actors retain individual sovereignty to decide for themselves.

Like individual intentions, collective intentions are commitments that help induce and provide an account for actions. But with collective intentions, in addition to committing to yourself you also commit with others, to a common purpose: let's keep the peace; let's resolve the Balkan crisis. The fact that participants commit explicitly to do something *together*, in Margaret Gilbert's words, to "emulate as much as possible a single body"[15] for the purpose of executing the intention, takes us out of the realm of strictly individual intentions. As such, following Gilbert, we could say that these are intentions by a plural subject.[16] That term is useful because it suggests there is a single commitment to act, and so a single locus of agency, yet more than one agent with authority over action. A plural subject is an emergent phenomenon in that it is separate from the actors who create it and cannot be reduced or disaggregated to their preferences and/or interactions.[17] At the same time, it does not subsume the intentionality of the individual actors. Some collective intentions are organized hierarchically to make unitary decisions, such as the state, where individuals fully cede sovereignty over their intentions, at least in some issues.[18] The anthropomorphized state actors of IR are themselves a case of collective intentionality.[19] But hierarchy is only one way to organize collective intentions, and many collective intentions do not involve fully or formally ceding authority.

To make the idea of a plural subject more concrete, consider a team—

---

15. Gilbert 2006b, 8; 2003b, 51.

16. Gilbert 1992, 2003a.

17. Sawyer 2005; Jansen 2005; Gibbs 2001.

18. Schmid 2008, 36ff. develops three models of collective intentions: corporate, influence, and team; Pettit 2003 focuses on corporate agency; Velleman 1997, 34 argues that hierarchically organized collective intentions are an easy case.

19. Wendt 2004 conceptualizes the state as a collective intention.

like the basketball team from chapter one—which is a particular kind of plural subject. A helpful, commonsense way to convey plural subjecthood is to consider a phrase they might use as they head toward the court: "let's win the game!" Winning requires the team to work together—the goal cannot be produced alone. Each player retains authority over the specific choices she makes on the court, but it does not make sense to reduce the game to a set of individual rational choices. Of course, without any choices on the court there would be no game, and without choices consistent with the collective intention, the team would not win. But the win (or loss) is accomplished by the team and not by any particular player or play.

Moving to world politics, a "team" like the Contact Group for Former Yugoslavia also can be considered a plural subject. Here, five states (the United States, Russia, Britain, France, and Germany) committed in 1994 to work together to end the Balkan conflict. While each retained authority over specific policy choices, each also treated its Balkan policy as a joint effort, which gave each some authority over the others' choices. For example, once the Contact Group existed, "lift and strike" could no longer be justified as a US strategy. It could not be rationalized within the context of the collective intention. If these states were working together to end the conflict, it would be inconsistent for the United States to take a unilateral action that its partners, particularly Russia, strongly opposed.[20] Conflict resolution belonged to the group.

These examples point to the two conceptual components of a collective intention.[21] First, like individual intentions, collective intentions are commitments. But because more than one actor is involved, they are joint commitments, which gives them a second feature that individual commitments do not have. Collective intentions must be fully out in the open or public among those who have committed together.

JOINT COMMITMENT.   To collectively intend is to jointly commit, to agree to do something together, as a body.[22] Anchoring collective intentions in the concept of commitment suggests that, like individual intentions, col-

---

20. Schwegmann 2000.

21. Gilbert 2006b, 46; 2003b.

22. There is disagreement in the collective intentionality literature on how explicit the initial agreement must be, but the notion that collective intentions rest on commitments is widely shared.

lective intentions are inherently normative; they constitute obligations, both to others and ourselves.[23] As discussed above, when we individually intend, we owe it to ourselves (our future selves, to be precise) to follow through. Joint commitments externalize that owing relationship to others. Invoking obligation raises two questions, the conceptual question of how it is constituted and the causal question of whether and how it produces effects. This section addresses the conceptual question. The causal question will be covered later in the chapter.

A joint commitment is an obligation to oneself (internal) and to those with whom one commits (external). Internally, a joint commitment creates the same obligation for each participant as does an individual commitment. In Abe Roth's phrase, these are "contra-lateral commitments": each participant's commitment is separate but directly corresponds to others' commitments.[24] The internal obligation can be broken down into three aspects. First, each participant commits to follow through on the intention. This means that for each, even if preferences change, the obligation to herself to follow through remains, just as it does for individual intentions. Second, for each actor, the joint commitment provides sufficient reason to follow through.[25] Both individual and collective intentions provide content-independent reasons for acting. What is considered normatively valuable is following through, acting rather than dithering or being weak willed. Third, like individual commitments, the constraints of a joint commitment on an individual's behavior are circumscribed. Joint commitments are specific to the task or issue at hand: the obligations are owed only to others who have committed to the collective intention, and only in respect to the particular intention to which they commit.[26]

So far, joint commitments create the same obligations for each actor that her individual commitments do for herself. But the fact that the commitment is to other people gives rise to an external obligation as well, which has to do with togetherness. The intuition is that if a group of actors agrees to

23. In making this claim I am taking a stand within the collective intentionality literature. Not all philosophers of collective intentions agree that they are inherently normative. I am thus siding with "normativists" such as Gilbert, Meijers, and Pettit, as opposed to those such as Schmid, Bratman, Miller, and Tuomela, for whom collective intentions are interpersonal but not normative. Even some who accept obligation as part of individual intending reject it at the collective level. See Tollefson 2004, 5–9.

24. Roth 2004.

25. Malle and Knobe 2001, 47; Schutz 1951, 162; Green 2007, 4.

26. Roth 2004, 386.

do something together, the actions of each become essential to the agency of the other. The link to agency means that a joint commitment is rooted in the same normativity as that of an individual commitment. There, intending is normatively valued because it is how we link ourselves to the future, and the need to stabilize the future is a condition of possibility for agency and thus for identity. In the case of joint commitments, actors have authority over or partially "own" one another's actions. They have entered into what Gilbert calls a relationship of owing. Where your capacity for agency rests on my contribution and mine on yours, I owe it to you to follow through by directing my actions toward what we have committed to do. You have standing to call me on it if I fail to do so.[27] One actor's weak will potentially undermines that capacity for every one of them to successfully execute the intention, so each is obligated to stay on course.

In a relationship of owing, each actor is accountable to the others for actions relevant to their goal. This suggests both that actors must act consistently with the intention and that they must be recognized by one another as doing so. As Gilbert puts it, when we are parties to a joint commitment, our right to expect actions from one another that satisfy that intention gives us a special "standing to demand explanations" if some members of the group choose not to conform.[28] We are sharing authority over the intention and so must authorize (or not) one another's actions as part of it. The individual intentions I form relevant to our joint intention must be compatible with it. To take an example that is common in the collective intentionality literature, I cannot intend with you to go for a walk together and then get in my car and drive away. I certainly can, in that I have the capacity to do so, but if I choose to do so I have undermined our agency. I have not fulfilled my obligation to you to execute the intention, and indeed I have prevented you from realizing a sense of agency when it comes to our walk. The United States could not have committed to the Contact Group and then actively pursued "lift and strike." Of course, it had the material capabilities to pursue that policy unilaterally, but doing so would have undermined the agency of the group. The joint commitment gave Contact Group members the standing to call the United States on its actions.

The external dimension of joint commitments suggests that they create a type of collective identity—by committing to a common project, individuals constitute a "we." But this is a plural subject only for this par-

27. Gilbert 2006b, 2003a; Roth 2004, 380.
28. Gilbert 2006a, 11; Gilbert 2000: 17.

ticular purpose: we will win this game, we will clean the park, we will end this war. Doing one thing together does not mean doing everything together, nor even does doing something together necessarily require *being* something together—we can intend to sing a song together without forming a choir.[29] Finally, doing something together does not require having the same values or identical preferences. Participants in a collective intention are obligated to one another in respect only to their commitment. As we saw above, intentions are not altogether divorced from values and preferences, but they are not determined by them either. Since collective identity usually is understood in terms of shared values and preferences, the "we" of a joint commitment is distinctively thinner. Commitments are not mere expressions of our desires, and they create reasons for action that are independent of those desire.

When discussing commitment in a contemporary IR context, the first thing that comes to mind is not obligation but the "commitment problem,"[30] which is assumed to plague all interstate agreements. Without a central enforcer to keep the pursuit of joint goals on track, it is hard for states to know whether others will follow through on their agreements. The main problem is time inconsistency.[31] The problem is that leaders cannot credibly commit to actions in the future, because both leaders and contexts of action may change, and in a changed context (e.g., an increase in relative power, a revolution) it might be more rational for a leader to renege on the commitment than to follow through. States therefore cannot trust that others will follow through and they cannot credibly commit to following through themselves. As a result of the commitment problem, many argue that any so-called commitments among states must be—in the language of rational choice—already incentive compatible, so that the commitment serves merely as a focal point.[32] If incentives are not compatible with commitments, or not reliably so over time, then external mechanisms such as sanctions and transparency arrangements must be created to channel behavior.

The commitment problem cautions against the idea that obligations among states could meaningfully affect their behavior, especially over time. But in a sense the social theory underlying the commitment problem has stacked the deck against commitment. As discussed above, the ratio-

29. Thanks to Anne Holthoefer for suggesting this analogy.

30. Fearon 1995. Also Powell 2006.

31. Time inconsistency is a problem for all commitments, not just interstate commitments.

32. E.g., this is how Goldsmith and Posner 2005 understand international law.

nal choice framework does not distinguish intentions—commitments to act—from motives, preferences, or interests. Commitments merely reflect preferences and have no content of their own. From here, it is not surprising that commitments have no independent behavioral pull, because the possibility that they could obligate has been excluded a priori. It is not surprising, then, that the concept of obligation has not received much attention in IR scholarship. While international lawyers have been talking about obligation for years, IR is only beginning to take the concept seriously. The special issue of *International Organization* on "Legalization in World Politics"[33] defined obligation as one of the three central features of international law, and this led to responses[34] that suggest that IR scholars now agree with international lawyers that obligation is somehow important, but it is still unclear exactly how obligation works among states.

The collective intentionality framework, particularly the concept of joint commitment, offers a way to think about the constitution and the pull of obligations among states. Moreover, the thin, action-oriented normativity of collective intentions makes it a productive anchor for global governing, because collective intentions can be created even among actors whose preferences might not be fully aligned or who do not share extrapolitical values and desires. Nothing about intending together makes individual motives or preferences irrelevant. But they do not fully account for choices. More importantly for now, the obligatory pull of commitment is wholly separate from their content. Joint commitments obligate actors for reasons internal to the notion of what it means to act together.

Note that I have not yet shown how external obligations could actually pull individual (or state) behavior at the microlevel or how such behavior instantiates and sustains collective intentions at the macrolevel, which are the propositions I make about states in the later chapters. I will take up the task of describing the behavioral pull in the last section of this chapter. For now, it is sufficient to note that collective intentions begin with the act of jointly committing, and to understand the obligation that such a commitment implies.

PUBLICITY.    A joint commitment alone does not constitute a collective intention. It must be out in the open, for all its participants to see; it must be public among them. It could be that each individual commits herself to

33. Abbott et al. 2000.

34. E.g., Finnemore 2000; Finnemore and Toope 2001; Reus-Smit 2003; Brunée and Toope 2010.

the same end, but if they do not know it then there is no collective intention, only an aggregate of individual intentions.

Positing a role for publicity in intentionality taps into a long-standing debate in philosophy, going back to Wittgenstein, over the extent to which intentions are matters of the mind and internal versus external and therefore public all the way down. For the purpose of understanding collective intentions, I believe that debate can be bracketed because whether or not we can get inside the minds of individuals to know their intentions, in the case of collective intentions, which are in most accounts irreducible to individuals, there is no physical body there into whose mind we might look.[35] The conceptual necessity of openness for collective intentions reduces the explanatory burden on individual psychology and mental states. Instead of asking whether stated intentions match beliefs and desires, the question for determining whether a collective intention exists is how people refer to and invoke their commitments and for what purposes, and how invoking their commitments relates to what they ultimately do.[36]

Publicity among participants is explicit in most accounts of collective intentions, although it has not received much analytic attention. The lack of attention might be because much of the collective intentionality literature presupposes a context in which openness among those who have committed can be taken for granted—such as two people going for a walk together or cleaning up a park. In any case, from the normativist account of collective intentions I have developed above, openness is necessary for commitments to govern action and for actors to realize their joint goals together because it enables participants to hold one another responsible for their actions. The term *publicity* seems to capture this link to the normativity of joint action better than the vaguer term *openness*.

In an IR context where there are incentives for secrecy and deception, publicity takes on even more salience. To my knowledge, Raimo Tuomela provides the only sustained discussion of this requirement, in his "bulletin board view" of collective intentions.[37] Tuomela distinguishes two equally

35. Bracketing this debate takes a stand in the collective intentionality literature. For Searle, a brain in a vat can have a collective intention. For Gilbert, Tuomela, Bratman, and others, the presence of others is necessary but internal states of mind are crucial. Gilbert, for example, stresses "readiness" as a precondition for entering into joint commitments. See discussion in Tollefson 2002.

36. See Krebs and Jackson 2007. This is not to endorse their strong claim that we cannot access motivational states, on which I remain agnostic; my claim is only about collective intentions.

37. Tuomela 2005.

necessary dimensions of openness, which he calls epistemic and ontic. The former, more familiar, term refers to what the actors know about their intention. The latter term refers to what the intention is, and it suggests that there must be some referent of the intention that exists in the real world. Here I will briefly define both terms and relate them to relevant IR scholarship in order to help assimilate what we already know about international governing to a collective intentionality framework.

Epistemically, in order to be a collective intention, a joint commitment must be common knowledge. Actors must know, and know that they each know, what they have committed to and how each is expected to follow through. There is an important sense in which acting together depends on the quantity and comprehensibility of information they all have. The bulletin board metaphor is useful because bulletin boards convey the same information to everyone. The information enables each actor to then decide whether to commit and whether to follow through.[38] Tuomela points out that collective intentions vary in their epistemic strength. A collective intention is "epistemically strong" when each can see, on a metaphorical bulletin board, that a group plan exists, who is party to it, and what the plan entails. As the quality and quantity of information decline, the intention weakens. It is difficult to sustain a collective intention without sufficient, symmetric information.

The epistemic requirement of collective intentions that all parties have the same information parallels the role of transparency in rationalist IR scholarship, understood as "the availability of regime relevant information."[39] The transparency literature in IR is concerned with how information affects a state's compliance behavior and a regime's effectiveness.[40] The argument is that transparency arrangements reduce uncertainty, which facilitates ongoing compliance. States become more confident of their cooperation partners since the partners' behavior is visible, and they are less likely to cheat because they know they will be found out.[41] But scholars of transparency disagree on the independent power of visible information to produce compliance. Theorists such as Ronald

38. Sugden 1993. Cf. Chant and Ernst 2007, 105–6.
39. Mitchell 1998, 110. See also Mitchell 1994; Lord 2006; Naurin 2006; Lindley 2007, 17.
40. Mitchell 1998, 113.
41. Mitchell 1998; Chayes and Chayes 1995. Some IR scholars argue that transparency can enhance the accountability of international institutions and even spur democratization. E.g., Payne 2001; Grigorescu 2007.

Mitchell and Abram Chayes and Antonia Chayes[42] take as unproblematic the notion that transparency facilitates compliance; while others such as George Downs, David Rocke, and Peter Barsoom[43] argue that greater information has no real impact on compliance. Daniel Lindley also takes a skeptical view, arguing that having accurate information about a state's capabilities and intentions and actions can enhance power politics as much as it can enhance cooperation.[44] In other words, many scholars argue that the effect of information by itself is indeterminate.

Turning back to collective intentions, like transparency arrangements, the information actors get from the "bulletin board" is crucial for but does not constitute their collective intention. Just as information does not alone produce regime compliance, it does not produce joint action. The epistemic requirements for collective intentions are important—you can't share an action if you don't know what's going on—but information alone does not capture what it is to act together. Something must exist in the world, for all the actors to see, that constitutes or instantiates the intention.

Tuomela calls this an ontic dimension, an aspect of the intention that exists separately from our knowledge about it. For Tuomela, the fact that the bulletin board is a board matters, in that it is something tangible that all participants can orient themselves toward and talk about. But the ontic requirement of a collective intention does not necessarily require a physical object like a board. Most collective intentions are instantiated not through objects as much as through practices, that is, behaviors with the same meanings for all participants,[45] especially practices of sharing authority over action. These practices can take a variety of forms and are more quotidian than they at first sound. For example, authority over one another's actions can be shared behaviorally, as in the intentionality of a basketball team or of pianists playing a duet. Authority over actions also can be shared through verbal, communicative practices. This mode of sharing implies an ongoing conversation about the commitment and the actions that could be relevant to it, such as criticism, justification, and reconciling actions to intentions. Ontic strength would be measured by the existence and density of this conversation. I

42. Mitchell 1998; Chayes and Chayes 1995.
43. Downs, Rocke, and Barsoom 1996.
44. Lindley 2007. Also Finel and Lord 1999.
45. Adler and Pouliot 2011.

will argue that among states governing together, talking together in forums serves this function of making real the collective intention. But for
now, the upshot is that collective intentions to do something together
are not just mental constructs in individual brains; they exist in the
world, in our practices.

To pull together this discussion, to intend is to commit, and to intend
together is to share a commitment with others. Collective intentions to
do something together have two conceptual components, joint commitments and publicity. Following through on commitments is normatively
desirable, and when acting with others, publicity is crucial both for constituting the intention and for following through. We know collective intentions exist when we see joint commitments linked to practices of sharing
authority over action.

## Governing Together in Anarchy

There is nothing inherently political about collective intentions. Indeed,
governing is a hard case. To govern is to make authoritative decisions
that steer power toward the public interest. It is intentional and collective, but what makes it a hard case for collective intentionality is that governing is a contentious process that can be difficult to sustain. In anarchy,
where even social order is an accomplishment, this sort of collective intentionality seems out of reach. To be sure, it is not difficult to imagine
states making commitments to one another, since they do so all the time.
What is difficult to imagine is that their commitments would have any discernible, discrete effects on the ground in the absence of enforcement.
That is, it is hard to imagine states following through or executing their
intentions.

This section applies the framework developed above to the case of
governing among states in anarchy, paying particular attention to the
challenge of follow-through. I first outline the difficulty violence poses for
governing and then derive the proposition about global governance that
guides the empirical chapters. When states in international society commit to do something together, talk in forums helps them follow through.
The effects of forum talk are mechanisms that instantiate the collective
intention and help produce outcomes consistent with it. The collective intention, in turn, is a macrolevel phenomenon that can guide state action
over time.

## Social Order and the Problem of Violence

The first step in applying a collective intentionality framework to global governance is to acknowledge the problem of violence and to recognize the role of international society in managing it.[46] All collective intentions to act together presume social order. But this presumption remains unstated in the collective intentionality literature and social order is taken for granted. Paradigmatic cases of joint action include going for a walk (Gilbert) or the store (Roth) together, or cleaning up the public parks (Tuomela).[47] What these have in common is that they are all relatively small, informal groups in which the actors are generally friendly (or at least indifferent) toward one another and interaction is optional. The stakes associated with their collective intentions are relatively low. These joint actions also take place in a rule of law setting where violence is generally not on the table.[48]

Governing differs from each of these paradigmatic cases in that social order cannot be taken for granted. When it comes to governing we cannot assume low stakes, or that actors see their governing as optional and voluntary, or that those who govern together are friendly or even indifferent to one another. Generally speaking, governing in the modern case is an activity made necessary when individuals who are interdependent and who expect their relationship to extend into the foreseeable future recognize that they face problems they cannot address alone. In such situations, decisions must be made about how to live together and what to do. They might disagree about a whole range of things: the definition and scope of the problems they face, their role as a group in solving them, and even the most basic questions of how to disagree and discuss problems.[49] And in political discussions the stakes are high because the resulting decisions can have an enduring impact and there always are winners and losers. A political group might share extrapolitical, communal ties that buffer it against the worst consequences of disagreement; but it might not. The political relationship itself is a relatively thin bond that does not require that actors share such

46. This section draws on Mitzen 2005.

47. Among political collective intentions, Wendt 2004 develops the intention of citizens to be a state together, and Ruggie 1998 develops the intention of the Western states after World War II to create a neoliberal economic order.

48. Searle 1995, 89–90, discusses war as a collective intention.

49. This definition of governing is drawn loosely from Galston 2010.

ties. Indeed, even as individuals come to share political institutions, they may choose to remain "strangers," permitting one another a sphere of privacy about extrapolitical values. As strangers, when they disagree they cannot fall back on deeper bonds to hold them together.

All of this suggests that violence is a live empirical possibility when it comes to governing. But insofar as the medium of governing is discussion and argument, the problem of violence is even harder to escape. This is because even in its ideal form argument is an unstable social practice. In its Habermasian formulation,[50] argument is defined as the exchange of reasons by participants who are oriented to reaching consensus and remain open to changing their minds if faced with better reasons. Because it only is possible to say speakers are holding one another accountable to reason if their agreements can be undone through future argument, each consensus they forge remains contingent. This inherent openness lends argument its instability. It must have the power to undo and remake consensus yet undoing any consensus raises uncertainty and insecurity and opens the door to violence. The instability of argument lies beneath all governing, from the boardroom to the town hall to states in anarchy. Whether in their real or ideal form, then, political discussions face a potentially slippery slope, from the conference table to the street, or even to the battlefield.

The slippery slope to violence is particularly in force in anarchy. In a domestic context, violence is not generally a salient problem. The state backstops social processes that might tear the group apart. It can be tempting to argue that functionally equivalent backstops now exist internationally, since globalization and the spread of democracy have been accompanied by a decline in interstate war. But the analogy falls short. Domestically the state's backstopping role is rooted in its power and the authority to enforce the prevailing social consensus. Those engaged in political argument yield to the state. At the global level, no supranational power or authority exists. As long as there is no world state to maintain order, the task falls to states themselves. This is not to deny the importance of systemic forces integrating societies transnationally, but to place them in context. Where we see governing deepen in the international system, it is made possible because of states and not despite them. If states cannot manage the problem of violence between them then global governing shuts down altogether.

With this in mind, I propose that global governing is made possible by

50. Habermas 1984; 1996.

international society. As Hedley Bull pointed out long ago, every social order evolves unique ways of solving the fundamental problem of regulating violence among members. Because states are a different kind of actor and are much less vulnerable than individuals, a society of states will be ordered by different types of institutions than a society of individuals. [51] Two premises of international society in particular stand out as contributing to the production of order. First, social order is promoted through the Westphalian rule that sovereignty means nonintervention. States have permission to remain strangers, that is, not to form an extrapolitical community of values. The idea is that trying to make the society of states conform to the same extrapolitical values had been a recipe for religious war and not for stability. Rules for managing interdependence, and not rules for living under god's grace, form the basis of international society. Second, social order is promoted by granting states the private right to violence and a monopoly on it. Taking away the private right to violence by instituting a world state could very well be destructive, since concentrating world coercive power in a single source would open that site up for political competition, while demoting the state similarly could increase violence in the system rather than stabilize it. Both community and consolidation were seen as destabilizing; sanctioning difference and privacy were seen across the centuries as the premise for a more durable international social order.

## Intentionality and the Forum Effects

A normative order organizing the use of violence is an important accomplishment and certainly a precondition for governing, but producing order and governing are distinct. Governing is about injecting social purpose to a social order; it entails intentionality. For states to govern together requires that they can hold one another to their commitments, which in turn requires an ongoing process of keeping violence in the background. The institutions of international society cannot reliably do this alone. In this section I propose mechanisms that can instantiate and sustain the collective intention. States can concert their power when they link their commitments to forums. Forums permit specific commitments and international society's norms to become more salient in interstate decision making, even where states contemplate the use of force.

51. Bull 1977.

This is a two-part claim about forums. First, a forum setting changes how states talk. It causes ways of talking and norms of speech that mimic the practice of sharing authority that we would see in any sort of joint action. Forums cause states to talk as if obligated. Second, those ways of talking can change state behavior outside the forum; they can lead states to follow through on their commitments and realize their goals or projects. The mechanisms that form the basis of my hypothesis are drawn especially from the work of Jon Elster as well as several IR scholars, rationalist and constructivist, who have extended Elster's insights and/or engaged with Habermas's work on communicative action. What's distinctive in my framework is to link the micromechanisms to the macrolevel idea of collective intentionality, an agency "beyond the state" that can pull state behavior.

It is useful to begin by defining the two central terms: forum and discussion. A *forum* is any locale where more than two actors who have entered into a commitment meet face to face to discuss issues of common concern. Among states, forums are locales where representatives from more than two states engage in face-to-face discussion. Forum is therefore a synonym for face-to-face discussion among those who have committed. These days when we refer to forums, even among states, we tend to mean forums that are visible and accessible to an audience of nonstate actors. I want to bracket that meaning for now in order to focus solely on forums in international society. The collective intentionality framework developed in this chapter does not presume an audience. It conceptualizes the pull of the commitment among those who have committed, which is a discrete problem that should be understood on its own terms before adding the phenomenon of audience effects.

What happens in a forum is a general form of group talk that can be called *discussion*. The deliberative democracy literature defines discussion as talk among actors who believe they face some need for coordinated or regulated action. Such talk can include reason giving, justification, rhetorical posturing, the verbal exchange of offers, and so on. Unlike deliberation, which can take place in silence, discussion requires the presence of others; it is fundamentally dialogic.[52] If all talk can be pictured along a continuum, ranging from a "cooperative" pole, where we would find the ideal of Habermasian communicative action, to a "conflictual" pole, where we would find (verbal) bargaining and strategic interaction,

---

52. Pure deliberation refers to addressing all logical possibilities for an action and can take place "in foro interno." See Bohman 1996. Fearon 1998 defines discussion.

then *discussion* is the term for group talk that encompasses the full range of this spectrum. It requires the presence of others but does not have the demanding precondition of Habermasian communicative action, that participants are oriented to listen and prepared to change their minds.[53] Parties in a discussion may come to agreement, but they may not. And if they do, their agreement will not necessarily be a reasoned consensus. It could be a compromise, a case of losing an argument or finding a lowest common denominator; or it could be a case of being rhetorically trapped.

With these definitions in mind, the question is, how could forum discussion produce actions consistent with a joint commitment that we might not otherwise expect (and are not reducible to interests and power)? Research in a variety of disciplines[54] supports the claim that appearing in a forum produces distinctive ways of talking and habits of speech, which in turn can lead to the type of behavior we associate with governing (or any collective intention). Four distinct effects have been isolated. The causal claims for each are probabilistic. Without forums we might see these ways of talking, with forums we are more likely to see them; and without these ways of talking we might see self-restraint and commitment-consistent behavior, with these ways of talking we are more likely to see it.

GENERALIZABLE INTEREST CLAIMS. The first, which has received the most attention among IR scholars since Jon Elster[55] articulated it in the 1990s, is that talking in public rather than in private affects the type of reasons actors give for their actions. In a forum, actors will tend not to make self-interested arguments, and they will tend to argue for a position slightly different from their ideal. This is because if a public argument looks too close to an expression of raw self-interest, others likely will not accept it as truly in the public or shared interest. So by avoiding self-interested claims actors can appear impartial and unselfish in front of others. The forum "launders"[56] idiosyncratic preferences, and actors then make "pseudo-arguments." They

53. See Fearon 1998. In appealing to a general, empirical phenomenon my approach is similar to that of Krebs and Jackson 2007. They focus on rhetoric, which they define broadly as all speech acts. Since I am interested in problem solving the term discussion seems more apt.

54. The intuition that face-to-face discussion enables people to cooperate better is buttressed by empirical work showing that such communication both increases the likelihood that players will cooperate and makes that cooperation more durable. Ostrom 2000. See Holmes 2011 for a review of this literature.

55. Elster 1995.

56. Elster 1995; cf. Abbot and Snidal 1998.

"ground their claims in principle [by] appeal[ing] to an impartial equivalent of self-interest."[57] For example, "This is in England's interest," would become "This is a great power interest," or "a matter of sovereign equality." The idea is that forums alienate participants from their private concerns. The positions they support are one step removed from their private intentions, at least when it comes to issues discussed in that forum.

Making public claims also has a compelling force. Once a speaker has taken a stand publicly it can be difficult to back down. Elster calls this the consistency constraint. A speaker looks too self-interested if she abandons a principle too readily rather than trying to reconcile things to the principles she has already taken a stand on.[58]

Why do these speech acts occur? For Elster, the tendency to generalize interest claims does not rely on the anticipation of material costs for being selfish, but on each speaker's sense that there might be genuinely impartial members in the discussion group. By generalizing her argument a participant tries to make it conform to some minimum definition of "normative rightness" that the truly impartial member(s) will accept.[59] More broadly, the desire to justify actions in terms acceptable to all implies a concern about public opinion. "A desire not to appear selfish before others is possible only if one has some concern for the opinion of others, and thus some desire to take into account their welfare (at least as far as this affects their opinions). Thus, a desire not to appear selfish presupposes a concern of sorts for a 'public' of those whose opinions matter, even if their votes may not."[60] This seems intuitively plausible, but it might not be necessary to appeal to individual psychology in order to account for generalized interest claims and the consistency constraint. For example, James Fearon argues that the norm of impartiality is inherent in the discussion situation. First, in a sense pursuing purely idiosyncratic self-interests is "at odds with the idea of having public discussion before making a choice that affects all."[61] By accepting the premise of participating in public discussion, you constrain yourself to offer certain kinds of reasons.

57. Elster 1995.

58. Elster 1998; Fearon 1998; Cialdini 2009, chapter three. Of course, holding tight to a publicly stated position is not always beneficial for a group. See Stasavage 2004, 672–73; Naurin 2003, 2006; Chambers 2004.

59. Elster 1995, 245.

60. Fearon 1998, 55. Also see Yack 2006, 424: "Political proposals cannot be persuasive unless they appear to promote the common good or advantage, since that is what brings and keeps us together to engage in collective deliberation and action." Cf. Eliasoph 1998.

61. Fearon 1998, 53.

NORM OF REASON GIVING.  Any forum can produce generalized interest claims. But in order for this way of talking to be part of a collective intention and not merely ephemeral, it must have staying power. This has at least two requirements. First, participants must expect to meet again. Second, staying power requires media: agendas, minutes of meetings that record the arguments and decisions made, publicists or reporters, as well as print and visual media such as pamphlets, newspapers, television, radio, and such.

When these two conditions are met, there is a second forum effect. Speakers tend to get habituated to practices of reason giving, and a norm develops to do so. When speakers become accustomed to giving reasons and demanding justifications, over time they come to rationalize similar behaviors. These practices of justification and reason-giving need not be indicators of truly democratic practices or true respect for one's partners, and they do not necessarily cause respect or democracy to grow.[62] It simply means that participants become habituated to the discursive practice of exchanging reasons. Additionally, the norm to give reasons does not mean actors feel obligated to justify publicly all of their actions. Forums tend to be constituted around particular commitments or problems. That means that only the behaviors the actors agree upon as collectively relevant come under scrutiny.

PUBLIC REASON.  A third effect of talking in forums is that it produces public reason. By public reason I mean a discursive structure that embodies the perceived consensus of a group on appropriate reasons for action in a given issue at a given time. It refers to language and arguments expressed in general, impartial terms that apply to all members of a group. The opposite of public reason is idiosyncratic or private reason, rationales that apply only to some restricted audience and cannot be adopted by the public as a whole.[63] What makes a reason or statement public has to do with a "standard of disclosure," not the location of its utterance. You can make public claims in secret forums; you can make idiosyncratic claims in public forums. Any reason can be made or transformed into a public reason.

Public reason on a given issue or problem may be comprised of con-

62. In democratic theory, discursive reciprocity is linked to mutual respect and is a requirement for deliberation; also, it seems for some that deliberation "grows" mutual respect or deepens democracy. See Sanders 1997 for a critique.

63. "Publicity here refers to the presuppositions of communication and not its actual scope; a conversation among friends may be just as public and open as the reasoned inquiry of the scientific community." Bohman 1997, 184.

tradictory norms and rationales, and as such may not yield a definitive answer (this is why discussion is needed).[64] Its importance is that it constitutes a framework for discussion about a given issue that endures beyond any specific decision situation. For example, public reason among the five great powers after 1815 was that revolution was destabilizing and sovereigns should be supported, although it was not public reason that they should intervene militarily to support all monarchs. Public reason today regarding sovereignty is increasingly contradictory. On the one hand the notion of sovereignty as a right to final authority is part of UN charter law and is regularly invoked; on the other hand a notion of sovereignty as a responsibility that can be revoked by the international community arguably is gaining ground.

Once public reason exists on a given issue, similar arguments will justify actions for all participants and actions will be seen as legitimate only if they can be justified in these terms. The implication is that when states repeatedly meet in forums oriented toward particular commitments, their public reason comes to define the meaning of actions outside the forum. Public reason manifests their (horizontal) obligations to one another, which are distinct from the (vertical) obligations to their own citizens. As long as the states expect to continue to participate in these interstate forums, their domestically derived intentions no longer exclusively guide their actions. The meaning of an action then is not provided by the state alone, but by the group of states. They are sharing authorship of actions relevant to their commitment. As noted above, the causal claim about these forum effects is probabilistic. When actors participate in public forums, repeatedly, they tend to rely on public reason to rationalize their actions or criticize the actions of others. They are more likely to couch their actions in public terms when they appear in forums than when they do not.

SELF-RESTRAINT AND COMMITMENT-CONSISTENT BEHAVIOR. The fourth effect of forum talk takes place outside the forum: forums can cause self-restraint in subsequent behavior. The idea is that public talk keeps the commitment salient, which can pull behavior toward it. Forums thus can have the effect of constraining or channeling the pursuit of self-interest.[65] This fourth forum effect is crucial to my claim that states can sustain their

64. Bohman 1996.
65. Elster 1995; Fearon 1998, 55.

collective intentions. Their forum discussion mitigates the problem of violence by generating structures of public reason; their public reason then channels collective outcomes while keeping the rationales for action open to debate. This forum effect also is crucial to my claim that governing together pulls state behavior from the top down, since the public reason surrounding a given commitment in a sense constitutes "the top." That is, public reason is an emergent property of the system rather than an expressed preference or interest of any individual actor.

Like the other forum effects, this effect derives in part from Elster's work. The argument is that when people speak in public, they will find themselves subsequently expected to follow through on commitments based on those rationales, lest they appear hypocritical and lose credibility among their conversation partners. Thus there is what Elster calls a "civilizing force of hypocrisy."[66] Social psychologists have long recognized the pressure people feel to act consistently. The pressure has both internal, psychological roots in the need to resolve cognitive dissonance, and external, social roots, at least in societies where consistency is valued as a personality trait.[67] Recent experimental research supports Elster's more precise claim that making commitments publicly disposes actors to follow through. Visible stands cause us to want to seem consistent. This effect of the forum means that speech acts can have causal power over action, even if they do not match the mental state in the speaker.[68] Since Elster's seminal work, several IR scholars have taken these insights to the international sphere, showing that even strategic or insincere talk among states, when done in public, can cause decision makers to act consistently with their public statements.[69]

While Elster anchors his mechanisms in individual psychology, Ron Krebs and Patrick Jackson argue that there is no need to appeal to psychology to understand the relationship between arguments made in public and the behavior that follows.[70] They define political debate as a struggle over meanings of a situation or problem, where no single actor can impose the meaning. In the contest to see which frame wins, each

66. Elster 1995.
67. Festinger 1957; Cialdini 2009, chapter three.
68. Velleman 1997 makes this argument about individual intentions. It also relates to work by Stasavage 2004 and Naurin 2003, 2006 on negotiation behavior.
69. E.g., Risse, Ropp, and Sikkink 1999; Lynch 1999; Schimmelfennig 2001.
70. Krebs and Jackson 2007.

side tries to legitimate its position using public language. The frames they put forward have to be familiar and acceptable rationales for the group.[71] Each speaker tries to get the rhetorical high ground, to "box out" the opponent's planned action or simply to make the opponent look bad. Actors can be "rhetorically maneuvered into a corner, trapped into publicly endorsing positions" and even taking actions they otherwise would not have done. This "skillful rhetorical maneuvering [doesn't necessarily] persuad[e] one's opponents of the rectitude of one's stance, but [denies] them the rhetorical materials out of which to craft a socially sustainable rebuttal."[72] In short, the emphasis here is on the context of the discussion as having the real causal power, rather than the motivation or psychology of individuals. Public practices produce these rhetorical framing contests, and the realm of action is bounded by the range of actions that fit the winning rhetorical frame.[73]

Krebs and Jackson are interested in the dynamics of framing contexts and in how they produce winners and losers; I am interested in the ability of results of the forum, whatever they are, to pull behavior and in how it manifests collective intentionality. My argument is that by providing a locale with the power to cause a certain type of talking and mode of interaction, forums keep obligations to one another salient, and this pulls behavior toward more talk and away from violence. Through the forum effects of discussion, the invisible hand of the balance of power becomes the visible hand of governing together.

There are two things to take away. First, forums are important. Collective intentions produce their intended outcomes more reliably than an aggregate of individual intentions, even if every member of the group shares the intention. Even if each state privately accepts a particular principle of public reason—say, sovereigns should be supported when there are revolutions—it would not constitute public reason and so would not be part of their collective intention to maintain stability, until jointly articulated and publicly accepted. Each may want privately to avoid war, but if those desires remain private they are less likely to be realized.

---

71. Krebs and Jackson 2007, 46.

72. Krebs and Jackson 2007, 42. See Goddard 2008/9 for empirical application.

73. Mattern's 2005 notion of representational force is similar to rhetorical coercion as Krebs and Jackson develop it, but for Mattern the conditions of success are the thick social ties of friendship, whereas Krebs and Jackson suggest that thinner normative environments actually leave speakers less room for maneuver and so we might be more likely to see speakers having arms twisted.

Second, analytic focus is shifted away from preferences and desires. Collective intentions do not depend for their achievement on high levels of collective identity or culture, and speakers need not become altruists or put aside strategic modes of interaction. Rather, as long as speakers appear in the forum and talk about their commitments, the forum effects dampen the effects of varying motives. It is not that individual desires are irrelevant, but when filtered through collective intentions they come to matter less. In global governance, good outcomes are possible without good intentions.

In sum, sustaining collective intentions among states in anarchy is a challenge. An important tool for doing so is forums. Forums causally produce the types of talking that one would see if actors are following through on their collective intentions. So by making joint commitments and linking them to forums, states are able to govern together.

## Talking about Talk in IR

The forum effects are rooted in claims made and shown by scholars in several disciplines, from which essentially all IR scholarship on the effects of talk has drawn. But at the level of theory, looking only at the IR literature, the particular claims about the power of public talk made above chart a course in between rationalist approaches, which focus on the instrumental use of talk and the material consequences to speakers of some speech acts, and constructivist approaches, which focus on persuasion processes and socialization as the desired outcome of these deliberative processes. From the standpoint of global governing, the rationalist approach is too thin while constructivist alternatives have been too thick.

Addressing rationalist approaches first, while the mechanism and speech acts that constitute the forum effects are consistent with rationalist assumptions, in my framework they produce a whole that is greater than the sum of its parts and has causal power over them. A rational choice perspective would reject the notion of top-down causal power, much less a power rooted in commitment, which seems to challenge its individualist ontology.[74] Insofar as my argument stresses commitments, a rationalist might interpret this through the lens of signaling, where signing on to a commitment signals cooperative intent. The more binding the better, but any commitment is a signal. In rationalist work, signals are behavioral, and costly signals are desirable because the sender can be more certain

74. Müller 2004.

the signal is interpreted correctly. To the extent that this work examines rhetorical moves and treaty making as signals (the costs being audience costs or reputational costs), my argument is consonant.[75] But to suggest that each forum conversation is no more than a signal (invoking public reason signals the cooperative type, perhaps, while disagreement or not showing up signals a revisionist) seems to me conceptual overstretch. It cannot be the case that everything a state does is a form of signaling. If conversations are mere signals, the rationalist would then have to specify what type of action would *not* count as a signal. It also seems odd to talk about a face-to-face conversation as an exchange of signals. As Friedrich Kratochwil stressed a long time ago, human language is a distinct type of signaling system, compared, for example, to animal signaling. Animals use sounds, but human language signals with symbols and concepts "whose communicative function is separate from the sounds used in signaling."[76]

In any case, to some extent I have controlled for the rationalist counterargument by focusing on the Concert of Europe case. Rationalist signaling arguments rely on the assumption that actors know the signals their choices send. But while today states know the signal they send by making commitments or showing up to a particular forum, it was not entirely clear what these signaled in the early Concert period. At that time the whole idea of forum talk was new and untested, and states did not know how to work it in to their strategic calculations. It is all the more surprising, and significant, that the forum had such effects. From here, when we find other instances where states with mixed motives acted consistently with their commitment in an environment where that commitment was linked to a forum, it is reasonable to consider my argument that states can execute collective intentions.

Turning to constructivist approaches, while my claim is that collective intentions, a macrolevel phenomenon, have causal power at the microlevel on the behavior of the units, unlike some constructivist scholarship, the framework does not rely on persuasion or norm internalization. My focus is on action and not preference change.[77] IR scholarship on persuasion as a mechanism for socialization tends to be rooted in a Habermasian framework.[78] While many acknowledge that true Habermasian communi-

---

75. E.g., Thompson 2009.
76. Kratochwil 1989, 6.
77. Checkel 2001. Also see Finnemore 1996.
78. Cf. Johnston 2001.

cative action is a "theoretical paradise" that is "empirically lost,"[79] international institutions are often analyzed as sites for argumentative legitimation[80] and persuasion.[81] Certainly in some cases talking the talk leads to
walking the walk, and a state's preferences change.[82] To take one example,
Nicole Deitelhoff[83] argues that specific design features of the International Criminal Court (ICC) cannot be explained without understanding
the deliberative process that led to the Rome Statute. There were true
persuasive processes in which actors changed their minds because they
were convinced by the power of principled arguments. Actors came to
shared understandings about what the ICC was for, which then gave rise
to a sense of the types of design outcomes that would be legitimate. For
Deitelhoff, what marks these negotiations as true persuasion processes is
that "law and morality" won out over "politics."[84]

Nothing in my framework is meant to rule out that states sometimes
get persuaded of things, or that they internalize norms. When these happen they can deepen commitments, which can be a good thing (or a bad
one!). Still, there are three reasons to distance the framework developed
here and its approach to interstate discussion from a Habermasian model,
and from the goal of internalization more broadly.

First, there are socially beneficial effects of talking that do not rely on
empathy or a sense of common weal. As Fearon argues, even strategic
actors can prefer discussion over acting in silence. Humans have a limited
capacity to know and cannot always identify all of the alternative courses
of action. Discussion lessens the impact of bounded rationality in complex
situations and "increase[s] the odds of making a good choice."[85] It helps
participants clarify the likely consequences of a decision and can lead to
brainstorming and imagining new alternatives that none of the participants could envision prior to gaining the perspective of others. All of these

79. Deitelhoff and Müller 2005. Also see Müller 2001; Diez and Steans 2005.

80. Crawford 2002; Johnstone 2003, 2004; Kornprobst 2008; Bjola 2009; Hurd 2008; Steffek 2003.

81. E.g. Risse 2000; Checkel 2001; Johnston 2001; Payne 2001. Slaughter 2004, too, links
face-to-face talk to a Habermasian story of argumentative persuasion. See Anderson 2005
for critique.

82. E.g., Risse, Ropp, and Sikkink 1999.

83. Deitelhoff 2009.

84. Deitelhoff 2009, 35.

85. Fearon 1998, 49.

beneficial effects are possible despite the fact that participants might have mixed or conflicting motives and are never fully "persuaded."[86]

Second, the premise of Habermasian communicative action oriented toward mutual understanding is that understanding—an "imagined consensus of all hearers"—is reachable. But many theorists question the premise that rational conversation can be assumed to converge on a unitary or singular rational opinion. Public reason in a diverse society necessarily grows out of a "many-sided common sense" rather than any unitary notions of reason, justice, or morality.[87] Moreover, even if we can agree that "arguments not identities" of speakers should determine the outcomes of discussion, and even if all social power could be neutralized in a communicative situation, it is quite possible that no consensus could be reached on how to solve a given problem. Politics at any level tends to involve discussions of complex problems on the ground, and it is not clear that complex problems could lend themselves to one ideal reasonable solution. In groups that lack shared values "reason underdetermines, if not basic values themselves, at least their relative weight and priority when they come into conflict. And they will conflict: value pluralism defines an inharmonious moral universe."[88]

Third, that premise also assumes that an imagined consensus of all hearers is a desirable ideal for international politics. But a focus on consensus conflates governing with socialization, and in the current international environment that means socialization to liberal cosmopolitan norms. This conflation is evident in some Habermasian influenced persuasion work in IR, where international persuasion processes are usually linked to narratives in which the nonliberal sovereign is persuaded to adopt liberal and supranational norms and rules.[89] It also is evident in Deitelhoff's argument that persuasion allowed law to triumph over politics in the ICC case. But as James Bohman and Craig Calhoun each have argued in a more general context, given the diversity, scale, and complexity of social life, deliberative processes should not be treated as an ide-

86. See Bohman, who defines dialogue as "ordinary deliberation," the exchange of reasons necessary for solving joint problems, in which "various claims are often mixed together so that it is difficult to tell in advance what type of reason will be convincing in any particular situation." Bohman 1996, 42.

87. Bohman 1997, 186; Fraser 1992.

88. Galston 2010, 396.

89. E.g., Risse, Ropp, and Sikkink 1999. See Diez and Steans 2005 for discussion of the use of Habermas in IR scholarship. Also Anderson 2005, 1292.

alized process aimed at unity or consensus. Rather, discussion should be treated, in Bohman's words, as a "form of cooperative social action to solve a problem, part of an ongoing dialogical process of settling common problems and conflicts."[90] Public discourse in a plural society—and international society is definitely that—must be able to sustain itself across different cultural values and ways of understanding the world. It must accommodate our "lines of difference" and accept that maintaining those differences is compatible with the public good.[91]

Jens Steffek extends this way of thinking to international politics. As he puts it, governing together in anarchy is about building bridges across states, not closing gaps between them.[92] Often among states agreeing to disagree is an accomplishment, and when there are agreements many are going to be what Steffek, following Cass Sunstein, calls "incompletely theorized," agreements where the parties agree on what to do even if not on the principle their action represents or expresses.[93] It is not always the case that states that face common problems must share common values too. The political problems that bring states together do not necessarily respect value divides. To capture the irreducible pluralism of international politics, it makes more sense to use a framework oriented toward the thinner normativity of acting together.

## Empirical Implications

This chapter has developed a framework for thinking about global governing as states concerting their power for common public interests, drawing on the concept of collective intentionality. When states commit to address particular problems together they can constitute a public power beyond the state with the capacity to steer international political outcomes. Having in this chapter conceptualized international public power and offered the hypothesis about the role of joint commitments and forum discussion in producing it, in the remaining chapters I explore three empirical claims.

The first is that there are preconditions for a set of actors to govern together. Governing cannot emerge whole cloth from just any aggregate of

90. Bohman 1996, 25–26, 34.
91. Calhoun 1998, 29–30.
92. Steffek 2005.
93. Steffek 2005. See Sunstein 1995.

individual actors. It requires social order, which means actors that share reliable institutions to mitigate the problem of violence. Chapter three charts the development of these preconditions in European international society, that is, the decline of communal bonds as the basis for political interaction and rise of bonds that were more impersonal and generalizable. The chapter also argues that the Vienna Settlement marks a key turning point that made governing together possible for states. The history covered is well-charted territory, but here it is combined in a new way, specifically to show how the practice of states forming collective intentions became possible in 1815. Because commitments and forums at first glance might appear to be epiphenomenal, that is, effects of some deeper cause that actually produces the outcome of the long peace, a key goal is to show that the main candidate for a deeper cause—thick transnational ties of class and culture—cannot account for the long peace. Such ties existed long before 1815 and did little to mitigate violence. Quite the contrary: those cultural norms rationalized and produced the war-prone system. Arguably the developments that muted the political relevance of family are what made governing together possible.

The second empirical claim has to do with the mechanism of the forum effects. When states commit to address a problem together, talking in a forum affects their speech acts and produces particular norms of speech. In chapter four, I show how the prospect of meeting in a forum affected how leaders of the Concert powers talked to one another. The focus in chapters five, six, and seven is more on how the sovereigns talked about and reacted to their forums rather than the conversations inside the forums. Once a commitment to address a problem together and the option of meeting existed, state leaders spoke and acted as if obligated to one another about those problems. They acknowledged the power of meetings to affect their behavior and did not want to meet if they did not want to act on the commitment.

Third, if I am right that governing together is a case of collective intentionality, then commitments and forums together should lead to collective self-restraint and actions consistent with the commitment. I show this in chapters four and five, where great power rivals were able to avoid war, manifesting a collective self-restraint that had not been possible in the eighteenth century and would not have been possible without their forum. These chapters each individually show evidence of the forum effects; taken together they lend some support to the macrolevel claim that the collective intention had some causal power.

Chapter five shows how a relationship of discussion developed among the Concert powers, which enabled them to keep their commitment and avoid war. Without a commitment such collective self-restraint was not possible, as I show in chapter six. The 1850s and 1820s cases have much in common: the same major states, roughly the same problem of containing a Russo-Turkish War, and similarly high levels of Concert discussion. However, the construction of a common problem and a commitment to address it together was missing in the 1850s. It is difficult to decisively demonstrate that this lack is what accounts for the difference in outcomes. But it is at least as plausible an explanation as competing explanations of the Crimean War and has the advantage of being more precise: it pinpoints the moment in diplomacy where a commitment could have made a difference and shows what that difference could have been.[94]

Taken as a whole, the goal of the empirical chapters is to tell a plausible story that the Concert of Europe was an instance of states governing together as an international public power. In other words, neither extrapolitical community nor bottom-up dynamics alone can account for the Concert's achievements. The story in turn supports my hypothesis that states can steer the international social order toward public interests through their commitments.

93. Bennett and Elman 2007, 175; Levy 2008, 10.

# CHAPTER THREE

# From International Society to Public Power

In this book I propose that there is a dimension of global governance constituted by states acting together as an international public power. When states commit to address a problem together and link that commitment to forums, they can concert their power toward public ends. My argument includes the claims that, first, international public power became possible in 1815 with the Vienna Settlement ending the Napoleonic Wars, and second, the great powers jointly, intentionally produced the long peace that followed.

This chapter develops the first claim. I first establish the historical preconditions for states to form a public power together, narrating the rise of international society between Westphalia and Napoleon. In this period, Europe evolved from a system of hierarchy under king and pope, where sovereigns competed for precedence, to an anarchical society of sovereign states, which increasingly was organized according to their relative power rather than relationships to god and one another. However, forming a society—being "conscious of certain common interests and common values ... [and believing] themselves to be bound by a common set of rules ... and share in the working of common institutions"[1]—is not the same thing as governing together—jointly directing state behavior toward shared goals and projects. Governing together entails the ability to take a first person plural or "we" perspective about the use of power. For it to be possible among the sovereign corporate units, these states must acknowledge a shared, public space among them and also commit

1. Bull 1977, 13.

to manage or steer it together. With this in mind, in the second part of the chapter I show how the Napoleonic Wars mark a turning point. The fact that their former balance of power practices could not defeat the Napoleonic threat made statesmen willing to experiment in the hopes of securing continental peace. The Vienna Settlement was then a creative leap, not predicted by any previous settlement. Prior to Vienna there was no way for the rhetorical ideal of European peace to have collective behavioral pull. I suggest in this chapter that a conjunction of contingent events enabled European statesmen to make these ideas concrete and to steer their social order.

The history covered in this chapter is familiar terrain, charted by historians, historical constructivists, and English School scholars. My purpose is narrow: to provide historical evidence of the rise of particular conditions among European states that made it possible for interstate commitments and forums to have the power I am proposing they have after 1815. The evidence in this chapter allows me to address two counterarguments for the nineteenth-century long peace that would make these factors epiphenomenal. First, some might argue that transnational thick ties of family and religion had sufficient causal power to produce peace in the wake of Napoleon even absent commitments and forums. But the chapter shows that these ties governed relations long before 1815 and did little to mitigate violence. Indeed, norms associated with those ties rationalized a competitive, war-prone system; arguably the institutional developments muting their political relevance are what made the peace possible.

Second, others might take issue with my argument that the peace was produced intentionally, arguing that societal institutions were sufficient to keep the peace as long as state interests were aligned. But one of the central institutions of international society as Hedley Bull defines it is great power management, which is a relationship of responsibility in which the most powerful states self-consciously produce order.[2] In other words, Bull's understanding of society smuggles in an aspect of intentionality. To the extent that international society includes this particular institution, then, I agree with the criticism. However, it seems worthwhile to keep normative integration, which can operate at the level of habit or practical consciousness, analytically distinct from intentionally governing together, which operates at the level of discursive consciousness. Recalling the antitrust law analogy suggested in chapter one, collusion among firms (coop-

2. Bull 1977, chapter nine, esp. 207ff.

erating to engineer a particular social outcome) is ascertained and distinguished from the mere pursuit of self-interest (where the social outcome is not intended or produced together) often by looking for evidence that firms actively attempted to reduce uncertainty about one another's behavior and one another's sphere of independent action. Communication and openness among the firms in question and information sharing are considered evidence of collusion, and the implication is that the actors are accountable for the social outcomes only in the latter case.[3] In this chapter I lay the institutional foundations for the possibility of collusion among the great powers to produce European stability.

## The Rise of International Society

It has been part of the disciplinary common sense in IR that sovereign states are the central actors in a balance of power system with ongoing communication and shared institutions, and that this system was born in 1648 with the Treaties of Westphalia. Yet it also is generally accepted that Westphalia was not a "switch" transforming medieval into modern relations.[4] In this section I dip into the history of European political relations from Westphalia to Napoleon. My stylized account stresses institutions that made concerting power possible among states: institutions enabling a secular practice of commitment among corporate actors and anchoring their ongoing communication.

### From Religious Hierarchy to Secular Anarchy

The modern states system grew out of and overlapped with a Europe ordered more by dynasty and Christianity than by territorial sovereignty and the balance of power. In the early modern period, absolutism and the divine right of kings dictated that kings held the land by God's will, and part of divine right was a sense that kings must protect and preserve their inheritance, by war if necessary. Manipulating one's inheritance through marriages and successions was the main means of securing control. Succession claims were considered legal rights, but because there was no ac-

3. Del Mar 2011, 111–12.
4. There is a large literature critical of the Westphalian assumption. E.g., Krasner 1999; Osiander 2001; Croxton 1999; Philpott 2001; Hall 1999; Teschke 2002.

cepted adjudicatory institution or procedure, negotiations over disputed successions often resulted in war.[5] War was considered a legitimate mode of dispute resolution and celebrated as heroic. Monarchs looked for opportunities to engage in it in order to achieve personal glory.[6]

European sovereigns considered treaties to be private contracts among kings that obligated particular individuals, not the state, and signers, not successors.[7] This meant the death of a monarch could profoundly affect the distribution power. Agreements among sovereigns were thus "one-shot" deals, and because they were neither enforceable nor self-enforcing, time horizons were short. To lengthen them, sovereigns looked to a variety of measures, especially religious guarantees. In the fifteenth and sixteenth centuries papal validation of a treaty was seen as the highest form of binding oneself, and the pope also had the authority to relieve a prince of his obligations to other princes.[8]

The basis of what we would call "international" law in medieval times was Christian theology, since Europe was held to be a unified Christian empire under God. F. H. Hinsley notes that the term "Europe" did not have a political meaning in the Middle Ages. Europe was a geographical space; the political unit was Christendom.[9] Guides to international law referred to several different types of political units—states, companies, and other groups, each with the capacity to make what we would call foreign policy and to engage in war, and individuals rather than states were the rights-bearing members. Natural law principles rather than actual practices stood as the authority for how Christendom should operate politically in most of this scholarship.[10]

The intra-Christian wars of the Reformation, however, were difficult to reconcile with this legal framework, since they essentially were wars over the validity of the framework itself. Over the course of the sixteenth century, Europe increasingly came to be populated by political units with

---

5. Hatton 1980, 15n39; Wolf 1951, 3.

6. Historical constructivists whose work engages with the early modern period include Nexon 2009; Reus-Smit 1999; Ruggie 1993. Also see Anderson 1993; Black 1999; Hinsley 1963. The classic history of Renaissance diplomacy is Mattingly 1955.

7. Dunn 1929, 9.

8. Nicolson 1954, 39–40. Other forms of guarantee also were attempted: pledging valuable possessions, calling on witnesses or external ratifiers, exchanging valuable hostages. See Satow 1925.

9. Hinsley 1963, 156.

10. Bull 1977, 29ff.; Anderson 1993, 47–48; Duchhardt 2000, 283–84.

different value systems, which called into question the notion of a universal community. The Reformation also heightened the sense of threat posed by universal monarchy, since shared values and interests with any potential hegemon could no longer be presumed.[11] The shift to a secular language of Europe and its balance of power in the sixteenth and seventeenth centuries can be seen as an effort to reground international law and establish shared rules that could stabilize relations for an increasingly diverse group.

The peace conferences at Westphalia were a turning point in this respect. They were institutionally innovative in that the participants neutralized the cities and put states in continuous communication, and in that the resulting settlement was recognized throughout Europe. The treaties also were guaranteed "horizontally" by fellow sovereign states (France and Sweden) rather than "vertically" by the pope or emperor.[12] Nonetheless, in many ways these "semi-chaotic assemblages"[13] reflected the practices of the time. Three years were necessary simply to sort through issues of precedence and method, leading not only to the necessity of convening two separate conferences (at Münster and Osnabrück) but also to the awkward method of proceeding entirely through written communication among delegates, carried between them by mediators.

After Westphalia, dynastic, Christian Europe increasingly coexisted with secular, balance of power Europe, and the patterns of war and peace making in this period reflected a mix of old and new. The period between 1700 and 1790 saw many different wars among various combinations of European powers.[14] Some were fueled by geopolitical rivalries (e.g., the Great Northern War), but many were rooted in disputed successions (e.g., the War of Spanish Succession).[15] The mix of old and new is particularly evident when looking at the rise of two institutions of international society, the balance of power and public international law.

11. Duchhardt 2000, 282; Little 1989.

12. Headlam-Morley 1927, 154; Satow 1925.

13. Langhorne 1981/82, 67.

14. Precise counts differ. For example, Rothenberg 1989, 201 identifies sixteen wars in this time period. Holsti 1991, 48, operating on a slightly different time span, counts thirty-three bilateral and multilateral European wars between the Peace of Utrecht and the Congress of Vienna (1713/15–1814/15).

15. Bukovansky 2002. See also Doyle 1992, 265; Cronin 1999, 45–46; Schroeder 1993, 50; Hall 1999, chapter four.

BALANCE OF POWER. The idea of the balance of power has a long pedigree in political thought, but it was not part of the broader European political discourse in the sixteenth and seventeenth centuries, and it is far different from the hierarchical and unified conception of Christendom dominant at the time of the religious wars.[16] After the Treaties of Westphalia, however, the idea that Europe was a single system operating according to a secular logic increasingly came to dominate the political calculations of the period.[17]

First, after Westphalia, "Europe" increasingly replaced a stress on Christendom in European diplomacy. Its components were seen as juridically sovereign and as independent, equal parts of this political whole. Europe increasingly was treated in secular terms as "the sum of its historical and political parts," a geopolitical unit rather than a geographical locale or synonym for Christendom.[18] Andreas Osiander[19] points to the Treaty of Utrecht (1713) ending the War of Spanish Succession as the first modern treaty explicitly to use the language of seeking stability through balancing or equilibrium. At Utrecht, the European system was treated as an "imaginary super-actor" whose stability was an "acknowledged official aim of the European actors." The notion that passion, greed, and private interests should be subordinated to this higher, common interest was an important legitimating idea used to get people to support specific policies and for face saving when actors were forced to back down.[20] Increasing secularization was evident in international treaties later in the century as well: religious oaths and references to natural law declined as references to Europe increased in texts of the eighteenth century.[21] It also was evident in the evolution of "peace schemes," which increasingly envisioned European peace through a system of relative equals.[22]

Second, from Utrecht on, the idea of Europe as a system, characterized by an "unavoidable, quasi-law-like connection and interdependence of states," began to be applied in European diplomacy.[23] There still was a sense of belonging to a "whole" whose primary interest was peace and

16. Vagts 1948, 85, 89; Little 2007.
17. Vagts and Vagts 1979, 558–59; Langhorne 1981/82.
18. Hinsley 1963, 157.
19. Osiander 1994.
20. Osiander 1994, 112–17.
21. Bull 1977, 33.
22. Hinsley 1963, 37.
23. Osiander 1994; Vagts 1948, 85; Vagts and Vagts 1979, 560; Little 1989, 2007.

in whose name all peace-minded diplomacy was aimed, only now that whole was treated as a system rather than as a community under God. Over the course of the eighteenth century, balance of power talk increasingly was linked to the mechanistic ideas then gaining currency in Enlightenment Europe. Historians differ on precisely when balance of power thinking became dominant and thinking in terms of dynasty yielded.[24] But as Paul Schroeder shows, balance of power thinking is reflected in eighteenth-century alliance behavior, where war loyalties largely were bargained according to generally accepted rules of "compensation." Alliances were business transactions, paid for and measured in terms of material gain. Any given war involved numerous such transactions, and the deals and combinations often could not be predicted.[25] There was no expectation of loyalty, not even familial, and states often were as suspicious of their alliance partners as of their adversaries. In fact, it was common practice for a state to leave an alliance midwar if it felt it could cut a better deal with the adversary than the deal it had made with its initial ally.[26] The balance of power system based on transactions among dynasts made the eighteenth-century system fluid, and especially during the second half of the century the system was competitive and zero sum. It was a system in which cooperation was difficult, eyes were focused on short-run, narrowly self-interested calculations, and no state could fully trust any other.

However, according to the mechanistic thinking of the time, this was not a bad thing. If each sovereign pursued her or his self-interest in the balance of power system, the interests of the whole would be the outcome. This meant that no state needed consciously to restrain itself or to speak in terms of any larger interest. The superactor of Europe may have appeared as a legitimating device at peace conferences, but at the level of day-to-day strategic practice, self-interest sufficed. Inis Claude would call this an automatic balance of power system.[27] That is, although the termi-

---

24. E.g., Ingrao 1994, 681–82, 689 argues that there is a sharp divide in 1763. Before 1763, states thought in terms of dynasty, not balance of power. Hinsley 1963, 169–73, 178 argues that by 1748 the secular balance of power had replaced the dynastic one. Schroeder 1994 assimilates the dynastic and balance of power logics and argues that what's going on throughout the eighteenth century is a disagreement on the ideal balance of power in Europe, which led each state to seek expansion.

25. Schroeder 1993, 49–50; Rothenberg 1989, 206.

26. Schroeder 1993, 61; Bruun 1965; Langhorne 1981/82.

27. Claude 1962, 46.

nology did not yet exist, the balance of power functioned essentially for these statesmen as an "invisible hand" of international politics.

PUBLIC INTERNATIONAL LAW. After Westphalia, the Christian moorings of international law increasingly came undone in favor of a law anchored by state practices. Legal thought increasingly gave a nearly unlimited right to sovereigns (but only to sovereigns) to wage war and to determine the justness of a war's cause, while law concerning the actual conduct of war increasingly tended to limit how war was waged.[28]

It is useful in this respect to consider the writings of Emmerich de Vattel. Writing in the mid-eighteenth century and responding to the need for a modus vivendi after the religious wars, Vattel begins with the assumption that states and not individuals are the rights-bearing units of the European system. These states were sovereign equals, existing in a state of nature where they were the sole judges of right and wrong and of their rights and obligations. Res publica Christiana, the single, overarching community, did not play a role: there is "by no means the same necessity for a civil society among Nations as among individuals."[29] Vattel's work exemplifies the sense developing among legal scholars that the anarchical system was a distinct type of social system and the balance of power was a "necessary object of policy."[30] Additionally, Vattel marks an important shift toward a positive law of nations,[31] that is, law based on consent and state practice. Vattel discussed aggressive war, preventive war, and intervention, and laid out a precise legal definition of neutrality as well as strictures regarding justice in war.[32]

The rise of states and state practice as authoritative is reflected in another noteworthy development of the eighteenth century: the midcentury publication of all interstate treaties since Westphalia by the Abbe de Mably, who "assert[ed] that this was the basis of Europe's public law."[33] By the late eighteenth century it became common to speak in terms of practice-based law—the public law of Europe or "international law."[34]

---

28. Duchhardt 2000, 284.
29. Hinsley 1963, 167–68.
30. Hinsley 1963, 167–68.
31. Bull 1977, 33ff.; Doyle 1992, 269.
32. Duchhardt 2000, 297–98; Simpson 2004, 32.
33. Hinsley 1963, 166.
34. Bull 1977, 33; Suganami 1978.

And by the time of the Napoleonic Wars there was a sense in legal and diplomatic discourse of a state system with laws premised on consent and practice. It is difficult to assess precisely how these legal changes affected state behavior in this period, but it is noteworthy that both Grotius's and Vattel's manuals were widely read among sovereigns, diplomats, bureaucrats, generals/military, and the emerging reading public.[35]

EUROPEAN SOCIETY.    As the Napoleonic Wars began, there was a mix of old and new. Old-style glorification of monarchical rule persisted. But there also was a movement away from a system based on vertical, religious relationships between sovereigns and God to one based on horizontal, secular relationships among sovereigns themselves. This movement is evident in the incorporation of Russia and the Ottoman Empire, neither of which were signatories to the Treaties of Westphalia, into Europe's balance of power system.[36]

The Treaty of Carlowitz (1699), which ended the Austro-Ottoman War, marks the first time that Russia and the Ottoman Empire were parties to a European congress and a European brokered peace treaty. From then on, and particularly after Peter the Great's victory in the Great Northern War of 1700–1721, which showed that Russia clearly had the material power to "shake the overall equilibrium of Europe,"[37] Russia was fully integrated in the European system. Importantly, Russia was not part of Europe due to any "feelings of friendship."[38] Russia's Orthodox Christianity was different from the Christianity of the other European powers, Catholic or Protestant, and many Russian cultural practices were alien to other Europeans. Russia was part of Europe's marriage system, but its sovereigns did not follow all of the rules.[39] The other European sovereigns respected Russia's power, but they still saw it as backward and even as culturally inferior.

Ottoman diplomatic integration into Europe was far more halting.[40] The Ottoman Empire was a regular participant in eighteenth-century European diplomacy, increasing its diplomatic connections, especially

35. Duchhardt 2000, 288–89.

36. England also was not a signatory of the Treaties of Westphalia and spent much of the century focused on internal conflicts. From around 1660, however, England played more of a role in continental affairs. Ogg 1970.

37. Neumann and Pouliot 2011, 125; Watson 1985; Neumann and Welsh 1991; Naff 1984.

38. Neumann and Pouliot 2011, 125–26.

39. Neumann and Pouliot 2011, 123, 128.

40. Mangone 1954, 24. Also Jelavich 1983, 54; Lewis 1968; Adanir 2005, 397.

with France, and joining alliances and signing treaties. However, Europeans still tended to treat and talk about the Ottomans as barbarians and infidels. For example, political thinkers of the eighteenth century who envisioned a European federation tended to balk at the inclusion of Russia, and excluded the Ottoman Empire. Indeed, the European union they envisioned functioned in part to preserve and defend the "reputation of Christianity" against infidels, especially "the Turk."[41] Still, the norms and rules of European interaction no longer excluded non-Christians a priori.

The differential incorporation of Russia and the Ottoman Empire relate to the criteria I am developing for governing together in two ways. First, the political solidarity of being a public together rests on a prior sense of interdependence and of sharing a set of rules and norms. In the European case, system consciousness was increasing, manifest in decision makers' balance of power discourse. War was prevalent, but ordered and contained: the power to make war now resided squarely with states whose sovereigns controlled the war decision, and war had clear, accepted causes and rationales. The goal was no longer to overturn the system but to keep it in balance. Second, being a public together is a thin political bond among strangers who do not necessarily share extrapolitical bonds. Among European sovereigns, dynastic ties and shared Christian identity did not disappear or become wholly irrelevant. Part of their relevance was the continued energy they gave to disputes and wars. At the same time, extrapolitical moralities of family or god no longer fully dictated political interactions. This was important in a period in which Russia and the Ottoman Empire were hard to exclude from the balance of power system. The new mode of interacting was aimed not at universalizing Christendom but at achieving a modus vivendi. The two Eastern powers were unavoidably part of the balance of power system and the rules for problem solving increasingly accommodated them.

### Diplomacy

Modes and norms of communication changed after Westphalia as well. Diplomacy had long been marked off as a discrete mode of communication with its own rules regarding representation and diplomatic activities.

41. Hinsley 1963, 34. These were not aggressive ideas, although they were exclusive. Hinsley points out that Abbé de St. Pierre included both Russia and the Ottoman Empire in the 1712 version of his peace plan, but dropped the Ottoman Empire in later versions. Also Mastnak 1998.

But in the sixteenth and seventeenth centuries, political communication was not systematic or regular. Many different kinds of actors had diplomatic representation—princes negotiated with such various actors as groups of merchants or even private individuals. Diplomats of the time often were merely "letter writers," without the power to commit the king, and sovereigns conducted foreign affairs themselves, in secret. Ambassadors on embassy could not be sure their religious practices would be tolerated by local sovereigns.[42]

Ceremony and issues of precedence heavily encumbered diplomatic practice in this period, and conferences after Westphalia at times were held up on such issues.[43] The pope and Holy Roman emperor were given precedence over all other princes, and at multistate gatherings, personal rivalries guided interactions more than sovereign equality. When convening conferences, states spent a lot of energy simply deciding where to enter and where to sit, who would sign first (often several copies of an agreement were made so that each party could sign on top), whether to proceed in writing, through informal discussions, or through speeches, and so on.[44] Disputes among ambassadors on these issues were sometimes settled by duels.[45]

Overall, the norm of diplomacy was more deception than communication. Diplomacy was seen as an "instrument of the aggressive, distrustful and untrustworthy monarchies which now completely dominated European political life, not as a restraint upon them."[46] States often used diplomats to undermine one another's regimes, representatives abroad often were in danger, and hostages were necessary to secure interstate agreements.

INSTITUTIONAL CHANGES. In the eighteenth century, institutional changes increased the separation of the personal from the political in European diplomacy. The evolution of diplomacy shows that the corporate body of the state was replacing the individual monarch as the sovereign subject of international law.

First, with the norm of extraterritoriality or diplomatic immunity, vio-

---

42. Anderson 1993, 4; Spruyt 1994; Wolf 1951, 5–6; Mattingly 1988, 23ff.; Nicholson 1954, 35.
43. Mangone 1954, 37–38; Langhorne 1981/82, 1990; Nicolson 1954.
44. Nicolson 1954, 42–46; Mangone 1954.
45. Doyle 1992, 268; Nicolson 1954, 63–64; Wolf 1951, 6.
46. Anderson 1993, 40; Nicolson 1954.

lence by and toward diplomats declined. By the early eighteenth century it became generally accepted among the states of Europe that envoys would not be murdered or imprisoned, and that weapons were not permitted in negotiations.[47] Second, diplomacy became increasingly secularized. Fewer clergy were used as ambassadors or mediators as the eighteenth century progressed, and French replaced Latin as the language of diplomacy.[48] A shared understanding developed that ambassadors officially represented the king or government. This was not always followed, but in general ambassadors had power to commit the state. Foreign affairs in the eighteenth century were autocratic—the king monopolized policy making and a good deal of secrecy remained. But diplomats could at least execute policy on the monarch's behalf—the exchange and recognition of formal powers was the first joint activity at conferences.[49]

Third, in the eighteenth century diplomacy began to be recognized as an official activity and a profession, not to mention a distinct sphere of activity—foreign affairs—within the state. This was a period of bureaucratization. Foreign ministries began to emerge within states and permanent embassies spread throughout Europe, regularizing communication among the major powers. Louis XIV's France was the forerunner, followed closely by Peter the Great's Russia.[50] Prussia, Sweden, Russia, Spain, and Austria followed, with England lagging a few decades behind. States attempted to standardize the training of diplomats and to draw ambassadors from this group rather than from the clergy or landed nobles, since the primary loyalty of this new official class was to the state itself.[51] The professionalization of diplomacy entailed a shift in its norms toward a greater stress on honesty and fair dealing. If not always evident in diplomats' practices, these norms were clearly evident in the manuals on diplomatic method that emerged in the seventeenth and eighteenth centuries. By the time Callières wrote in the late eighteenth century, diplomacy was seen as a core institution of the society of states whose goal was to "reconcil[e] conflicting interests and ambitions and facilitat[e] coexistence."[52]

47. Mattingly 1988; Hatton 1980, 7–8; Langhorne 1981/82, 65–66; McKay and Scott 1983; Ruggie 1993, 164–65.

48. Wolf 1951, 7; Doyle 1992, 268.

49. Doyle 1992, 268; Wolf 1951, 4, 7.

50. Nicolson 1954.

51. McKay and Scott 1983, 206.

52. Anderson 1993, 46.

CONFERENCES AND CONGRESSES.[53]    Alongside the trend of professionaliz-
ing communication was a complementary trend toward multilateral, face-
to-face meetings to end wars and/or construct peace settlements. Precedence and method issues made such meetings difficult to convene and
run, however, and they did not necessarily result in binding agreements.

At Oliva (1660), for example, it took a month of written exchanges for
negotiators to agree to engage in verbal discussions rather than proceed
(as at Westphalia) through written submissions.[54] At Nijmegen (1676–79)
participants insisted that their representatives enter the room, sit, and sign
the agreement at exactly the same time, on identical chairs. Procedurally,
the advance at this conference was to "declare . . . that titles assumed or
omitted by any ruler did not prejudice the rights of anyone."[55] This prevented sovereigns in conference from asserting broader dominions than
they in fact held—such as the emperor calling himself the Duke of Bur-
gundy, the King of Spain referring to himself as the King of France, and
so on. Additionally, the city was neutralized for the conference, citing the
precedent of Westphalia.[56] At Ryswyck (1697), the agreed-upon procedure was written submissions, supplemented by private discussions and
two formal meetings per week. However, Louis XIV's nonrecognition
of William III as ruler of England led to a second level of secret meetings between French and English ambassadors, rendering the conference
meaningless.[57]

Precedence issues were more easily resolved at the next two major
European conferences, Carlowitz (1699) and Utrecht (1713), but even
with precedence out of the way, conferences did not always accomplish
their tasks. At Carlowitz, four doors were built so all delegations could
enter simultaneously, which accommodated their precedence concerns;
from here participants finally agreed to proceed informally in a neutralized "conference village." At Utrecht, participants agreed to enter
the conference room and sit in no fixed order and to sign treaties alpha-
betically.[58] Yet even with precedence out of the way, conferences did not

53. This section draws heavily on Langhorne 1981/82, 67–75. Also see Lossky 1970.

54. Langhorne 1981/82, 69.

55. Langhorne 1981/82, 70.

56. Langhorne 1981/82, 70; Roelofsen 1980, 112–13; Hatton 1980, 8.

57. Langhorne 1981/82, 70–71; Lossky 1970, 169–70.

58. Only the emperor was still concerned with precedence, and the conference allowed
him to enter the room before the other delegations and to sit opposite a mirror rather than
directly face any other sovereign. Osiander 1994, 108ff.; Langhorne 1981/82.

always accomplish very much. As one publicist, noted by Gerard Mangone, pointed out, "nothing happened [at Utrecht] but Compliments ... and everything (else) that might retard the Conclusion of the Great and Good Work" of peace making.[59] Utrecht meetings took place while the War of Spanish Succession was still being fought, and its multilateral aspect broke down within two months. Everyone wanted France to proceed with written submissions, while France wanted verbal discussion. As a result, separate, private negotiations led to a series of bilateral treaties.[60] After Utrecht, the conference trend died down in the eighteenth century, and several wars ended without them.

As discussed above, eighteenth-century sovereigns were struggling to find some arbiter of their interests in a Europe where the supranational authorities of church and emperor were no longer recognized. The conferences were attempted in a sense as a substitute, but they did not always work. Jeremy Black points out that

> the Congresses of Cambria and Soissons were linked to the development of a system of collective security involving reciprocal guarantees. . . . [However, t]hey failed to produce a satisfactory solution to the problems affecting European relations, essentially because the irreconcilable interests of the major powers were made more apparent through the process of negotiation. The arbiter of disputes remained the battlefield.[61]

A meeting at Aix-la-Chapelle (1748) was called to end the War of Austrian Succession, but the multilateral aspect was minimal. Prussia and Austria had made peace in 1745; this was an attempt to generalize the peace to Europe. But the participants were suspicious of one another's intentions and wary of convening. Britain and France called the Aix-la-Chapelle meeting, and a series of "bilateral deceptions" by France secured the agreement.[62] The Seven Years' War ended without a general congress because France rejected the idea. There was instead a small set of meetings at Augsburg (1762) to settle only the German questions, which lasted six weeks and included one representative from each of the German states.[63]

59. Mangone 1954, 23.
60. Langhorne 1981/82, 72–73; Osiander 1994, 122; Mangone 1954, 22.
61. Black 1999, 326.
62. Langhorne 1981/82, 73.
63. Langhorne 1981/82, 74.

Conferences at Focsani and Bucharest in 1772–73 between Russia and the Ottoman Empire, with Prussian and Austrian mediation, failed to produce a peace. Finally, the Congress at Teschen (1779) was called to end the Austro-Prussian war. Russia and France offered to mediate the settlement and then guaranteed the final outcome. Procedurally this was an entirely informal congress among the four states, which simply reviewed the text of a settlement that already had been negotiated.[64]

In sum, by the time of the Napoleonic Wars multilateral congresses to end wars were not uncommon, but they were not treated as tools for managing international conflict, settling disputes, or solving shared problems. Congresses took place after wars to divide the spoils. Public international law played little role, and private interests dominated negotiations. The resulting settlements tended to be collections of bilateral agreements rather than comprehensive settlements for Europe. Perhaps most importantly, while they did take place periodically, there was by no means a settled expectation that congresses would be held following crises or wars.

A VISIBLE SOCIETY.    The relationship of being a public together requires not only that participants share basic rules and institutions (society), but also that they communicate with one another about the terms of common life. This suggests that their power has to be broadly visible to one another. The trends in diplomacy and conferences outlined above made their power more visible.

First, to summarize the above, permanent embassies and the dampening of competitive norms in diplomacy helped create a distinct realm for conversation among states.[65] Tracing through the multilateral congresses, the waning of precedence issues and decline of references to familial bonds in joint discussions can be interpreted as the emergence of a norm of sovereign equality. Conferences could proceed only once hierarchy and private personal bonds had been neutralized or at least subordinated. Of course, meeting face to face could not guarantee that actors would come to agreement, much less an agreement that represented any "collective" interest or that would be treated as binding. Conferences in the eighteenth century often were unsuccessful simply because interests clashed. Still, the ability to engage in discussions, bilaterally and in groups,

64. Langhorne 1981/82, 74–75; Mangone 1954, 25.
65. Improved roads in Europe also helped make ongoing communication easier. Langhorne 1981/82, 65–66.

became taken for granted among European sovereigns in this period. The conference was an accepted diplomatic tool.

Second, increasingly the work of these forums was given permanence and made visible beyond the small group of decision makers. Treaty printing and record keeping of international events was more common in the eighteenth century than the seventeenth, and a sporadic practice arose of designating official secretaries at conferences to keep records of the events.[66] Such record keeping, along with the large delegations that attended conferences, raised the visibility of international politics to those outside the narrow sphere of the king and court. One could not say that there was civil society in all of the European great powers of the time, much less a Europe-wide public capable of forming opinion on international affairs.[67] But, for example, the English translator of a study of the conference at Nijmegen speculated that its primary audience might not be "public persons who could benefit practically from the study of Nijmegen peace," but rather those who would read out of a sheer "love of speculation and knowledge."[68]

The audience for political affairs expanded beyond "public persons" mainly through the development of the weekly newspaper and the advent of the political pamphlet. Regularized postal routes helped to make possible the transmission of information throughout the continent.[69] By the end of the seventeenth century, around the time of Nijmegen, several European states had weekly newspapers.[70] The news contained in the papers was largely of political events, and sometimes consisted of the reprinting of political documents. A major function of the newspaper was to facilitate intercourt communication, and as such newspapers were seen as a "service industry" for rulers. But group subscriptions and public readings of the news widened the sphere of those capable of talking about politics beyond the court and even beyond the literate few.[71] The political pamphlet was a seventeenth-century innovation that also became common in the eighteenth century.[72] In other words, actors outside of official

66. Anderson 1993, 86–87.

67. Goldstein 1983.

68. This was published only in English, according to Hatton 1980, 14.

69. Gestrich 2006.

70. Weber 2006, 397.

71. Weber 2006, 408ff.; Anderson 1993, 37–46.

72. Nicolson 1954, 54. For a study of the role of the political pamphlet in consolidating royal power in seventeenth-century France, see Sawyer 1991.

decision-making forums of the state were beginning to know about and discuss the affairs of the state, and there was more attention to the need for public support of political decisions.

The eighteenth century saw several publications on international politics meant for a wide audience. These included peace projects and news magazines devoted to more general criticism of foreign affairs.[73] The Abbé de Saint-Pierre, secretary to the French delegation at Utrecht, published his two-volume *Project to Establish Perpetual Peace* in Europe in 1713, with new editions and a third volume in 1729 and 1738.[74] Rousseau edited the volumes and in 1765 published them with commentary including his own vision of a European federation for peace. In 1795, with the French revolutionary wars underway, Kant published *On Perpetual Peace*. This sold exceptionally well in the 1790s, and a new edition was published the next year, along with translations in French and English.[75] These were not Europe's first visions of federation, to be sure, but are noteworthy in their wide dissemination and in their prescriptions for European-level mechanisms. Other scholars and critics emerged, especially in France. While focused mainly on domestic politics, several attacked the diplomatic system and the militarist and personalistic values that dominated eighteenth-century foreign affairs. These critics denied that foreign policy was "the center and culmination of political activities," assailed the system of treaties and alliances as deceitful at its core, and called for openness in foreign affairs.[76] Whatever the impact of these ideas on statesmen, their prominence points to the sense in which war and the conference diplomacy surrounding it were becoming more broadly visible. Foreign affairs remained the realm of princes, but the world of power politics was generating a critical literature.

Equally important, these developments contributed to a sense among decision makers of a "public" audience whose opinion mattered in international politics. Black notes that a concern to "influence public opinion" predates the development of any real mechanisms for political voice: in the eighteenth century "public opinion developed as a category in political thought, although there was uncertainty about what constituted such opinion and about its impact on high politics."[77] Osiander points out

73. Weber 2006.
74. Hinsley 1963, 35–36.
75. Sacks 1962; Mangone 1954, 23–24; Gilbert 1951, 14–15.
76. Gilbert 1951; Hinsley 1963.
77. Black 1999, 493–94.

that the terminology of public and public opinion, while absent from the discourse of Westphalia, figured prominently among decision makers at Utrecht. He states that several actors noted a concern for public opinion, but that alone it did not provide reason enough for action.[78] Harold Nicolson adds that at Utrecht, participants recognized that a prince's interests could be different from those of his people, and that sovereigns either needed to bring their publics along or else do things in secret.[79] Habermas famously associates these developments with the rise of the public sphere at the domestic level, which transformed domestic political authority.[80] These developments show that in that period international affairs similarly came under public scrutiny.

In sum, in the late eighteenth century, states had the capacity to talk to one another in an environment where their decisions were increasingly visible both to one another and to an audience of "nonpublic persons," who were aware of and attentive to how states use their power. My primary interest here is in the former—the public of decision makers and the public power they create through their commitments and forums. But the public of nonpublic persons, that is, the audience of great power politics and those affected by great power decisions, is crucial. Decision makers refer to and care about newspapers and public opinion, and they talk as if they face a discipline from public opinion. This is true of autocrats Alexander and Metternich as much as liberals Castlereagh and Canning.

## Creating a European Public Interest

By the start of the Napoleonic Wars in 1792, European leaders were participating in a balance of power system based on the state's corporate personality, Europe had a diplomatic system that permitted ongoing conversation, and states' leaders periodically met after wars in multilateral conferences to craft settlements. A state's foreign affairs were becoming visible to foreign courts and were discussed in terms of the public's interests and with occasional reference to an abstraction, "public opinion," that all seemed to use in a similar way. Still, European leaders did not treat their relations with one another as if their states faced shared problems that required collective regulation. Certainly war was not

78. Osiander 1994, 104–5.
79. Nicolson 1954, 70.
80. Habermas 1989.

treated as a shared problem. At peace conferences and congresses the desire for a tranquil Europe was sometimes mentioned, and in this sense leaders shared an interest in continental peace. But collective violence and individual hegemonic aspirations were not seen as shared problems requiring joint preventive action. Rather, a state's foreign policy was treated as a set of private, individual choices. These choices had systemic consequences, but being aware of system-wide consequences is different from constituting violence as a shared problem requiring a collective solution.

This changed as a consequence of the Napoleonic Wars. The devastating wars followed by the experience of the Final Coalition of 1813/14 helped solidify the idea of a European public interest, and linked that interest to the practice of collective discussion among the most powerful states. Several historians and IR scholars connect the practices of the Final Coalition to the Vienna Settlement provision of great power consultation.[81] My account of the events builds on this work but draws out how the Vienna Settlement made it possible for the great powers to constitute themselves as an international public power.

*Privacy Becomes Costly*

There is no reason to assume that actors who share a social system will choose to collectively manage any issue, much less the use of violence. Moreover, several factors in eighteenth-century Europe likely contributed to keeping violence a matter of sovereign right rather than collective responsibility. First, on the whole, war was felt to be cheap and unproblematic. At least until midcentury, war was treated simply as another tool in a state's arsenal.[82] Second, the dominant understanding of the balance of power was that the individual pursuit of self-interest generated collectively harmonious outcomes without the need for explicit coordination. Indeed, in an invisible hand system explicit cooperation can undermine rather than promote the common good. Finally, behavioral norms of self-help, mistrust, and competition inhibited the leap into collective solutions. Great power violence simply was not seen as a shared problem.

The Napoleonic Wars changed this, creating the shared sense that great power violence posed a kind of problem that their balance of power prac-

81. E.g., Schroeder 1994; Langhorne 1981/82; Dakin 1979; Holsti 1992.
82. Schroeder 1994 and Black 1994 make this point.

tices could not address. For most of the period in which France sought hegemony, responses to Napoleon were governed by alliance norms similar to those of previous wars in the eighteenth century. From 1792 to 1812, coalitions against France formed and faltered, compensations were negotiated, and peace and marriage treaties were signed.[83] Yet rather than bring the system into balance, increasingly the continent came under French control. No coalition could stop the agile threat of Napoleon, especially because alliance partners did not always agree that Napoleon was the main threat they faced.

To give a schematic sense of how their balance of power norms translated into practice: when France first declared war on Austria in 1792, Russia took advantage of the diversion to invade Poland. Prussian-Austrian rivalry prevented cooperation against either France or Russia, as Prussia deserted a brief alliance with Austria to focus on securing gains from Russia. The three Eastern powers

> were all preoccupied with internal affairs and mutually suspicious of each other over plans further to divide Poland. Austria, moreover, was involved in an indecisive war with the Ottomans, complicated by unrest in Hungary and Belgium, and Russia was fighting both the Ottomans and the Swedes. Great Britain, the traditional rival, was resolved on a policy of peace. It regarded all wars as inimical to trade and British financial interests.[84]

In short, European states did not treat Napoleon as a threat to "Europe" in any holistic sense. Instead, the threat to Europe was an aggregate of the individual threats Napoleon posed to each of them. And for each of these states, Napoleon was just one factor in their threat environment; each also was considered a threat by the others.

In 1793 the distinctiveness of the Napoleonic threat began to become clear when France launched an offensive into the German states and declared war on Britain, the Dutch Republic, and Spain.[85] This prompted

---

83. Scholars of the period disagree on the precise number of coalitions—ranging from around four to as many as seven. All describe the same history; they differ on when defection constitutes final destruction of the coalition and when joining on amounts to a whole new coalition. Because my purpose is to show the overall pattern, I stick to a broad notion of coalitions and divide them into four. See, e.g., Black 1994; Whiteneck 2001; Rothenberg 1989.

84. Rothenberg 1989, 205. Also see Bruun 1965, 253.

85. Ingrau 1994, 691.

Britain to assemble a large coalition. But the allies had different political and military goals, and this first coalition soon withered. Prussia, Spain, and several German states withdrew by the end of 1795, and after a successful Italian invasion Napoleon was able to compel Austria to the Treaty of Campo Formio in 1797.

The Second Coalition (1798–1802), of Austria, Britain, the Ottoman Empire, and Russia, fared no better. Prussia did not join, and although Britain fought to secure a commitment that the allies would sue for peace only as a group, Russia, Austria, and even ultimately Britain refused to bind themselves.[86] They then proceeded separately. Russia removed its forces in 1799 and revived its armed neutrality against Britain. Austria, despite a substantial British subsidy offered in the hopes of keeping the alliance together, was compelled by France to sign the Treaty of Lunéville in 1801. Left alone, Britain signed a treaty at Amiens in 1802.

The Third Coalition (1805–7) of Russia, Britain, and Austria was as unsuccessful as the previous two, but it stands out because this is the moment when ideas for a postwar European order began to be discussed, particularly in an exchange between the Russian czar, Alexander, and the British prime minister, William Pitt.[87] In 1804, Alexander sought an agreement with Britain to act together against Napoleon and jointly keep the peace afterward, stating that "if Russia should . . . mix in the affairs of Europe . . . it should be for the purpose of establishing 'an order of things that produces a real benefit for humanity and assures . . . the European states a permanent peace.'"[88] Alexander's goal was to "counter the French appeal to European public opinion pretending that they are the harbingers of freedom and to show that . . . it is the allied powers who aim to promote a return to freedom and order in Europe."[89]

Pitt responded with the State Paper of 1805, in which he amended Alexander's proposal by making it concrete. Pitt sought a specific division of territory and added that this "would still be incomplete and 'imperfect, if the restoration of peace were not accompanied by the most effectual measures for giving solidity and permanence to the system.'"[90] He

---

86. Bruun 1965, 257; Whiteneck 2001, 158–59; Rothenberg 1989; Schroeder 1994.

87. Ragsdale, 2002, 138–40. On the 1804/5 proposals, see Schroeder 1994, 257–62; Webster 1931, 53–63.

88. Alexander's instructions quoted in Ragsdale 2002, 148. See also Delfiner 2003, 134–35.

89. Czartoryski's memoirs, II, quoted in Gulick 1955, 105–6.

90. Gulick 1955, 144.

called for a "general agreement and Guarantee for the mutual protection and securing of different Powers, and for re-establishing a general system of public law in Europe."[91]

As far-sighted as these ideas were, however, they soon were undermined. France defeated Austria at Ulm (1805), the combined Austrian and Russian armies at Austerlitz (1805), and Prussia (who had refused offers to join the coalition) at Jena (1806), and European states lost any cohesion. Napoleon then abolished the Holy Roman Empire once and for all by creating the Confederation of the Rhine (1806), and he was able to coax Russia into an alliance through the Peace of Tilsit (1806), at which point Alexander dropped his equilibrium idea.[92] Even as Napoleon planned his 1812 invasion of Russia, he had the formal cooperation of Austria and Prussia. As Gunther Rothenberg points out, in terms of the behavior of the major European powers against Napoleon, "at one point or another all of the states, except for Great Britain, were opponents or allies of the French, joining or leaving coalitions, and on occasion changing sides, under different circumstances and for differing reasons."[93]

During most of the war years, then, the powers were so absorbed in individualistic balancing practices that it took a long time to discern the depth of threat that Napoleon posed. Then, once it was clear, they could not do anything about it.[94] Each state pursued its interests individualistically, and even as several began to speak the language of public law and European interests, they did not act on that public interest. No practices in their diplomatic tool kit could make it concrete. Meanwhile, a determined hegemon was exploiting the rules of the game and in the process remaking the game board altogether.

## The Final Coalition

When Napoleon was defeated (the first time) it was only because the strongest powers were able to work together for a sustained period of time. As many scholars have pointed out, techniques of the Final Coali-

---

91. Gulick 1955, 144; Langhorne 1981/82, 76; Dakin 1979, 16; Hinsley 1963, 193–94.

92. Gulick 1955, 106.

93. Rothenberg 1989, 200.

94. There is a debate over why the coalitions were unable to balance Napoleon. For recent contributions, see Dwyer 2008; Haas 2005; Whiteneck 2001. Earlier discussions include Langhorne 1981/82, 1990; Schroeder 1994; Ingrao 1994.

tion were a key model for the postwar order. What's significant through my theoretical lens is that the Final Coalition experience led these allies to appoint themselves as guardians of Europe's common interest and to commit themselves to uphold that interest, especially through direct consultation.

The Final Coalition took shape once Napoleon had regrouped after his disastrous Russian campaign. At this point, in 1813, Prussia and Austria joined the alliance with Russia and Britain. Britain's foreign minister, Robert Stewart Castlereagh, negotiated the coalition, and troops from Prussia, Austria, and Russia, along with Sweden and Saxony, together defeated Napoleon at the Battle of Leipzig in October. However, despite its victory even this coalition threatened to splinter, since each state had a different vision of what it meant to impose peace on France. Britain therefore sent Castlereagh to the continent in December 1813, with instructions to stay for six weeks and safeguard British interests in any settlement.[95] Instead, Castlereagh stayed for more than a year, which put the decision makers of the four major allies, Castlereagh (Britain), Klemens Wenzel von Metternich (Austria), Karl August von Hardenberg (Prussia), and Alexander (Russia, who left Russia in January 1813 and did not return until August 1814[96]) in nearly constant contact for the first time.

One of the first actions after Castlereagh's arrival was that the allies bound themselves to make peace only as an alliance: there would be no separate negotiations with Napoleon.[97] The focus in this period was more on each other than on Napoleon.[98] Castlereagh had laid the ground for this move in his September 1813 Project of Alliance, which was circulated among the allies around the time of the Battle of Leipzig, and which was itself inspired by Pitt's State Paper of 1805.[99] Castlereagh called for the allies to work together to defeat Napoleon, to hold all negotiations subject to "common consent," and to maintain a "perpetual defensive alliance after the conclusion of the peace."[100] That winter, despite ongoing mistrust

95. Webster 1931, 187, 193ff.; Gulick 1955, 142.

96. Bridge 1979, 34.

97. Bruun 1965, 273.

98. Langhorne 1981/82, 79–80; Gulick 1955, 133.

99. E.g., Gulick notes that when Parliament criticized the Vienna Settlement in 1815, Castlereagh showed Pitt's 1805 letter "as a kind of scriptural justification for his own policy and action." Gulick 1955, 145.

100. Dakin 1979, 21; Langhorne 1981/82. Until Britain joined the coalition it consisted of nine separate treaties of various combinations of the allies. Gulick 1955, 133.

among the allies (e.g., in January Metternich reportedly "still considered Napoleon a lesser evil than the Tsar"[101]) the allies stuck together.

In February 1814 discussions at Chatillon, the allies referred to themselves as great powers, or "powers of the first order,"[102] and took on the shared responsibility to manage the continent. This was a newly claimed status, great powerhood, linked to a new responsibility, to manage the continent. They "explicitly claimed to negotiate with Napoleon in the name of Europe as a whole," and in the Treaty of Chaumont (March 1814) they agreed to keep the peace of Europe for twenty years, an unprecedented commitment in the modern states system.[103] The allies talked as if not "mere envoys of the four courts 'but as men entitled to treat for Peace with France in the name of Europe, which is but a single entity.'"[104]

In other words, finally the allies were able to concert their actions long enough to defeat Napoleon. To be sure, what happened in 1814 was not the birth of a pacific union, or a change at the level of motives, from competitors to friends, or even the growth of trust. Rather, a combination of three things made it newly possible for these rivals to stick together. There was, first, the constant contact among decision makers; second, the arrogation of the new role as guardians of Europe; and third, the precise commitment to one another to keep the peace. This combination had not been attempted before, not in these wars or in earlier ones.

## The Vienna Settlement

Two months later, after Napoleon's abdication and the Bourbon restoration, in the (First) Treaty of Paris (May 1814) the four allies, joined by Sweden, Spain, and Portugal as well as France, called for a second, general congress to meet at Vienna "within two months" in order to come to a final agreement on provisions of the settlement. The treaty established peace; the congress's goal was to make that peace durable by neutralizing all foreseeable threats. The goal, then, was both to satisfy all of the main powers and guard against a resurgent France, a powerful Russia, and the new, continent-wide threat of revolution. Beyond this ambitious, broad goal, the call for a general congress included no stipulations about who

---

101. Dakin 1979, 23; Langhorne 1981/82, 78.
102. Anderson 1993, 187.
103. Schroeder 1994, 501; Holsti 1992, 35–36; Langhorne 1981/82, 79.
104. Holsti 1992, 35–36; Anderson 1993, 187.

should attend or what the agenda should be. However, the allies agreed among themselves that they alone would retain final decision-making authority. In a secret clause to the Treaty of Paris, the four powers (Britain, Russia, Austria, and Prussia) agreed that final control of the European equilibrium would remain in their hands.[105]

The Congress of Vienna met from September 1814 until June 1815. It remained in session even as Napoleon escaped from Elba and the Quadruple Alliance reconstituted itself to put down the threat; and the signatories of the First Treaty of Paris (except Spain) signed the Vienna Final Act. The congress achieved agreements that were unprecedented in scope, covering issues from territorial boundaries to the slave trade, the German and other constitutions, and the free navigation of rivers.[106] Like most postwar agreements, it divided the spoils of war. The balance of power continued to be the operating principle, and frontiers were decided based on defensibility and population concentrations (the latter determined with the help of a statistical committee).[107] After Napoleon's defeat at Waterloo, the allies signed the Second Peace of Paris and also renewed their Quadruple Alliance with an eye toward combating any future threat from France.

Taken together, the Vienna Final Act, the two Treaties of Paris, and the Quadruple Alliance—called the Vienna Settlement—established the great powers' intention to govern together. Three interlocking aspects of the Vienna Settlement in particular enabled their commitment to have the force of a collective intention: the association of the general European interest with the treaty through the Vienna Final Act, the designations of state rank and responsibility, and the commitment to future consultation on their common interests.

PUBLIC POWER.    The first innovation was that with the Vienna Settlement the great powers constituted themselves as a public power for Europe. At Chaumont and afterward, they referred to themselves as powers of the

---

105. Peterson 1945, 533–34, 550; King 2008, 50–51; Holsti 1992, 35–36; Anderson 1993, 187. "The relations from whence a system of real and permanent balance of power in Europe is to be derived, shall be regulated at the Congress upon the principles determined by the allied powers among themselves, and according to the general provisions contained in the following articles." Langhorne 1981/82, 80, quoting Hertslet 1875, 18.

106. Woolf 1916, 26.

107. Holsti 1992, 40. For accounts of the negotiations, see Langhorne 1981/82, 1990; Schroeder 1994, chapter twelve; Nicolson 1946, chapters eight and nine.

first order, charging themselves with the responsibility for maintaining the settlement. They authorized themselves to act on the interest of a European public that transcended the membership of any single state. The Vienna commitment institutionalized a system in which hierarchy based on material power conferred a special status and role. They constituted themselves as guardians, acknowledging that their authority derived from their power. By agreeing together they created a type of authority that was new in the European system. Metternich in 1814 wrote:

> This Congress could not model itself on any predecessor.... The Powers which made the Treaty of Paris will determine the meaning which they wish to attach to the word Congress, and will also decide the form which would seem most appropriate for reaching the goals they have set themselves. They will use this right of determination ... to the good of Europe as a whole.... Thus the Congress is brought into being of itself, without having received any formal authority, there being no source which could have given any.[108]

This was the birth of great power management, and it involved two moves: taking on the role of managers, linking the role to their relative power; and removing or delegitimating other authorities. First, the allies who had defeated Napoleon assigned themselves the role of directing the Vienna Congress and gave themselves the responsibility to carry out its mandates. Castlereagh wrote that "the 'conduct of business must practically rest with the leading powers.'"[109] His concern was not the legal one of whether a given state had signed a given treaty, but relative power: powerful states should determine the shape of Europe. Genevieve Peterson notes that this may be the "first expression of the idea of great powers, with rights as such, distinct from any derived from treaties."[110] Still, while rooted in capacity, the prerogative was intimately linked with responsibility. As Castlereagh put it, they had "not only a common interest but a common duty to attend to."[111] As they took on the right to set the terms of the postwar order, the allies took on the duty to serve as its guardians.

Although technically all eight signatories[112] of the Treaty of Paris had

---

108. Langhorne 1981/82, 80–81.

109. Peterson 1945, 534, quoting from British Foreign Office Peace Handbook #153, 149.

110. Peterson 1945, 534, 550.

111. Quoted from Richardson 1999, 51.

112. Britain, France, Prussia, Russia, Austria, Spain, Portugal, and Sweden.

called for this congress, the four strongest powers (i.e., the powers that defeated France) sought to constitute themselves as a directorship. To this end, before most delegations arrived at Vienna, the Quadruple Alliance met informally to set up the congress structure. They put off the type of general opening ceremonial session that was often seen in post-Westphalia conferences and proceeded to make most decisions as an informal committee. On France's arrival Talleyrand argued his way into the inner circle, and once France was accepted the five became the informal steering committee.[113]

The Congress of Vienna never officially opened, in that the usual rituals—exchanging credentials and settling precedence and procedural issues—were never done. "The members of this imaginary Congress never met together in the same room.... No plenary session was ever held."[114] Many states had come to Vienna expecting a European assembly or parliamentary style Congress. And, altogether, there were 216 principalities and states represented, which came from those who had fought in the war as well as from neutrals.[115] Nonstate interest groups were represented as well, and all expected that their concerns would be heard.[116] Instead, the four allied powers, usually with France and sometimes with Spain, Portugal, and Sweden, met with one another. Friedrich von Gentz, chosen as secretary, referred to the five powers—the allies plus France—as the "real and only Congress" because only these states discussed all of the issues. The Committee of Five met forty-one times, while the eight signatories of the Paris Treaty met nine times and the full congress never met at all. Thus, although the Congress of Vienna hosted more delegations representing more interests than any prior postwar conference, decision-making authority remained within a tight circle of the materially strongest powers.[117]

The fact that the operative hierarchy was based on material power and not the transnational authority of the church was evident in the allies' reaction to Alexander's proposal of a Holy Alliance, which would have

113. Technically, the addition of France was specifically to handle the Polish-Saxon question. But the committee effectively ran the congress as a whole from January 1815 on. Nicolson 1946, 141–47; Schroeder 1994, 523.

114. Hazen 1917, 15–16.

115. Peterson 1945, 550.

116. Nicolson 1946, 129–33; Webster 1969, 76–79.

117. Hazen 1917, 17.

committed the great powers to adhere to Christian principles in their public relations. In September 1815, before the Second Treaty of Paris, Alexander circulated the Holy Alliance agreement. Austria, Prussia, and Russia signed, and eventually all European leaders signed on except Britain, the Ottoman sultan, and the pope. But other sovereigns did not take this statement of religious principles seriously; at least it was not given political weight but seen rather as an expression of "conscience," not politics or diplomacy.[118]

The alliance's arrogation of a managerial role was new and caused much controversy. Bavaria, Sardinia, Denmark, and the Low Countries protested the fact that they could not meet with the allies and that any allied decision was presented to the larger group as a fait accompli, which they could only choose to ratify or reject.[119] The secondary powers, Portugal, Sweden, and Spain, had somewhat of a greater role in that they were admitted to deliberations of the five, but they, too, could only ratify or reject. Thus several provisions in the Final Act were not heard much less ratified by the Committee of Eight, and few of its protocols were signed by all eight.[120] In June when the eight convened to sign the Final Act, Spain and the Netherlands refused, resentful of the role the great powers had taken for themselves.[121]

If there was going to be leadership at the congress, it is not surprising that the most powerful states assumed that role. Nonetheless, it is noteworthy that they took on a leadership role at all and that the role was self-consciously meant to be one of leadership. In other words, they took steps to legitimate their domination to the lesser states.[122] For example, the Vienna Final Act institutionalized sovereign equality. Vienna was the first international congress where neither the pope nor the Holy Roman emperor played a role. The congress designated a Committee on Diplomatic Rank, which explicitly rejected the proposal that certain states had

118. Hinsley 1963, 202–3, 211.

119. Peterson 1945, 539, 546–50, 551–52; Hazen 1917.

120. Peterson 1945, 549; Hazen 1917.

121. Hazen 1917, 18; Peterson 1945, 549.

122. Although plenty were cynical: Gentz, the representative from Austria, said of the Congress of Vienna: "The grand phrases such as 'the regeneration of the political system of Europe,' 'a lasting peace founded on the just division of strength,' were uttered to tranquilize the people, and to give an air of dignity and grandeur to this solemn assembly; but the real purpose was to divide among the conquerors the spoils taken from the vanquished." Caldwell 1918, 62.

"rights of antiquity" superseding sovereign equality and adopted instead a classification of diplomatic representatives and the broad rule that all treaties and agreements be signed in alphabetical order of the French spelling of the state's name.[123] March 1815 was the first classification of diplomatic agents in international law. States accepted shared definitions and a shared hierarchy among representatives, from plenipotentiaries, to ambassadors, to chargés d'affaires, and so on.

Giving all states a nominally equal voice in international affairs was seen as a way of stabilizing the settlement, and interstate politics overall. It made diplomacy easier. Extrapolitical standards, ceremony, pageantry, so-called rights of antiquity, and prerogative now had no official place. It also enhanced stability by making the settlement legitimate to smaller, less powerful states. Note that at this time, sovereign equality was under-stood as a right to survival and recognition: the right to be seen and not necessarily the right to be heard. As Gentz put it in 1806, "true equal-ity, and the only equality attainable by legitimate means, consists in both cases, in this, that the smallest as well as the greatest is secured in the pos-session of his right, and that it can neither be forced upon him nor en-croached by lawless power."[124] This is not a notion of equal voice, or the right to have a say in managing crises on the continent.[125]

Castlereagh made this argument to a Prussian delegate at Vienna, Baron Humboldt. Smaller states were not generally entitled to have a say in all European affairs, but the decisions of the congress had to be made legitimate. For Humboldt, the concern for legitimacy was misplaced. Humboldt protested that because Europe is not a "constitutional whole," while the congress's decisions certainly affected all states, the bottom line was that the congress was no more than "a mere collection of negotia-tors in one spot" and not "a European Assembly,"[126] so the great powers needed to remain as flexible as possible to do whatever actions would be needed at any time to keep the balance. Castlereagh's counterargument did not reject Humboldt's premise of the great powers' special role, but

123. Peterson 1945, 546. The rules were adopted specifically for dealings among the eight signatories of the Paris treaty, but they came to anchor diplomacy from here out. See also Nicolson 1946, 216–18; Schroeder 1994, 578–79.

124. Gentz cited in Peterson 1945, 553–54.

125. For a critique of the Vienna Congress for its meaning of sovereign equality, see Peterson 1945. See Schroeder 1994, 576 on the importance of not reading contemporary defi-nitions of rights and freedoms into this time period.

126. Peterson 1945, 535–36.

focused on the importance of treating smaller states "with respect" and thereby to get "a sort of sanction" for great power decisions and actions. The final settlement had to be acceptable to all in order to be stable. He pointed out that protests from smaller powers are more manageable in an assembly than on the battlefield. Castlereagh also specified that smaller states should be allowed in on negotiations that affected them.[127] The four thus took some steps to acknowledge the status concerns of the larger group, without giving them actual decision-making power. In 1818 at Aix, the powers agreed that

> where the affairs of non-participating states were involved such meetings "shall only take place in pursuance of a formal invitation on the part of such of those states as the said affairs may concern, and under the express reservation of their right of direct participation therein, either directly or by their plenipotentiaries."[128]

PUBLIC COMMITMENT.    The second innovation was the Vienna Final Act, a single treaty that pulled together all of the individual agreements made at the congress, so that upholding the Vienna Settlement meant upholding each of the separate treaties, and violating any amounted to violating the whole settlement. Umbrella treaties of this sort were not unheard of but were not common practice, and legally speaking they were unnecessary.[129] Supplementing a treaty in general was a way of adding weight or gravity to the agreement, but the more common way of doing so was through a guarantee,[130] where a strong third party, usually a mediator to the settlement, pledged to enforce the terms of the treaty.[131]

127. Peterson 1945, 537; Dunn 1929, 69–70.

128. Quoted in Langhorne 1981/82, 87.

129. Headlam-Morley 1927, 161

130. Headlam-Morley 1927, 158. The term is used in many peace treaties to refer to what Headlam-Morley calls a defensive alliance, that is, a promise to help one side or the other should they get attacked. He notes that Vattel also points out that the word is used casually sometimes. Headlam-Morley points out that it is in all but one of forty-nine treaties in the eighteenth century. The term "guarantee" had become an "ornamental expression which lawyers like to put into documents." Headlam-Morley 1927, 157. That number is supported by Satow 1925.

131. Satow 1925; Headlam-Morley 1927. Such treaties replaced other modes of securing compliance used in the early modern period, such as hostages, or oaths on the cross. Although the practice of hostages to secure a treaty can be found as late as 1748, according to Satow, it was not common in that period. Satow 1925.

The Vienna Final Act self-consciously was not a guarantee. The possibility of a general guarantee of the post–Napoleonic War treaty had first been introduced in Pitt's 1805 State Paper, and it was discussed at several points in the Vienna negotiations.[132] In 1814, Castlereagh sent a circular to the ambassadors about the "general accord and guarantee" to come, and asked Gentz to draft an official declaration.[133] After Napoleon's escape, however, the idea of having the allies formally guarantee the Vienna Settlement was dropped.[134] There is no written record of the process of leaving the guarantee behind, but Congress of Vienna documents rarely use the term "guarantee," and when it does appear it is not used in a legal sense.[135] Still, even without the formal guarantee it was an umbrella treaty, and this was another technique of enhancing a commitment. As Hinsley puts it, the Final Act united all of the frontiers of nearly all European states in a "single instrument, no part of which could be infringed without invalidating the rest; and it gave every signatory the right—though not, indeed, in the absence of a guarantee clause, the duty—to uphold its terms."[136]

The Final Act made the Settlement a public commitment by constituting a public interest and by doing so publicly. First, the goal of the Final Act was to create a European whole that was greater than the sum of its parts. In the preamble, it states:

> desirous to embrace, in one common transaction, the various results of their negotiations, for the purpose of confirming them by their reciprocal ratifications, [they] have authorized their plenipotentiaries to unite, in a general instrument, the regulation of superior and permanent interest, and to join to that Act as integral parts of the arrangements of the Congress the Treaties . . . , as cited in the present Treaty.[137]

132. Pitt had proposed that Britain and Russia guarantee the European settlement, and this was the sense that Castlereagh also used in February. Dakin 1979, 30–31.

133. Dakin 1979, 30–31.

134. The last use of the term that Langhorne finds is in a May 1815 circular by Russia. Langhorne 1981/82, 84.

135. They speak of "definite and formal obligation" to help another state if that state's territory is threatened, and at the follow-up congress at Aix-la-Chapelle (1818) they pledge to "observ[e] the principle of the right of nations which . . . can alone effectively guarantee the independence of each government and the stability of the general association. Headlam-Morley 1927, 159.

136. Hinsley 1963, 194. See Ikenberry 2001, 110–11, who argues that British concerns about Alexander's credibility as a partner caused Castlereagh to back off from the guarantee.

137. Quoted from Headlam-Morley 1927, 161.

That is, each individual agreement was given the additional endorsement of being part of the overall plan for continental peace and stability. Through the Final Act, European stability was made indivisible, and it was made the responsibility of all signatories—which began with the four allies, but extended outward until it included all of the political players in Europe.

The treaty's concern was narrow: stability among the states of Europe proper. In Paul Schroeder's words, "The Vienna settlement . . . shielded Europe, fenced it off from extraneous quarrels."[138] Its positive agenda was left rather vague, but the Concert had a fairly clear "negative agenda": neither America nor the Ottoman Empire, areas of special interest to Britain and Russia respectively, appear in the treaty. Regarding America, in 1814 Britain was negotiating an end to the War of 1812 but did not want Europe weighing in. In the Treaty of Ghent (1814), difficult issues were glossed over, no territory changed hands, and the rest of Europe had no say. "Britain chose to protect its interests in the New World by keeping Europe at bay."[139] The Ottoman Empire also was kept out, although in this case the "fencing off" was odd, since unlike America and as discussed above, it had long been a player in the European states system. In addition, the Ottoman Empire had joined a coalition against Napoleon and then had been engaged in war with Russia from 1806 to 1812, and the Balkans had been a theater of competition throughout the Napoleonic Wars. Still, Ottoman holdings were not brought under the Concert's purview. The bilateral 1812 Treaty of Bucharest ending the Russo-Turkish War was considered the last word on Ottoman relations with Europe, and that treaty was explicitly left out of the Vienna Final Act.[140]

Second, the Final Act was also a public commitment in that it was made in public—in front of a large audience of fellow states and Europeans. Because the invitation to the congress had been vague about the agenda beyond noting that matters of general interest would be discussed, all European states sent delegates—and even the Ottoman Empire sent an emissary. An estimated one hundred thousand people visited Vienna during the Concert.[141] "With their families and retinues, the delegations sent to the Congress swelled Vienna to a bursting point. Never had modern Europe witnessed the collection of so many crowned heads

138. Schroeder 1994, 575.
139. Schroeder 1994, 573–74.
140. Hinsley 1963, 199.
141. Peterson 1945, 550; Mangone 1954, 35.

and their distinguished diplomats in one place."[142] While most states had no voice in the terms of the treaty and most did not sign it immediately, ultimately it was broadly and officially accepted. In other words, the Final Act cemented the agreements and united them, in front of a European-wide audience.

PUBLIC FORUMS.   The third innovation—perhaps most important in a practical sense—was the consultation provision. In November 1815 the Quadruple Alliance signed the Second Treaty of Paris. This particular treaty focused mainly on punishing France,[143] but in a separate Treaty of Alliance on the same day, the four powers further solidified the Chaumont commitment to keep the peace for twenty years.[144]

This latter treaty included the stipulation in Article Six that they should meet to consult on their common interests and for the general tranquility and prosperity of Europe. In Article Six they agreed

> to facilitate and to secure the execution of the present treaty, and to consolidate the connections which at the present moment so closely unite the four Sovereigns for the happiness of the world, *the High Contracting Parties have agreed to renew their meetings at fixed periods ... for the purpose of consulting upon their common interests,* and for consideration of the measures which at each of those periods shall be considered the most salutary for the repose and prosperity of Nations and for the maintenance of the Peace of Europe.[145]

Like the Vienna Final Act, this alliance treaty had some characteristics of a guarantee. It was a separate treaty that referred to the prior treaty and restated the importance of maintaining its terms. But like the Vienna Final Act, it did not use the language associated with international legal guarantees. In the treaty negotiations Alexander had proposed that "the powers should guarantee the whole Vienna Settlement, by a reciprocal guarantee of all their territories as well as by meeting from time to time to survey the internal affairs of all the European states."[146] Castlereagh and

---

142. Mangone 1954, 35.

143. The Second Treaty of Paris was more punitive toward France than the first had been, in that it shrank France's boundaries, demanded an indemnity, and called for a five-year occupation.

144. Dakin 1979, 31.

145. Hertslet 1875, italics added.

146. Sked 1979, 4–5.

Metternich, however, each opposed words that mandated intervention. Thus in the treaty, intervention was explicitly called for only in order keep the Bonapartes out of French politics. This is a very circumscribed trigger for enforcement, especially in light of the more general sense in which guarantees had long been used.

In lieu of a general guarantee, the allies agreed to Article Six, whose wording was "careful . . . but without legal precision,"[147] and gave each of them the right to be consulted.[148] "This article . . . was an attempt to perpetuate the practice of conference diplomacy which had come into use during the final phase of the Napoleonic Wars. It did not, however, define precisely when and for what specific purposes these international conferences should be held."[149] Thus the signatories were left free to react to perceived threats to European stability in their own ways. They could call for a meeting, ignore, consent, and so on.

Stepping back and viewing the Vienna Settlement as a whole—from the initial treaty at Chaumont through the Second Treaty of Paris and the Quadruple Alliance—it is clear that the allied powers considered what they were doing to be without precedent. These leaders knew what they were *not* doing: they were not creating a European parliament, assembly, or federation; they were not guaranteeing the distribution of territory agreed on in June 1815 in the sense of promising to enforce any treaty violation. There was no pretense of solving the problem of war by imposing themselves as a supranational authority. But they nevertheless found ways to give the settlement additional gravity, to move Europe beyond the eighteenth-century balance of power. They committed to consult one another on public interests, with that commitment situated in a spot—as a separate treaty meant to deepen the alliance commitment to the Vienna Settlement—where one would expect to find a guarantee. They thus linked that novelty—the consultation commitment—to their role and the perceived needs of the system.

The mechanism of interstate consultation and its link to pursuing public interests is taken for granted today. But as E. V. Gulick points out, a call for great power consultation to maintain an alliance of peace had never been stated so explicitly in an international treaty.[150] While no one could have known the success of the strategy of consultation in advance,

147. Dakin 1979, 31; Headlam-Morley 1927; Satow 1925, 298 on criteria for a guarantee.
148. Headlam-Morley 1927, 161; Langhorne 1981/82, 81.
149. Dakin 1979, 30.
150. Gulick 1965, 641.

Castlereagh clearly had high hopes. Robinson, his privy councilor and treasurer of the navy, wrote that Castlereagh earlier had lamented the lack of

> an habitual confidential and free intercourse between the Ministers of the Great powers as a body; and that many pretensions might be modified, asperities removed, and the causes or irritation anticipated and met, by bringing the respective parties into unrestricted communications common to them all, and embracing in confidential and united discussions all the great points in which they were severally interested.[151]

## Conclusion

International public power—governing together among the European great powers—first became possible in 1815 with the Vienna Settlement. It became possible, first of all, because of characteristics of the European diplomatic institutional setting that deepened after Westphalia. But although these conditions were perhaps necessary, they were not sufficient. Characteristics of the settlement itself made it for the first time possible that the rhetorical ideal of European peace could have behavioral pull among the great powers.

Why did they do it? As Hinsley notes, it is impossible to isolate one single cause:

> The impressive thing about the behavior of the powers in 1815 is that they were prepared . . . to waive their individual interests in the pursuit of an international system. This fact is not rendered any less impressive by the reason that they were prepared to waive their individual interests because it was in their individual interests to do so; they were seeing for the first time that self-interest required cooperation.[152]

Reflecting on the innovation of the Vienna Settlement, and especially on the role of Castlereagh's diplomacy in producing the Final Act and the Quadruple Alliance, it is tempting to attribute the innovation to Britain's ideology and/or its material power. This is John Ikenberry's[153] influential

151. Webster 1931, 199.
152. Hinsley 1963, 197.
153. Ikenberry 2001.

argument. Ikenberry proposes that Britain, the strongest state after the wars, proposed that the great powers turn to institutions as a way of locking in the settlement, thereby restraining its own power as much as that of its allies.[154] Support for Britain's key intellectual role is found in Pitt's State Paper of 1805, where he argued for the alliance to become a sort of federation guaranteeing the postwar order, and in Castlereagh's reliance on the Pitt document. Because of their domestic habits and institutions, Ikenberry argues, liberal states turn to institutions to manage their international relations.

Ikenberry is certainly correct that Britain played a crucial role holding the final coalition together—both through its presence on the continent and materially, through subsidies[155]—and Castlereagh was a creative diplomat particularly in this period. But there are limits to the "British liberalism" explanation. First, when it comes to the ideas of great power management and consultation, credit needs to be shared more widely. Each of the major decision makers was schooled in Kantian and newfangled democratic ideas. There is evidence that despite their autocratic domestic environments and fear of democratic mechanisms at the domestic level, both Metternich and Alexander were committed to the idea of some sort of European federation.[156] In fact, when it came to international politics it is surprising how "democratic" their vision for interstate politics was in comparison to their domestic programs.

Second, we should not discount the role of international experience (versus domestic institutions). After all, Pitt's paper specified a guarantee, whereas the allies specified no more than consultation. A plausible account of the innovations is that they were a pragmatic attempt to generalize the type of behavioral cooperation the great powers had achieved in 1815. Coalition politics certainly had not been easy. Schroeder argues that the allies' learning process was

> not merely uneven, spiral, and tortuous, filled with relapses; it was driven by powerful coercive factors, and needed to be. Europe's leaders ... did not actively look for new and better ways of thinking about international politics and

---

154. Ikenberry 2001, 80.

155. Ikenberry 2001, 94.

156. Sofka 1998; Kann 1960; Schroeder 1994. Alexander's tutor as a child was a Swiss liberal, La Harpe, and they corresponded into adulthood. Caldwell 1918, 51. See Delfiner (2003, 129–30) on Alexander's liberal education and cosmopolitan advisors. Hinsley mentions that Gentz had studied under Kant. Hinsley 1963, 193.

practicing it; nor did they willingly accept them. They were forced into systemic thinking by repeated failures, the exhaustion of alternatives, their inability to make any form of the old politics or any combination of the old and the new politics work—and finally, by the ruthless imperialism of [Napoleon].[157]

But once victory was achieved, each saw the role of consultation in getting them there.[158] In particular, "[Castlereagh's] experience with what is now called summit diplomacy had left him a firm believer in 'the habits of confidential intercourse which a long residence with the principal actors has established and which gives facilities to my intervention to bring them together.'"[159] This is not to discount the novelty of the consultation provision or to diminish its importance but to point out that an equally plausible narrative can be constructed from an "international society" rather than a "'democratic regime-type" perspective.[160]

Finally, there is some irony to attributing the innovation to Britain and linking it to liberalism, given Castlereagh's strategy. He departed from Pitt by abandoning the guarantee and looking instead to consultation. After the Final Coalition, Castlereagh became more confident in the idea of preserving peace "by discussion and agreement instead of by the threat of armed force. This device had now become in his mind a far better instrument than Pitt's idea of a guarantee, which he had advocated at Vienna."[161] But he kept his plans and negotiations close to the vest, and did not report regularly to parliament while at Vienna.[162] He had been instructed by the Cabinet not to sign on to a system of periodic conferences, which was called "new and . . . very questionable."[163] In other words, Castlereagh did not pursue the strategy of joint commitment and consultation necessarily out of an appreciation for his domestic political structure and ideology, and he did not do so with the blessing of parliament. It

157. Schroeder 1993, 68.

158. See Kissinger 1957, 122, 139.

159. Quoted in Bridge 1979, 34.

160. This critique seems to be supported by Schroeder, who notes that "it is a great mistake to see the Anglo-Russian programme of 1805 as the forerunner and model for the settlement of 1814–5," because in 1805 these two states "proposed to impose on Europe a settlement they had concocted while making Europe . . . fight and pay for it. In 1815, these same two powers . . . worked out a settlement with the rest of Europe." Schroeder 1994, 262.

161. Webster 1931, 480, quoted in Langhorne 1981/82, 84.

162. Webster and Temperley 1924.

163. Bridge 1979, 38; Nicolson 1946, 261–62.

is reasonable to conclude, then, that his actions reflect a pragmatic commitment rooted in his experience with the coalition.

In sum, two mechanisms had enabled the allies to stick together until Napoleon's decisive defeat—an explicit joint commitment to maintain the peace of Europe together and direct consultation. These now were formalized in the settlement as anchors of the postwar order. The Vienna Settlement established the territorial boundaries of all of the states of Europe and set boundaries on sovereign privacy, and it demarcated an agenda of public or European concerns. Even more importantly, the settlement created the possibility of the great powers pursuing that agenda together by designating them as governors, and it established a tool, the consultative forum, for governing. These states committed themselves to replacing the individualistic norms of the eighteenth-century balance of power system, where European order was produced by an invisible hand, with self-conscious, collective management, that is, with a more visible hand.[164]

The Concert of Europe is widely acknowledged in IR scholarship as the first security institution. In the minimalist interpretation, the Concert is viewed in bottom-up terms: self-interested states, with a common interest in avoiding war, created a particular institutional mechanism, the consultative meeting, which added transparency and information. In the maximalist interpretation, the Concert is characterized as an authority structure, but the constitution of that authority and how it was exercised has not been fleshed out. My interpretation of the Concert leans more to the maximalist, and with the framework of chapter two in mind, the innovation of the Concert stands out more sharply. Not just the consultative meeting, but meetings in the context of their commitment made possible a top-down dynamic of concerting their power toward the pursuit of common, public goals.

164. What Inis Claude would call a manual balance. See Claude 1962, 46.

# CHAPTER FOUR

# More Than Mere Words

*Publicly Managing the Vienna Settlement,*
*1815–22*

The Vienna Settlement could have been a flash in the pan, a brief respite between great power wars. Its comprehensive Vienna Final Act created an equilibrium of power among the self-proclaimed great powers and in lofty language promised continental stability for a long time to come.[1] But as the five great power signatories looked forward from 1815, it was not clear that the settlement augured any change in their familiar competitive practices. First, the intentions, capabilities, or both of their partners seemed opaque if not threatening. Austria and Britain, the settlement's main architects, saw France and Russia as threats and considered holding them in check as a key goal.[2] France was keen to remedy what it saw as a biased balance and appeared increasingly capable of launching a new war of conquest.[3] Russia, too, seemed to have expansionist aims, having ended the Napoleonic Wars in an extremely strong position. Russia was the sole power not to contract its army after Napoleon's defeat, and the army was three times its prewar size.[4] Russia had ongoing tensions

---

1. Schroeder distinguishes between the equilibrium created at Vienna and the balance of power system that it replaced. See Schroeder 1994, vii; cf. Ingrao 1994.

2. Bridge 1979, 36.

3. Bridge 1979, 34–35; Schroeder 1994, 522.

4. Kagan 1999, 2, 28ff. Alexander maintained a "two power standard" for Russia's army, i.e., it must be the size of Austria's and Prussia's combined. Kagan 1999, 34; Flockerzie 1992, 221.

with the Ottoman Empire (also called the Sublime Porte, or the Porte), and while the Ottoman Empire was not included in the Vienna Settlement, any gain in Russian influence there clearly would alter the European balance. In addition, the Russian czar, Alexander, was known to be an unsteady alliance partner.[5] In this postwar environment, it seemed as possible the great powers would fall back to their old practices as adopt new ones. While a deep crisis like the Napoleonic Wars can open space for new and creative thinking, if old habits are highly institutionalized they tend to reassert themselves. After a brief lag, meanings, practices, and relationships settle back down and the old order gets restored (albeit with some modification).[6]

The second reason it was not clear the settlement augured change was that nothing like the consultative meeting had been tried before as a tool for keeping the peace.[7] The provision to meet was neither part of a formal treaty guarantee nor linked to a quasi-legislative body, which meant meetings would neither technically trigger the use of force nor necessarily lead to binding political decisions. The act of joint discussion, the face-to-face exchange of opinions among fully empowered representatives, seemed to carry some weight over and above regular diplomacy. But the nature of that "weight" was not at all clear.

One might think that great power meetings would reduce uncertainty about intentions, and contemporary analyses of the Concert treat consultation this way.[8] But that assumes, even if implicitly, that decision makers knew how to use their forums strategically, and this was not the case in 1815. Rather, great power consultation was like any other new, untested technology—when first introduced it was not incorporated into strategic thinking.[9] From an individual perspective it was difficult to know how to employ great power forums for the benefit of one's own policy goals; from an interaction perspective it was difficult to figure out why another state would call for a meeting, to ascertain how fellow strategic actors were figuring it into their own calculations. Consultation had been proposed as a tool to help them prevent continental war, but it was not clear to any

5. E.g., Reinerman 1974.

6. On habit, see Camic 1986; Sewell 1996. For discussion in an IR context, see Mitzen 2006; Hopf 2010.

7. Several scholars discuss the difficulty these states faced. E.g., Langhorne 1981/82, 86.

8. For example, see Lindley 2007; Ikenberry 2001; Kupchan 2010; Jervis 1986; Lipson 1994.

9. Weldes and Laffey 1997.

of them how meeting together in peacetime could accomplish that end. It is not surprising, then, that key players—Metternich, Castlereagh, and others—did not expect their agreement to last very long.[10]

But it did: the great powers avoided fighting one another until the Crimean War. In that intervening period of some forty years, when crises arose the great powers often turned to discussion. I argue in this chapter that what made the Vienna Settlement more than mere words was its link to consultation. Their commitment had given each of the five powers the standing to call a meeting, which put every continental crisis potentially under their purview. As I argued in chapter two, when parties collectively intend to do something together, and when their joint commitment is fully out in the open among them, the commitment can pull their behavior. Each party stands in a relationship of obligation to the others and has the standing to hold them accountable for actions relevant to the commitment. The forum enables that mechanism of accountability to kick in, because the public context has a causal power to produce ways of talking, and even actions, that are publicly acceptable. The Vienna commitment and the forums together, then, made it possible for the great powers to keep the peace together.

In this chapter, tracing the diplomacy of 1820–22 surrounding the Spanish, Neapolitan, and early Greek revolts, I show that the option to meet enabled the settlement to hold, and that without it war would have been far more likely. The power of the forum provision is first evident in the process through which the powers found themselves at a congress in 1821 at all. Metternich was trapped by his own rhetoric into holding a consultative meeting when he would have preferred to act unilaterally and without the input of the other great powers. It is next evident in the meetings themselves, as deep disagreements among allies were contained within the terms of the settlement and neither spilled out from the conference table nor ended the alliance.

Finally, the power of the forum provision is evident in the great powers' ability to restrain Russia's response to the Greek revolt. In 1821, the Greeks revolted against Ottoman authority in the Balkans. The revolt generated pressure on Russia to intervene on behalf of the Greeks, which the other powers feared. Through the end of 1822, however, no great power intervened. I argue that a major factor in averting intervention was that the powers were able to interpret the revolt through the lens

10. Dakin 1979, 32.

they had just applied to the other, European revolutions. The Greek revolt became a liberal revolt against a legitimate sovereign, which meant
the great powers should support the sovereign. Making this interpretation stick required invoking the European interest, but the strategy only
worked because a concrete referent for that public interest existed: the
forum. The combination of great power forums and shared, public reason
made the collective interest in European stability visible. Ultimately the
liberal revolution lens was an awkward fit for the Greek revolt, for reasons that will become clear in chapter five. But through the end of 1822,
it was contained within this discursive framework. Forum talk, in the context of the Vienna Settlement, pulled Greece and the Ottoman Empire
into Europe and Russia away from declaring war.

In each episode, I trace the role of their commitment and forums in
producing great power self-restraint (commitment-consistent behavior).
The argument of this chapter is consistent with interpretations of the
Concert as a form of political authority;[11] the contribution is to illustrate
a mechanism for how the Concert commitment could be authoritative in
practice. I enhance the plausibility of my account of these events through
counterfactual analysis and by comparing it to accounts that stress individual preferences, relative power, or deeply held collective identity. My
aim, however, is not to disprove these other accounts. There are many sto-
ries to tell to account for the nineteenth-century long peace, and no single
overarching truth. But in my view, our understanding of the Concert is incomplete without acknowledging the role of the great powers' collective
intention to keep the peace, that is, their new capacity to work together
for a common, public purpose.

## 1820–21: Revolutions and Responses

The Vienna Settlement created a new category of problems: some problems are in "Europe's" interest, an interest distinct from that of any particular great power and shared by all. Invoking general interests in peace
treaties by itself was not new, the novelty was in the practice associated
with upholding it. The powers should consult and agree on how any European problem should be addressed. This tie between European problems
and great power forums led to great power self-restraint. In 1820, there

11. E.g., Schroeder 1994; Holsti 1992; Dakin 1979.

were four liberal revolutions in Europe: Spain, Portugal, Piedmont, and Naples. The meetings at Troppau, Laibach, and Verona had the same purpose of minimizing the destabilizing international effects of the revolutions. These meetings worked for two reasons. First, because public problems required public meetings, actors spoke differently when addressing a conflict. The prospect that a crisis could be a common problem led the great powers to justify their stance toward it with respect to the public interest. Without the option of meeting, it is reasonable to assume that there would not have been such attention to the potential impact of a given revolt on Europe as a whole, rather than its impact on any given individual state. The forum—a locale linked to their commitment, in which parties woud be visible to each other—added stakes to this label. Second, once a public frame was linked to a crisis, participants acted in ways consistent with their joint commitment. Disagreements were domesticated by being couched as differences in interpretations of the Vienna Settlement. This modified selfish behavior and kept the alliance together. I argue that if there had been no option to meet, no practice associated with the category "public problem," the outcome would have been meaningfully different, and the prospects for maintaining the settlement would have been diminished.

### Getting to Troppau

The first spontaneously called meeting of the allies[12] took place on Austrian territory, in Troppau, from late October through December 1820. It came about only because of the joint commitment at Vienna. The fact that each of the five powers had the standing to call a meeting when "European" interests were at stake ultimately trapped Metternich into holding a cabinet-level meeting with the full alliance to discuss a revolt in Naples, which was in Austria's sphere of influence.

A SPANISH STEP.    The road to Troppau began not in Naples, however, but in Spain. In January 1820, a contingent of Spanish troops revolted against their king, Ferdinand VII; by March the revolutionaries had compelled Ferdinand to accept a liberal constitution. Alexander suggested that the Quadruple Alliance be "activated" through a joint meeting of Russia,

---

12. The 1818 meeting at Aix-le-Chappelle (Aachen) was a "pre-arranged ceremony for winding up the military occupation of France, settling her debts and readmitting her (with some reservations) among the great powers." Crawley 1965, 669; Phillips 1934a; Dunn 1929, 68; Satow 1917, 79–80.

Austria, Britain, and Prussia, to craft a common response in case the king fell or the revolution would not die out on its own.[13] A meeting over Spain would have been the first use of the consultation provision, and the alliance was divided. Prussia proposed that the allies meet in Paris to jointly mediate.[14] France had drafted an individual letter of sympathy and aid for the Spanish king but then acquiesced to Alexander's suggestion for a conference, as long as it would be held in Paris.[15] Austria and Britain each opposed a joint response. Local intelligence from their ambassadors maintained that the revolution did not seem contagious.[16] Metternich supported "magisterial inaction,"[17] not wanting either France or Russia to act under the guise of a "European" intervention. Britain avoided taking a public stance. Castlereagh did not support the revolution but instructed his ambassador not to interfere with Spain unless the king's life was at stake or Spain attacked Portugal.[18]

In the spring the British cabinet asked Castlereagh for a memo on the situation.[19] This response, Castlereagh's State Paper of May 5, 1820, was circulated to the allies once the Cabinet adopted it. In it Castlereagh made specific arguments about the situation in Spain and general arguments about the conditions under which it was appropriate to "concert" their actions and the function of the alliance as a whole.

First, he argued that Spain's instability did not justify activating the alliance because it did not threaten to spill over to other states. The Spanish king had accepted the constitution and, while it was not ideal that the constitution had resulted from a military revolution, there was no "direct and imminent danger [of Spanish aggression against neighbors] which had always been regarded, at least in this country, as alone constituting the case which would justify external interference."[20] Each power should therefore feel free to advise Spain on its own, but "these warnings need not be made in a corporate character which would rather tend 'to offend than to conciliate or persuade.'"[21]

Second, the State Paper suggested a particular interpretation of what

13. Schroeder 1962, 25; Webster 1925, 228; Bridge 1979, 39–40.
14. Webster 1925 229–31; Schroeder 1962, 27; Schroeder 1994, 608.
15. Webster 1925, 230–31.
16. Webster 1925, 228.
17. Bridge 1979, 40; Webster 1925, 232.
18. Webster 1925, 233; Schroeder 1962, 27.
19. Webster 1925, 234.
20. Webster 1925, 238.
21. Webster 1925, 238.

meetings were for. Great power conferences are for "execut[ing] a purpose already decided upon," not for "fram[ing] a course of policy under delicate and difficult circumstances."[22] Anything decided upon in a joint conference must be backed with force. Words alone, coming from the great powers from a conference, will seem like no more than meddling. Therefore, a common principle is best forged through "confidential communications between the cabinets."[23]

Third, the State Paper also suggested the function and limits of the alliance: building from the principle of nonintervention and recognizing that each power had a different form of government, the alliance is meant only to combat military threats to stability. The alliance "never was . . . intended as a union for the Government of the world, or for the superintendence of the internal affairs of other states."[24] Rather, "what is intended to be combated, as forming any part of the duty as Allies, is the notion, but too perceptibly prevalent, that whenever any great political event shall occur, as in Spain . . . it is to be regarded almost as a matter of course, that it belongs to the allies to charge themselves collectively with the responsibility of exercising some jurisdiction concerning such possible eventual danger."[25] Concerting their power should not be a routine response to instability all over Europe. Because no representative government could agree to the principle of routinely interfering in the internal affairs of another government (in other words, it cannot be generalized to the alliance), "the sooner such a doctrine shall be distinctly abjured as forming in any degree the basis of our Alliance the better."[26] "Constitutional differences between the Allies" mean that only the great dangers will be those allies can work together on.[27] Britain will intervene "when actual danger menaces the system of Europe: but this country cannot and will not act upon . . . speculative principles of precaution."[28]

After the State Paper was circulated, calls for an allied conference stopped. The other powers each adopted Castlereagh's frame and attempted to justify their recent behaviors in light of it. Prussia backed off

---

22. Webster 1925, 237.
23. Webster 1925, 237.
24. Webster 1925, 238; also see Ward and Gooch 1922–23, appendix A.
25. Webster 1925, 238–39.
26. Webster 1925, 240.
27. Webster 1925, 238.
28. Webster 1925, 240.

its initial enthusiasm for mediation and for a general guarantee.[29] France apologized for its efforts at a secret mission, with the foreign minister going so far as to note with regret that "it was from neglect of the principles [of the State Paper] that all the troubles of the last five years in France had sprung."[30] For his part, Metternich did not simply refuse a meeting on the Spanish revolt, but praised Alexander and contributed his own principled statement about revolutions. "Foreign action has never either arrested or controlled the effects of a revolution."[31]

Stepping back, what stands out is how this diplomatic exchange, culminating in all five powers acquiescing to the State Paper, shored up the alliance by clarifying its role. The shared rationale for the alliance had been narrow and nonideological, oriented toward preserving European stability and not policing domestic regime type. This meant that a revolt in Europe was not necessarily a European revolt and did not necessarily warrant the great powers' collective attention. Moreover, the allies had decided against guaranteeing the settlement. Crises on the continent called for meetings, they did not automatically trigger great power intervention.

The arguments of the State Paper held the day not necessarily because any of these statesmen were persuaded or had internalized a shared meaning of the alliance, but because the State Paper gave the allies little rhetorical room to maneuver. It relied on rationales that all five of them agreed on, and not many rationales fit that requirement. The State Paper reminded them of the extent and limits of their shared commitment in a way that none of them could publicly reject without appearing as if undermining the treaties. In the face of the uncertainty about how to respond to the Spanish revolt, once the State Paper was known to all the great powers, it had the power to rhetorically trap[32] or coerce[33] them into publicly endorsing Britain's position. That position had a behavioral implication: abstain from intervening in Spain.

It was difficult to argue against the State Paper without also arguing against the Vienna Settlement. Consider the counterfactual possibility that upon circulation of the State Paper Russia had publicly invoked the

29. Webster 1925, 242.
30. Webster 1925, 244.
31. Schroeder 1962, 28.
32. Schimmelfennig 2001.
33. Krebs and Jackson 2007, 42.

Holy Alliance or France had publicly raised its Bourbon connection as a justification for action. Either of these would have sent a clear signal that they were willing to undermine the authority of the Vienna Settlement in the name of other authorities—religion, dynasty—that could not be generalized to the full alliance. In addition, once Castlereagh linked Britain's nonintervention stance to its own representative government, as a fellow and more fledgling democracy France could hardly disagree without raising suspicions.[34]

This diplomatic exchange took place only because of the great powers' experiment at Vienna. Without the stipulated link between European problems and joint consultation, it would not have been necessary for the five allies to agree on a definition of the Spanish revolt. Each could have maintained a private understanding. The problem they would have faced, if each acted on its private understanding, would have been that none could have had full confidence that the others would accept it. With a publicly shared meaning of the revolt, in contrast, a speaker who gave a rationale inconsistent with the Vienna Settlement's principles would have been exposed as a revisionist. Only because of the State Paper could the great powers convey their status quo intentions; only because of the forum provision was it necessary to call for a shared interpretation in the first place.

REPERCUSSION IN ITALY.    Shortly after that exchange, in July 1820, revolution broke out in Naples, and the Italian revolutionaries proclaimed the Spanish constitution. Unlike the Spanish revolt, this one was a surprise. Spain's regime had been unstable, but Ferdinand I's regime in Naples was considered one of the most stable of the Italian governments.[35] The revolt put moderates in charge, which meant there was no direct threat of contagion. According to the rationale of the State Paper, this was not a situation requiring great power attention.

In Metternich's view, however, the Naples revolt posed an existential threat to Austria and to the Habsburg Empire. The Italian states were in Austria's sphere of influence, and a peaceful transition from absolute to constitutional monarchy might have had a domino effect. If successful in Naples, constitutional revolution could spread throughout Italy; if successful in Italy, it could spread to the German states. Just one year earlier, Metternich had radically suppressed freedom of association and the

34. Webster 1925, 241–42.
35. Schroeder 1962, 32; Webster 1925, 259ff.; Bridge 1979, 40.

press in the German states in order to keep out revolutionary ideas. Now, preserving German stability seemed to require preventing any successful revolutionary precedent in the neighborhood.

In other words, for Metternich, the Naples revolt required attention, but only from Austria. The stability of the Habsburg Empire was a private, not a public, European problem. He favored a unilateral Austrian intervention to restore Ferdinand I's absolute monarchy. In the summer of 1820, Metternich followed a policy of nonrecognition and built up troop strength in Lombardy-Venetia. He secured the informal approval of the German and Italian states. Among the great powers, Prussia approved. Perhaps more surprisingly, Britain also conveyed support. Italy lay in the sphere of influence explicitly granted to Austria in the Vienna Settlement. Britain pressed Austria to act quickly.[36]

Rather than take quick decisive action, however, oddly enough Metternich began to talk the talk of the alliance commitment. He took a public stance on Naples, generalizing his interest in the revolt and deriving those interests from his earlier circular that had responded to the State Paper. Metternich argued to Russia and France that while foreign intervention is not generally capable of stabilizing revolutionary situations, the Naples revolt was a particularly dangerous problem, and it was in Europe's interest to put it down quickly. Metternich instructed the Austrian ambassador in Paris to tell the French that this revolution "was too dangerous for any power to be thinking of special interests. Louis and his ministry ought rather to be busy making sure that they did not share the fate of their fellow Bourbons in Spain and Naples."[37] Austria was the great power best poised to resolve the situation, particularly since its survival was most immediately threatened, and Metternich intimated that the measures would be best taken unilaterally. "It is not in the form of conferences of the five Cabinets that [Austrian survival] can be assured."[38]

Metternich framed Naples as a European problem but was arguing that acting in Europe's interest did not require either a great power meeting or any joint action. Merely conveying to one another their shared perspective was enough; this could be accomplished entirely through correspondence. In Metternich's view, a public expression of unity would not

36. Britain based its support on an Austro-Neapolitan Treaty of 1815 that "debarred Ferdinand from introducing constitutional changes without Austrian consent." Bridge 1979, 40.

37. Schroeder 1962, 46.

38. Schroeder 1962, 50.

add value. Needless to say, this frame allowed him to rely on Vienna Settlement rationales while acting without allied input much less constraint.

None of the great powers would publicly support the idea that Austria could act for their common interests without linking its actions to a great power meeting. Russia and France maintained that when it came to European problems, each of the great powers should have a voice in whatever steps were taken. Russia even admonished Metternich that had they met earlier regarding Spain they would not be in this situation, and Alexander insisted on a "full congress on the model of Aix-la-Chapelle."[39] France suggested a cabinet-level congress and supported the idea of "collective intervention." A French circular to the other foreign ministries stated that since France was more affected by happenings in Naples than Austria, France should convene the congress.[40] Britain approached Naples as a private Austrian problem and continued to handle it the old way, relying on bilateral diplomacy and balance of power rationales. Britain demanded that its continued support for Austrian unilateral intervention remain private, however. It refused to publicly condemn the revolution much less attend a conference to discuss its perils.

Metternich then proposed to hold a congress rather than act unilaterally, but at least initially neither Russia nor Britain was satisfied.[41] His first proposal was for ambassadors of the other three allies to be invited to observe a bilateral meeting of the Austrian and Russian sovereigns. When Alexander rejected this, Metternich proposed an informal conference between himself and the great power ambassadors at Vienna, to approve a plan that was to be adopted in advance: joint recognition and condemnation of the state of revolt, nonrecognition of the new regime, formation of a permanent center in Vienna to monitor revolutionary developments throughout Europe, and full powers to the ambassadors to commit their states. Since the conference would consist of allied ambassadors meeting with Metternich, the conference would be "strictly limited in competence and under Austrian auspices, and committed in advance to moral support of Austria."[42] In other words, the meeting would have the semblance of great power consultation, but basically would amount to a Greek chorus

39. Bridge 1979, 41; Schroeder 1962, 53.
40. Bridge 1979, 41.
41. Bridge 1979, 42
42. Schroeder 1962, 52.

for Austrian policy.[43] Dissatisfied, Alexander continued to press for the alliance to meet at the top level and lobbied hard to convince both France and Britain to send fully empowered representatives.

Metternich ultimately yielded to Russia's demands and agreed to hold a "full dress congress" at Troppau.[44] His ties to Castlereagh were important, but England was an ocean away and Russia (and to a lesser extent France) the more immediate threat. Metternich was uncertain about Russia's intentions, and the rationale he gave was that he could not risk Alexander "abandon[ing] the moral tie which unites us and set[ting] himself up again as the power protecting the spirit of innovation" in Europe.[45]

The great powers inched toward their first experiment under the consultation provision. With the prospect of a congress, alliances shifted. Britain distanced itself from a collective policy and from an interventionist policy more generally by sending an observer rather than an empowered representative. This influenced France. Without Britain's full participation, the congress would consist of the three autocratic powers and France. If France acquiesced to an Austrian intervention under those circumstances, to any observer France would seem to have supported that conservative policy while Britain would seem aloof. While eager to regain influence in Italy and to have the alliance devote attention to causes other than restraining France, the French regime did not want to leave Britain the sole beneficiary of political gains from any further spread of constitutionalism. France followed Britain's lead and sent only an observer to Troppau.[46]

### The State Paper as Rhetorical Trap

The diplomatic exchange resulting in the Troppau Congress shows that the Vienna Settlement's consultation provision made a difference. The settlement gave each great power signatory the standing to demand a meeting; once a meeting was proposed, others owed the speaker a response. This contestation about what constituted a European problem otherwise might not have happened. It might otherwise have been possible for, say, Russia to intervene in Spain, claiming to act in Europe's interest, and/or Austria to intervene in Naples, making the same rhetorical claim. Instead,

43. Kissinger 1957, 25; Schroeder 1962, 105.
44. Bridge 1979, 42.
45. Schroeder 1962, 54–55.
46. Bridge 1979, 42.

the claim, "European problem," was associated with a practice, "group meeting." No single great power could successfully categorize a problem as "European" without agreement from the others, as Alexander found out, nor could a single great power sever the link between problems and meetings, as Metternich discovered.

The puzzle in this period is why Metternich held a meeting about the Naples situation at all, since he preferred to act alone? Metternich's interest was unilateral intervention in Naples, and he had the capabilities and the support of a major ally. He did not want a great power meeting, and it is difficult to think of any reason he would have acquiesced to a "full dress congress" other than being trapped by his own rhetoric and constrained to act consistently.

Metternich's response to the State Paper had been a principled, public stance against great power intervention. His goal was to prevent action on Spain, but in agreeing with Castlereagh he had argued that the alliance existed to protect the European interest in continental stability. It was not about using their power to quash revolution. The principled stance boxed in France and Russia, and they abandoned calls for either a meeting or concerted action on Spain.

Had Metternich abandoned the principle that foreign intervention could not solve the problem of domestic revolution only a few months later, when faced with the Naples revolt, he would have been exposed as blatantly parochial. Contradicting himself in this way also could have served as a pretext for others to abandon course as well, with several possible destabilizing effects. First, Russia could have used the opportunity to take a stand on Spain. Already Russia had troops in northern Europe, and a unilateral Austrian intervention in Naples would divert Austrian armies to the south, leaving the Habsburg Empire exposed to what would have been an irritated Russia. Even a verbal protest from Russia could give hope to central European revolutionaries that Russia might defend constitutional aspirations against Austria. Second, France could have taken advantage of the opportunity by resurrecting the long-standing rivalry between these two great powers. That rivalry was primarily dynastic, but another axis of rivalry was that these two states had rival principles of rule. If Naples became a constitutional rather than an absolute monarchy, France would be its more rightful protector.[47]

To hold Russia and France in check, Metternich adopted a European frame. But drawing the Naples revolt under the purview of their commit-

47. Bridge 1979, 41.

ment then gave the other powers standing to determine how it was combated. Metternich could not de-link European interests from great power meetings. No other power would publicly agree that they could act together for Europe merely by resorting to the usual diplomatic channels. It required the new tool of peacetime face-to-face public talk. It is therefore fair to say that the rhetorical move of Europeanizing the revolt set in motion a chain of events that led to a meeting of all the sovereigns.

From here, the link between public interests and forum meetings enabled them to tame their security dilemma, so that Austrian intentions in Naples did not seem as opaque and indeed seemed to emanate from the group. Austrian troops were on the ground, but Europe had intervened. Such collective self-restraint was not possible in the eighteenth century and would not have been possible without their forum.

There are two plausible alternative accounts of why Metternich agreed to meet. First, some might argue that he considered the meetings to be "cheap talk" that would not affect his ability to achieve his goals. The evidence suggests this was not the case. If meetings were cheap talk then we would expect him not to care whether one was held or not. Instead, he fought not to have one regarding Spain, and for as informal a meeting as possible regarding Naples with a great power precommitment to his preferred policy. These moves suggest that Metternich worried that talking together among sovereigns would be costly. By linking his self-interests to the general interest in European stability, Metternich brought his treaty partners along, reducing the risk of Russian or French destabilizing or competitive reactions. But pulling Naples into the sphere of European concerns added daylight between Austria's individual intentions and its actions, which gave the other powers a say over how this absolutist empire would act in its own sphere of influence.

Second, some might speculate that Metternich called for a meeting to signal Austria's benign, nonexpansionist intentions,[48] or as a way to increase transparency about the motives of his fellow great powers.[49] But neither of these contemporary interpretations of the functions of institutions captures what was going on in this first case. Metternich was backed into a meeting, suggesting that he did not choose it in order to signal or get information. Moreover, there simply was not enough shared information about what meetings were for—calling a meeting did not send an unambiguous signal.

48. See Thompson 2006 on why powerful states choose multilateral options.
49. Jervis 1983; Lipson 1994; Lindley 2007.

*Troppau and Laibach Congresses*

While Metternich had agreed to a congress, he intended to keep Austrian policy in Naples unconstrained. This he was able to do, but only with great effort and a little luck. Metternich convened the congress in a small isolated Austrian town where he could control information and keep proceedings secret, and he set the agenda and planned the details. The delegates assembled at Troppau in late October. The three Eastern powers sent their sovereigns along with foreign ministers. Britain and France sent only observers without full powers, meaning that each was required to refer to his home government before voting.

Metternich opened the group discussion, reading a memo on the conditions of Europe and the problem of revolution. The debate was framed in terms of treaty obligations to the alliance. The central question was whether the great powers should formulate a general statement against revolution and a procedure for the great powers as keepers of the peace to follow. Did the Vienna Settlement give rise to a right or even an obligation to intervene in the domestic affairs of revolutionary states, based on either the great powers' own assessments of a threat to stability or a request from the legitimate sovereign for help?[50]

This question was posed to the full group, but most of the diplomatic work took place behind the scenes. The end product, the draft Troppau Protocol, reflected Metternich's heavy influence.[51] Russia had favored a general principle of intervention, or at least a discussion of the Portuguese and Spanish situations and not just Naples (a Portuguese revolt had broken out in August). Russia also circulated a memo early in the conference stipulating that any Austrian intervention could only take place after an allied attempt to reconcile king and people, with the goal of creating an order that would support an "authentically national desire."[52] After private bilateral meetings between Metternich and Alexander and secret meetings among the three Eastern powers, however, any reference to national desires was gone.

The resulting draft protocol of mid-November was more a general statement than a specific response to the situation in Naples. It gave all European sovereigns the right to ask for help from the allies in the event of a revolt,[53] appealing to a general right of great power intervention that

50. Schroeder 1962, 64.
51. Satow 1917, 83–84.
52. Bridge 1979, 43.
53. Bridge 1979, 43; Webster 1925, 294–95.

it derived from the treaties of 1814, 1815, and 1818. The draft protocol justified Austrian intervention in Naples and also included a letter to the Neapolitan sovereign, Ferdinand, inviting him to invite the allies to help him restore his legitimate government. Finally, it called on the three powers to inform Rome, Turin, and Florence of their plan, and to invite Britain and France to contribute their good offices.

The protocol did not emanate from and could not be generalized to the full alliance. The interpretation of the Vienna Settlement it offered was at odds with the interpretation all five powers recently accepted when they expressed support of Castlereagh's State Paper. And it did so as if all five had agreed: the Eastern powers submitted an already-signed declaration to their allies.

Once they were made aware of the draft protocol, the question was whether Britain and France would withdraw their observers from the congress. To do so would register a rift in the alliance and seem to end the experiment in great power management. They did not. Instead, Castlereagh had the British ambassador at Troppau read a statement reiterating the State Paper arguments, which put on record British opposition to the protocol's interpretation of the alliance as the "armed guardian of all thrones." Britain still quietly supported an Austrian intervention but made clear that it would not even commit publicly to nonrecognition of the revolutionary Naples regime and warned against allied intervention in Spain and Portugal. Britain also demanded that the Eastern powers remove the signatures of France and Britain and that the protocol be made less formal.[54] Metternich backed down.

But Metternich's agreement was mere words. The Troppau Circular the ministers of the three eastern courts received was not the revised and downgraded version. It presented the statement on intervention as if it were an agreement reached by the full congress, glossing over the differences between East and West.[55] In January 1821, the *London Morning Chronicle* published the text of the circular. Other papers soon followed, and Europe's literate public suddenly was aware that an agreement to protect thrones was reached at Troppau—an agreement that looked to be signed by all five powers.[56] Britain and France suddenly were aware that the Eastern powers had acted duplicitously: for the last month the major courts of Europe all had the impression that France and Britain

54. Nicolson 1946, 268; Webster 1925, 296, 298, 300–306.
55. Webster 1925, 306, 316–17.
56. Webster 1925, 320.

supported both intervention in Naples and an intervention doctrine derived from the Vienna treaties. The Netherlands, which had recognized the revolutionary regime, expressed dismay at Britain's apparent conservative turn. The Prussian minister used the circular in Madrid to generate fear of impending great power intervention in Spain.[57]

This time Castlereagh voiced British protests beyond congress channels, making clear that the allies were not in unison and potentially undercutting Metternich's policy. He made public in diplomatic circles the State Paper, adding additional arguments against intervention. He also for the first time spoke openly of the need in Naples for a moderate constitution.[58] These steps were the most visible airing of the rift among the allies. Up to now, disagreements had remained within the private circle of the five powers, and Britain had not voiced concern for the form of government for states in Austria's sphere of influence.[59]

Metternich's response to this tumult was perhaps the most surprising. According to Charles Webster, "so alarming were the rumors that reached Vienna" that Metternich published both the Troppau Circular and Castlereagh's response in the Austrian press.[60] Austria had a highly developed surveillance system and strict censorship laws recently authored by Metternich himself.[61] It is not clear why he would choose to publicize a disagreement among the great powers.

Despite the pre-congress publicity, the actual Laibach meeting differed little from the meeting at Troppau. All five powers participated and sent essentially the same delegations, with Britain and France remaining observers. The congress met in Austrian territory under the full control of Metternich. Its agenda was similarly sealed off from outside influences, and the main work was done in three power meetings and through private meetings in which Metternich always was involved. And, as he had at Troppau, Metternich tried to make the intervention appear to emanate from the full alliance using broad language in the plenary sessions that left open the possibility that Britain and France agreed to both an Austrian intervention in particular and an intervention doctrine more generally.[62]

57. Webster 1925, 320–21.
58. Schroeder 1962, 112; Webster 1925, 319–22; Satow 1917, 83–84.
59. Schroeder 1994, 611; Satow 1917, 83–84; cf. Bridge 1979, 45.
60. Webster 1925, 324.
61. Schroeder 1962, 60, 243; Kissinger 1957, 278.
62. Schroeder 1962, 104–5, Webster 1925, 314–15.

At Laibach, Metternich created the semblance of a fair process. He had invited the affected sovereign, Ferdinand I, to invite the great powers to intervene.[63] He also invited parties in Italy that would be affected by Austria's intervention in Naples: the pope and the rulers of Sardinia-Piedmont, Tuscany, and Modena.[64] On February 6, Austrian troops crossed the Po River and two weeks later the plan for Naples's government was announced.

The three powers alone had authorized the Austrian intervention.[65] They then agreed on a three-year occupation of Naples. At the final plenary session the powers resolved to reconvene in Florence, in September 1822, to monitor the progress and impact of the occupation. At this point, France, Britain, and the Italians left. By early April, Italy was pacified, and shortly after this the remaining powers departed from Laibach. On May 12, Russia, Austria, and Prussia updated the European courts.

From the start, Austria intended to intervene unilaterally, and this is what it did. The formal presence of the Italian delegations at Laibach did not translate to political voice. They were not included in the main deliberations. Metternich even wrote Ferdinand's speeches.[66] The plan for Naples's government was framed as Ferdinand I's own initiative. The Italian states were invited to acquiesce, which they did.[67]

## Collective Self-Restraint

While Metternich acted on his intention to intervene unilaterally in Naples, he modified the way he pursued that intention in order not to alienate his allies. His individual intention was filtered through their joint commitment. He hosted a congress of sovereigns to debate an intervention he had planned to take unilaterally. The actual intervention was brief and bloodless, its main repercussion was the similarly restrained intervention in Spain, and the alliance remained sufficiently intact that the powers would work together on the Greek and other questions still to come.

The disagreement among the great powers was nontrivial. It followed the major fault line among the alliance partners, domestic regime type.

63. Webster 1925.
64. Satow 1917, 84; Dunn 1929, 74.
65. Dunn 1929, 74.
66. Bridge 1979, 44; Schroeder 1962, 106.
67. Schroeder 1962, 97.

Tethering that disagreement to their treaty commitment made a difference, and it was made more possible by the tie to forums than it otherwise
would have been. Because of the Vienna Settlement and the provision for
meetings, great power leaders spoke and acted as if they were obligated
to one another regarding those problems. They did not want to meet if
they did not want to act on the commitment; if they did want to act, holding a meeting was a way to prevent destabilizing reactions. The forums
thus make possible self-restraint in a case where we otherwise might not
expect it.

Imagine the counterfactual. Had the powers not met and determined
that the Austrian intervention was in the public interest, it is possible
that Austria would have intervened unopposed. But it is reasonable to
think that this would have alienated both Russia and France, possibly
spurring stronger French action in Spain, potentially with Russian help,
and possibly French competition for influence in Naples. The evidence
thus is consistent with the argument that the Vienna Settlement commitment, especially because of the link to forums, enabled great power self-
restraint.

*Alternative Arguments*

RESTRAINT?    Some analysts of the period treat the heated airing of ideological differences between East and West as the end of the alliance. In
Harold Nicolson's words, with the Troppau Protocol "the Concert of
Europe had disintegrated; the Holy Alliance had succeeded in destroying
the Quadruple Alliance; the Conference System had failed."[68]

What this interpretation overlooks is that being able to contain great
power competition as an interpretive disagreement about treaty interpretation is an accomplishment. As vehement as Castlereagh's protests were,
he consistently framed them—in print, in covering letters to his ambassadors, and at home in parliamentary debate—by reiterating British commitment to the alliance.[69] If this was Britain continuing the old balance
of power practices, it was an awfully soft mode of balancing, especially
compared to the balancing practices of the eighteenth century.[70] Castle-

---

68. Nicolson 1946, 269. Crawley 1965, 674–77 also emphasizes the ideological divide as
rending the Concert. Cf. Haas 2005, chapter three.

69. Webster 1925, 319–28.

70. On soft balancing, see, e.g., Pape 2005; cf. Brooks 2005.

reagh did not threaten to break from the alliance and was satisfied with the inclusion of a paragraph noting the British protest as a sort of obiter dictum tacked on to the final statement at Laibach. Rather than sever the alliance or prompt the still-intense rivalries events in Italy and Spain triggered, the main conflict between Britain and the autocratic powers was played out verbally.

References to treaty interpretation are worth drawing attention to for both historical and analytical reasons. Historically, squaring state action against international law and precedent was a relatively new practice in the European states system. Andreas Osiander points out that one hundred years before, at the Utrecht peace conferences, no major actor relied on treaty or custom to anchor his claims, and no actor was criticized for violating treaty or custom. The principle of "Pacta sunt servanda," much less arguments over specific interpretations of treaties, did not play a role in the arguments or treaties signed.[71] Subsequent developments in the eighteenth century brought change, as a more secular practice and treaty-based law took over from its Christian and natural law predecessors. References to Europe rather than Christendom and to custom rather than natural law rose in the period between Utrecht and Vienna. But it had not long been regular practice to debate a potential policy by reconciling it to rival states against treaty commitments. This practice of reconciling present behaviors with past, reflecting on practices and placing them in a shared history, reflects a thickening of international society. Carrying out competition through argument, without ever a threat to resort to war, marks a significant change.

From the standpoint of my theory, what stands out is the fact that the disagreement was handled through words and not deeds. And they disagreed about what it means to guard the European peace, but all agreed that great powers have that role, and that they have it together. As Friedrich Kratochwil and others have long stressed, even dissent, if it is expressed within the terms of the shared commitment, can be part of upholding the commitment.[72] Metternich certainly pushed his agenda, but he did so without dropping the commitment to the alliance. By arguing in its terms, they enacted and reproduced their commitment and made it possible for their commitment to guide action—in this case to produce collective self-restraint.

71. Osiander 1994, 100–101.
72. Kratochwil 1989.

COLLECTIVE? Others read the events of this period as evidence not of the Concert's breakdown but of the fact that it never existed. Far from showing the demise of the alliance, Austrian intervention is part of the equilibrium dynamics of the Vienna Settlement. Underneath the epiphenomen of congress meetings and diplomatic disagreements, the invisible hand of the balance of power, operating at a structural level, produced this restrained outcome.[73] Austria acted within its sphere of influence and other great powers allowed it, just as it would have in the eighteenth century.

What this account overlooks is the extent to which Metternich's efforts to seem as if acting for the public interest injected uncertainty into the process and made a successful intervention less likely. Metternich talked and acted as if committed to the alliance even as he worked to stretch its remit. The author of the Carlsbad Decrees published the State Paper that undermined his own interpretation of the alliance; the staunch opponent of constitutional monarchy, much less democracy, invited the Italians in order to seem as if acting fairly.

Regarding the appearance of fairness, inviting the Italians made the process seem fairer, and involving all affected parties in discussions of public affairs had been a goal of the Vienna Settlement. These invitations were not necessarily "cheap talk." First, it was not clear the Italian delegations would fall in lockstep with Austrian goals. Russia and France had each suggested papal mediation rather than Austrian intervention in Naples, and the Papal States had not yet fully endorsed the Austrian policy. It certainly was possible that a papal representative could cause trouble at the joint sessions, especially if France or Russia supported him.[74] Metternich had already secured Italian permission for the intervention over the summer; by inviting the delegates he was only opening up an opportunity for trouble.[75] Second, it was not clear Ferdinand I *could* fall in lockstep. By all accounts he was a singularly incapable ruler. Although Metternich was committed to restoring absolute rule in Naples, "Even [he] and Gentz were shocked and embarrassed at the perfidy and cowardice of their miserable client,"[76] and found themselves writing his

---

73. Slantchev 2005.

74. Metternich had had problems with the Papal States prior to Troppau as well. Schroeder 1962, 107, 58–59.

75. This ultimately was not a problem. Schroeder 1994, 612.

76. Webster 1925, 314.

speeches.[77] Third, and finally, through November the moderate constitutionalists were in charge in Naples (which is when Metternich decided to invite them).[78] By the time the invitation was received, things had taken a more radical turn and reactionaries were not able to take advantage of the invitation.[79] This worked to Metternich's advantage, but he could not have known this when he made the decision regarding the invitations. Extending the invitations only added complications and uncertainty to his policy. What it did, however, was make the process seem fairer and more deliberative, more palatable, perhaps, to the Western observers. He was able to get the outcome he wanted, but only through keeping a tight rein on his guests.

The self-imposed constraint to appear as if acting in the public interest added work for Metternich. It made it harder to be duplicitous and required vigilance: he had delegates under police surveillance, he monitored the British press, he coached Ferdinand and Alexander; he tried hard to keep the British ambassador away so he could renege on commitments while privately placating Castlereagh; and he kept the French delegates in competition with one another. Luckily for Metternich, the disagreement with Britain was over the public rationale for policy and not the policy itself.[80] Luckily, the British representative was unable to follow up on Castlereagh's call for a constitution, and luckily Alexander, who earlier would have been apt to take up that call, was by that point firmly in Metternich's pocket. In the short period between Troppau and Laibach there had been a mutiny in Russia, which made Alexander wary of revolution and more supportive of Metternich.[81] Because of these unforeseeable contingencies, Castlereagh's arguments for mediation to give Naples a moderate constitution came to nothing.

### 1821–22: Grouping Alexander

I have shown that there were discernible effects of having linked their Vienna Settlement commitment to the tool of forum consultation. But the argument that the great powers' commitment pulled their behavior

77. Schroeder 1962, 105–6.
78. Schroeder 1962, 33–34, 98–100.
79. Schroeder 1962, 102; Webster 1925, 310.
80. Kissinger 1957, 265.
81. Bridge 1979, 43.

through its link to forums is more apparent in the period just after Troppau and Laibach, as they reacted together to the Greek revolt in the Balkans. In 1821–22 the great powers collectively kept Russia from intervening on behalf of the Greeks, which all felt would have led to European war. They accomplished this by adopting a definition of the Greek revolt that kept it within the parameters of their public reason: maintain the settlement, support sovereigns, avoid European instability. Given the ambivalent relationship between the Europe and the Porte and the ambiguous position of the Balkans on Europe's frontier, every aspect of the strategy was awkward. Given the insults to Russian national interests on top of the continual Ottoman atrocities, containing Russia was by no means certain. None of these states wanted to destabilize Europe, but it was not clear they could prevent war. I show that Russian restraint was possible because of two things: the great powers came to share a definition of the Greek revolt, they each knew that the others held that interpretation, and they knew that they would be meeting about it. This Europeanized the Greek revolt, which prevented Russian intervention.

In this section I show that Russia's choice not to intervene in the first two years of the revolt can be traced to the great powers' collective intention to maintain European tranquility. I first show that Russian interests in the revolt were mixed. There were strong interest-based arguments for and against intervention, and strong legal arguments for and against intervention. I then show that the allies attempted to keep the revolt a European problem first through private bilateral diplomacy, which did not work, and then through a public strategy linked to a conference, which did work. Because there was a forum, their commitment pulled behavior. Without it, it is reasonable to conclude that Russia would have intervened.

Scholarship on Alexander's decision in this case tends to attribute the cause of restraint to Alexander's and/or Metternich's personality and motives. Either Metternich duped Alexander or Alexander was singularly attached to the idea of Europe and put collective principles before his national interests. On these accounts, to the extent that the forum mattered at all, it was to make these interests more transparent. After showing how the great powers Europeanized the Greek revolt, I compare my account to those that stress personality, diplomacy, and transparency.

### Greek Revolt: Europe's Problem?

In March 1821, while the powers were still at Laibach, a Russian army officer of Greek descent, Alexander Ypsilantes, declared a Greek revolt against Ottoman rule. This problem was not as straightforward as the revolts discussed earlier in the chapter. It was not obvious that this was a European concern at all. First, because the Ottoman Empire was not party to the Vienna Settlement, technically even its European holdings—the Balkans, home to most Ottoman Greeks—were not under great power purview. While Russia and the Porte had fought a war during the Napoleonic period, from 1806 to 1812, the Treaty of Bucharest ending that war had not been brought under the umbrella settlement at Vienna. Russo-Turkish relations were treated by all the great powers as private bilateral matters rather than public European issues.

Second, in this case the incentives were to intervene on behalf of the rebels, not the sovereign. This was true especially for Russia. Greeks were co-religionists as Orthodox Christians, and the czar's main foreign policy advisor, John Capodistrias,[82] was Greek. Russia also had long-standing designs on Ottoman territory, and since Catherine the Great's reign had followed a policy of using its connection to the Greeks to gain presence in the Balkans. Catherine had aided the Greeks in a 1770 (unsuccessful) revolt at Navarino, then secured special treaty-based protection for them as Orthodox Christians in the Treaty of Küçük Kaynarca in 1774.[83] More recently, Turkish noncompliance with the Treaty of Bucharest had kept Russo-Turkish tensions high throughout the 1810s.[84]

Nevertheless, upon hearing of the revolt, Alexander denounced it, disavowed connections to the Greeks, and authorized the sultan to crush the revolt. He even consented to a temporary Ottoman occupation of the Principalities. Alexander now deeply feared revolution, and easily was convinced by Metternich's arguments that the Greek revolt was part of a general European conspiracy headquartered in Paris that threatened all thrones.[85] Alexander had Capodistrias draft the allied declaration against the revolt, and it was publicized immediately. With neither Russian nor local support among the population in the Principalities, Ypsilantes's revolt soon petered out.

Meanwhile, however, a revolt broke out on the mainland and several

---

82. In this period his name was Iannis Capo D'Istria. In 1827 when he accepted the presidency of Greece he anglicized his name. To simplify I shall use the anglicized name throughout the narrative rather than switch midway.

83. Schroeder 1962, 168; Jelavich 1991, 50–51; Anderson 1966, 8.

84. Anderson 1966, 59–60.

85. Jelavich 1983, 211, 223–24; Marriott 1940, 196–97; Woodhouse 1998 (1968), 132–34; Kissinger 1957, 288–89; Vinogradov 1981, 6–7; Temperley 1923, 87; Bridge 1979, 45.

islands, which engaged every stratum of the Greek population. Although
less organized than the crossing of the Pruth, it quickly gathered momen-
tum. The Ottomans responded forcefully, arresting and executing prominent Greeks, massacring Christians, pillaging churches, and hanging the
patriarch of the Greek Orthodox Church. The sultan neither condemned
the atrocities nor protected Greek or Russian property in Constantinople.[86] He also began to intercept ships in the Turkish Straits, the Bosporus and Dardanelles, which lay entirely under Ottoman control. The
Straits linked the Black Sea to the Aegean and thus to the Mediterranean
Sea. This hurt Russia more than any other European power. Between
1774 and 1821 Russia had greatly expanded its grain exports to western
Europe. This trade relied both on Greek shipping and merchants and
on the ability to get from the Black Sea to the Mediterranean. With the
Greeks in revolt and the Ottomans intercepting ships, Russia was effectively cut off from the European market. By 1824, fewer than five hundred ships left Odessa, compared to over three thousand per year in 1818
and 1819.[87]

In March, Metternich successfully had convinced Alexander that the
Greek revolt was no different from revolutions elsewhere in Europe.
But with explicit insults to Russian interests and prestige multiplying, the
European frame was increasingly awkward for the czar. Unlike European
revolutions, here the sovereign seemed more of a threat than the revolu-
tionaries.

The great power consensus began to fracture, and as the czar left Laibach in May 1821, he took two steps away from it. First, Alexander made
clear to Metternich and the British observer that he no longer saw the
Greek revolt as a European concern but as a bilateral one between Russia and the Ottoman Empire.[88] Second, the Russian ambassador to France
privately floated the possibility of a separate alliance, hinting that Russia might be willing to give land in Belgium and a protectorate over the
Morea (the Peloponnese peninsula in southern Greece) in exchange for
help in a European war. The overture formally was refused, but later in
the year the ministry that opposed the Russian plan fell and the new

---

86. Marriott 1940, 205; Seton-Watson 1968 (1937), 51–52; Nichols 1961, 53–54. Both
Greeks and Ottomans committed atrocities, but Ottoman actions were more widely discussed. Schroeder 1994, 616.

87. Anderson 1966, 60.

88. Nichols 1961, 53–54.

ultra-royalist ministry seemed possibly amenable. The other powers worried about the formation of a great power coalition separate from the alliance.[89]

Not just Russia but Prussia also chipped away at the Laibach consensus by circulating a memo among the powers arguing in favor of Russian intervention. This memo rejected the initial Concert interpretation of the Greek revolt and argued that the sultan was not a legitimate sovereign. The Prussian government soon backed off, but the memo raised uncertainty about whether the alliance would hold up.[90] These developments played into the hands of the war party in Russia, which included such influential members as Capodistrias.[91]

Over the summer of 1821, with the great powers no longer in one another's company, the situation became increasingly tense. Russian correspondence with both the Ottomans and the allies focused particularly on the insults to the Greeks as fellow Orthodox Christians. Alexander issued an ultimatum demanding that the sultan restore Orthodox churches, respect Christian rights, and allow Russia to help pacify the Danubian Principalities (Moldavia and Walachia / present-day Romania) on its southern border). The rights of religious protection Russia demanded were rights that it had claimed (and the other great powers had recognized) since the late eighteenth century. That is, Russia was at least equally concerned to protect Christians as to maintain its rights in the Principalities. Russia gave the sultan eight days to respond, at which point Russia would have the right to go to war. When the sultan did not respond, Russia suspended relations in August.[92]

At this point it was not clear what Russia would do. Russian interests pointed in two equally plausible but opposite directions. There was a strong interest in war. First, for balance of power reasons Alexander had the temptation and capacity to go to war. Russian trade was harmed, Russian nationals and Orthodox Christianity were insulted, and the Bucharest Treaty was being violated. Moreover, Russia was materially the strongest of the great powers, and it had the potential backing of two allies, France and Prussia. Second, Russian treaty commitments buttressed

89. Anderson 1966, 58; Schroeder 1994, 618–19; Nichols 1961, 54.

90. Kissinger 1957, 291.

91. Nichols 1961, 55; Schroeder 1962, 177.

92. Jelavich 1983, 213–14; Marriott 1940, 206–7; Anderson 1966, 61; Jelavich and Jelavich 1997 (1977), 47; Nichols 1961, 54–55.

the argument for war. The sultan was violating the Treaty of Bucharest and none of the allies contested Russia's rights to secure compliance with that bilateral treaty. Additionally, Russia's summer protest invoked its status as protector of Christians, a long-standing legal right. The Russian ultimatum had acknowledged the sultan's right as a sovereign to crush the rebels. But it distinguished between Greeks as rebels and Greeks as Christians and argued that Russia could not permit Christians to be punished. Basically it left Russia plenty of room to intervene.[93]

A third factor tilting Russia toward war was that the Balkans were not necessarily subject to the rules of the Concert. The integrity of the Ottoman Empire was not under the informal collective watch of the Concert, and the stipulation that the powers meet to maintain its stability did not apply. According to their own rules, the four allies had little pressure to bring to bear in order to encourage Russian self-restraint beyond the traditional, behind-the-scenes tools of diplomacy, good offices, and mediation. Without the Concert's watch Russia could be perfectly collective minded and *still* have no responsibility to its allies when it came to the Balkans. Indeed, that was Alexander's view as he left Laibach. He said as much to Castlereagh in correspondence in the summer.[94] From this perspective Alexander could rationalize both seeking an alliance with France and unilaterally breaking relations with the Ottoman Empire. In sum, even containing the conflict fully within the frame of public law, recognized treaties, and alliance commitments, Alexander had the right to go to war.

Despite those incentives, however, there is evidence that Alexander was interested in avoiding war. He feared the implications of a war over the Greek Question. Like the other great power leaders, he believed that revolution anywhere in Europe would have a domino effect on European thrones. And he believed the Greeks were European enough, or at least the Balkans were close enough to the rest of Europe, for the dominoes to start falling. Thus when Capodistrias privately pressed for war, Alexander strongly disagreed: "If we respond to the Turks with war ... the Paris directing committee will triumph and no government will be left standing. I do not intend to leave a free field to the enemies of order. At all costs means must be found of avoiding war with Turkey."[95] He forbade Capo-

93. Schroeder 1994, 619; Vinogradov 1981, 7–8.
94. Webster 1925, 373.
95. Anderson 1966, 61.

distrias from mentioning war in any dispatches and assured the British ambassador that Russia did not want war.[96]

## Europeanizing the Conflict in Private

The potential connection to European revolution was the only thing keeping Alexander from helping the Greeks. Austria and Britain, the powers that most feared Russian expansion in the Balkans, played up the European dimension of the Greek Question. In the summer their diplomacy was bilateral. For example, in July Castlereagh wrote Alexander a personal letter, arguing that the Balkans were part of Europe and under the "charge" of the great power guardians, and that the Greeks were Europeans. But while as Europeans the Greeks deserved sympathy, they also were rebels. From the perspective of their guardianship of Europe, Castlereagh argued, the balance of power had to come first. Britain and Russia therefore must sympathize with the sultan.[97] Metternich relied on the same premises in his bilateral diplomacy with Russia. In several private notes to Alexander he argued that acting against the Greeks was crucial to European safety. Metternich flooded Alexander with reports of revolutionary conspiracies in Europe, arguing that revolution, not the Ottoman Empire, was the real enemy. Intervention against the Ottomans for the Greek cause would encourage more revolution and could pull down the institution of monarchy altogether.[98]

Both Castlereagh and Metternich were following a rhetorical strategy of putting the Balkans in Europe and defining the Greek Question as European. They referred to the Vienna Settlement as if these same diplomats had not all been there in 1815 and agreed to leave out the Ottoman Empire. This brought the Greek revolt under the umbrella definition of the revolutions plaguing Europe. Not only were the Balkans now part of the settlement, but also the Greeks were now "Europeans." Diplomatic communication also downplayed Russia's special connection to Orthodox Christianity. From a European perspective, Russia's relationship to the Greeks was no different from that of the rest of the alliance members.

The rhetorical strategy of these diplomatic initiatives was essentially the same one the Concert powers had followed at Laibach, and it was

96. Kissinger 1957, 296.
97. Webster 1925, 360–61; Kissinger 1957, 294; Bridge 1979, 46.
98. Kissinger 1957, 293; Anderson 1966, 59.

even broadly in line with the terms of Russia's own ultimatum to the sultan. The difference was that these summer initiatives were *private*. Each pursued the strategy unilaterally and was uncertain of the others' commitment to it. They spoke in terms of public law and European interests, but they did not propose a meeting among the powers. Other aspects of each of their behavior also undercut their shared agenda. For example, Britain had a long-standing friendly relationship with the Porte, and the British ambassador at Constantinople had not joined in a joint allied protest against Turkish atrocities in May. His reticence raised the possibility that Castlereagh's initiatives were insincere.[99] Sitting in Saint Petersburg, surrounded by a strong war party and armed with balance of power temptations and international legal support, Alexander found it difficult to "see" the European interest in supporting the sultan as a fellow sovereign. With Prussia and France seemingly unsteady in their own support of the European interpretation, and with Russia questioning British and Austrian intentions, private diplomacy seemed unable to avert a war that would certainly alter the European balance and destroy the equilibrium they had constructed at Vienna.

*Making Europe's Interests Visible*

Then, during a set of meetings among Metternich, Castlereagh, and their respective sovereigns, held at Hanover in October 1821, Austria and Britain committed to pursue a joint strategy. Convinced that the five-power alliance could restrain Russia, they agreed to work toward peace on the basis of the Vienna Settlement. This meeting and the resulting strategy were calculated to send a benign, concerted signal to Russia. The Concert powers would make it possible for Alexander to see Europe's common interest in the issue.

The Hanover strategy built from the strengths of the existing diplomacy in two ways. First, it clearly distinguished a sphere of private, bilateral Russo-Turkish concerns from the sphere of common, European concerns. Austria and Britain wrote to Alexander in late October, advocating the same strategy of splitting the Russian grievances into two strands, treaty violations versus the Greek Question.[100] As in the summer notes, they agreed that Treaty of Bucharest grievances were bilateral, and as

99. Schroeder 1962, 175.
100. Nichols 1961, 56.

such each offered their country's mediation and good offices. The Greek Question, however, they argued, was a European issue. Here, while they certainly should try to persuade the sultan to treat his Greek subjects better, the great powers must grant the sultan the sovereign right of nonintervention.

Second, they ignored Russia's special relationship to the Greeks as Orthodox Christians and demoted religious ties. Russia continued in its diplomacy to invoke its right to protect Orthodox Christians in the Ottoman Empire, which had been written into the bilateral Treaty of Küçük Kaynarca.[101] But the other great powers did not reference it. Instead, they generalized the bond using the shared language of Christianity and European civilization. Castlereagh argued that we are all Christians, while Metternich spoke of the humanitarian sympathy that all the powers share with the Greeks. Like dynastic ties, religious ties cut across sovereign boundaries. They offered an alternate axis of division, alliance, and rivalry than that of the Vienna Settlement, with its reliance on an equilibrium or balanced distribution of power. In other words, religious ties represented rival principles to the norms of sovereignty and nonintervention that anchored European public law in general and the Vienna Settlement specifically. They were private, not public, reasons.

Moreover, Britain and Austria would be directly threatened if the principle that sovereigns could intervene for co-religionists was generalized. Both these powers had sovereign control over large groups of Muslim subjects—the Habsburgs in the Balkans and the British in India. The rule agreed to at Küçük Kaynarca could not be generalized without undermining the object of the alliance. From a European perspective, religion was a societal and not a political tie. It could not serve as the basis of a treaty legitimating intervention. Metternich's note stressed the importance of the peace achieved at Laibach and referred both to the peace at Vienna and the alliance role in Europe.[102] In the allies' eyes, Küçük Kaynarca was irrelevant. The Greeks were first of all rebels and only secondly Christian brothers.

In sum, the Hanover strategy built from the premises of the summer. The goal was to shore up Ottoman sovereignty and bring Russia into the allies' fold by calling on the allies to ignore the Greeks while delegitimating the type of treaty that would infringe on Ottoman sovereignty.

101. Jelavich 1991, 57.
102. Kissinger 1957, 300.

But there were three important differences that made this also a strategy of Europeanization, and that therefore enabled the allies to restrain Russia. First, Metternich and Castlereagh took steps to avoid the perception that they were forming an anti-Russian alliance. Alexander knew that Britain and Austria were meeting at Hanover, and he knew that relations between those two countries recently had soured. A reasonable inference would be that they were meeting with the sole purpose of aligning their power against Russia. Why else would they suddenly bridge their differences, except in the face of the common threat of Russia? Alexander therefore sent the Russian ambassador at London to join the meetings in order to assure his allies that Russia was not planning war.[103] Realizing that their meeting was prompting suspicion of a separate alliance, and that issuing a joint communiqué, no matter how benign, might seem to corroborate those fears, Metternich and Castlereagh agreed to act separately.[104] Thus the Hanover strategy differed from the summer strategy in that Russia knew there was concerted action by two of its allies, and knew that they were making efforts to appear nonthreatening.

Second, the two powers decided that if the bilateral diplomacy did not work, they would convene a special conference. They already were scheduled to meet in Florence to follow up on Laibach, but Britain was not planning to attend. By holding a special pre-congress meeting to discuss these "Eastern" issues, the powers could secure British participation without jeopardizing its anti-interventionist Concert stance.[105] Third, Metternich and Castlereagh informed Prussia and France of the strategy, mentioning the pre-congress meeting. The aim of the meeting would be to use the name of Europe and the notion of European interests to deny Russia the right to intervene on behalf of the Greeks. That is, they agreed to "humor [Alexander] by appealing to his idealism"[106] about Europe, which also meant appearing to Russia in a united front rather than as a potential countercoalition.

The combination of defining the issues in public language, not just the broad language of international law but the specific rules reflecting the Vienna commitment, linking the solution to a public forum, and involving the entire alliance made the Hanover decisions a public strategy. These

103. Nichols 1961, 55.
104. Webster 1925, 373–74.
105. Nicolson 1954, 269.
106. Nichols 1961, 57.

moves strengthened their collective intention to maintain European tranquility together both epistemically and materially. Epistemically, it made the collectiveness of the strategy known to all; materially it linked the collective aspect to a Concert meeting. From here on, the Greek Question was treated as a general interest, and any state's self-interest when it came to the conflict in Greece was defined through the collective European interest. That the Concert frame, including a specific set of arguments and the prospect of meeting in the Concert forum, restrained Russia is evident from the set of meetings in February 1822 and the congresses of Vienna and Verona in autumn 1822.

### Grouping Alexander

The Hanover agreement was tested in winter 1822 when Alexander sent Count Dmitri Tatischev to Vienna in the hope of securing Austria's secret cooperation on Greece.[107] Tatischev was instructed to persuade Austria (and Prussia) to support a second Russian ultimatum threatening the sultan with war. Historically, Austria had demonstrated that it had designs on the Balkans, and in the eighteenth century Russia and Austria had periodically cooperated on the issue. As such, the strategy seemed viable. Between March 8 and April 19, Tatischev met with Metternich. But rather than Austria signing on to the Russian strategy, Tatischev accepted the Hanover strategy. Alexander agreed.

The Bucharest violations would continue to be handled bilaterally, as a Russo-Turkish concern. Russia would restore diplomatic relations with the Ottoman Empire once it had evacuated the Principalities.[108] The Greek Question, on the other hand, was to be demoted to a humanitarian concern shared by the European powers. Metternich drafted the formal notes reporting the outcome of their meetings to the full alliance, stressing the bifurcation of Russia's grievances. The agreement also stipulated that if the sultan complied with the Bucharest demands, then Russia would keep diplomatic relations intact, "entrust[ing] its humanitarian demands on behalf of the Greeks to Europe, which would enforce them by diplomatic pressure on the Turks."[109] If the sultan did not comply with the Bucharest issues, however, Austria would sanction a limited Russian war.

---

107. Anderson 1966, 61.
108. Schroeder 1994, 620; Nichols 1961, 59; Kissinger 1957, 301.
109. Schroeder 1994, 620–21; Kissinger 1957, 304.

But Metternich pledged this support if and only if the full alliance agreed. Austria also requested that Alexander attend the pre-congress meeting along with Britain and the other allies.

The strategy appeared to work. The sultan accepted Russia's four points and Russia reestablished diplomatic relations. The Ottomans began to evacuate in May, and in July the sultan appointed two Romanians as governors of the Principalities. In August the sultan declared that he had met the requirements.[110] The evacuation proceeded slowly, and the sultan backtracked by closing the Straits to grain commerce.[111] Still, there was a sense that the treaty violations were being tackled.

The humanitarian issue, on the other hand, was spinning out of control. On April 22, 1822, the Ottomans massacred nearly the entire population of the island of Chios, in the Aegean, and sold whoever remained into slavery. But while the massacre received wide press coverage in the summer, the allies did not communicate officially about it.[112] The war party in Russia had been silenced. Alexander's public, political ties to Europe were defeating his other bonds. A good measure of how Europeanized Russia had become on this issue was that Capodistrias resigned in midsummer. Frustrated by the Russian relationship with Austria and agonized over the Greek condition, he left Russia for Geneva and began to work exclusively for the Greek cause.[113]

The final test of the Hanover understanding occurred in the fall with the two scheduled congresses. As with previous congresses, the European allies invited the affected parties. But unlike the Italian monarchs, the sultan refused to attend a conference of European powers to discuss issues felt to be at most bilateral with Russia. Even discussion seemed to infringe on Ottoman sovereignty. Instead of attending, the sultan's advisor on foreign affairs met privately beforehand with a trusted British mediator and empowered him to report on their discussions to the others.[114]

In late September the five European powers assembled to discuss the Greek Question. This informal congress consisted mainly of a circular— a note circulated to the participants—by the Russian foreign minister, Count Karl Robert Nesselrode, and the response by the allies. Russia com-

110. Nichols 1961, 60.

111. Jelavich 1983, 214; Kissinger 1957, 307–8.

112. Seton-Watson 1968 (1937), 52.

113. Schroeder 1994, 620; Woodhouse 1998 (1968), 141; Anderson 1966, 61; Jelavich 1991, 63–65.

114. Seton-Watson 1968 (1937), 98.

plained that the sultan continued to violate treaty obligations, and further complained that the British mediator was biased toward the Ottoman Empire. At the August meeting this particular mediator had not protested when the Ottomans accused Russia of instigating the Greek revolt.[115] Russia demanded that before diplomatic relations could be fully restored the Ottomans must evacuate the Principalities and allow the evacuation to be verified externally, and they must negotiate with Russia to restore free navigation in the Straits and Black Sea.[116] Russia also called for the sultan to guarantee toleration and amnesty for Greeks who wanted to stay in the empire or else show "by a series of deeds" that Christianity would be respected and the Greeks would be well treated.[117] In response, the Duke of Wellington (Arthur Wellesley), representing Britain, explained that Britain's mediator had received reliable intelligence that Russian agents were favoring Greeks, particularly in the Principalities, and this had influenced his attitude.[118] When the intelligence was verified, Russia backed down. Alexander denounced the pro-Greek agents in his service and dismissed the pro-Greek consuls in the Principalities.

Thus the discussions at the pre-congress meeting brought Russia around even more firmly to the European interpretation of the Greek revolt. After these meetings, the Russian diplomatic and consular staff in the Balkans was purged of Greek sympathizers explicitly in the interest of peace with the Ottoman Empire.[119] That European frame continued at the main congress at Verona: the Greek cause was completely disavowed. First, the Greeks were excluded. Metternich had moved the congress from Florence to Verona specifically to bring attendance and information flow more strictly under his control, and his efforts effectively kept the Greeks out. The Greek provisional government had submitted a formal appeal to all the powers for representation at the congress, and had sent two representatives. But the two were turned back.[120] Instead, representatives of each of the Concert powers met during the main congress to go over the Russian memo once more. Russia reaffirmed it and Austria approved. Britain's foreign minister was at this point George Canning, who had taken over after Castlereagh's suicide in August 1822. He instructed the Duke

115. Schroeder 1962, 192.
116. Nichols 1961, 62.
117. Anderson 1966, 62.
118. Nichols 1961, 63.
119. Nichols 1961, 60–62. Cf. Schroeder 1994.
120. Schroeder 1962, 225; Seton-Watson 1968 (1937), 99; Nichols 1961, 65.

of Wellington, the British representative, not to discuss any connection between Greek and western European revolts.[121] Even Alexander was more interested in discussing the possibility of sending a European army to Spain than intervening for the Greeks.[122] In the words of Friedrich von Gentz, the secretary of the congress: it was "remarkable ... that after all the stormy discussions ... diplomatic maneuvers ... and excitement which this famous insurrection has produced in all the nations of Europe, not one voice has been raised in favor of the Greeks at the Congress of Verona."[123]

Later in the month this small group met twice more, and the French, Prussians, and British approved the Russian note. Russia then permitted the British mediator to remain in charge of diplomacy between Europe and the Porte, with the Russian note as his instructions, and left for Constantinople in December.[124] By those instructions the Greek Question was completely subsumed under the Concert logic. In other words, the Hanover strategy had worked. "Alexander ... was restrained from declaring war on the Porte for the sake either of the Sultan's Greek subjects, or the Danubian Principalities, or Black Sea commerce."[125] From a European perspective, where Greece was merely one of many revolts festering on the continent, it was the least interesting and least likely to topple the central thrones of Europe.

By the end of 1822, the diplomatic work left to be done was to monitor progress on evacuation of Principalities, facilitate Russo-Ottoman negotiations regarding Black Sea commerce, and leave the sultan to deal with the Greek situation on his own. The Concert powers would not intervene or even monitor. They would respect the sultan's sovereign rights. Europe had spoken out against the revolt, and the sultan was free to put it down.

### International Public Power

The Hanover strategy pulled the Greek revolt under the purview of the Vienna Settlement commitment; and the commitment, combined with the option of the joint meeting, pulled Russian behavior. In order to preserve European peace, Alexander put the alliance commitment ahead of the interests of his state. Paul Schroeder calls this decision to refrain from war

121. Temperley 1923, 87.
122. Schroeder 1962, 202–4, 225.
123. Nichols 1961, 65.
124. Nichols 1961, 64; Schroeder 1962, 224.
125. Nichols 1961, 65.

a "triumph of diplomacy over the use of force," where Russia had "foregone concrete material advantages for the sake of moral principle."[126] Russian restraint certainly was a diplomatic triumph. But what made it possible in this instance is what Schroeder develops elsewhere—namely, that the Napoleonic War years had made it so that "systemic thinking and action [could become] a rational choice, effective in practical terms."[127] A "network of ideas" at the collective level broke through the eighteenth-century ideas, and thinking and acting from the perspective of the whole became possible.[128] By drawing attention to the power of the public commitment I am building on Schroeder's insight, linking the systemic thinking he discusses to the political practice that made it possible to realize public goals on the ground. I believe the evidence above supports my interpretation. My account also generates insights that go beyond those of the three main alternative explanations for Russian restraint.

First, some interpretations of this early period focus on the motives of the three main players—Castlereagh, Metternich, and Alexander. For example, Korina Kagan[129] (echoing Henry Kissinger[130]) argues that Russian restraint was due to Alexander's exaggerated fear of revolution and Metternich's skillful diplomacy. According to Kagan, Britain and Austria "exploited" Alexander's "paranoia," and their remarks to Russia that this was a branch of the European revolutions were hypocritical. Similarly, Daniel Lindley argues that this was a pure "deception campaign" by Metternich and Castlereagh, who used Concert norms to dupe Alexander. This deception was made easier by avoiding the forum and using the non-transparent Hanover strategy of private intersovereign communication.[131]

While there is some merit to these interpretations—Metternich and Castlereagh did play on Alexander's romanticism—they rest on monolithic accounts of each of these decision makers' motives that do not hold up to close scrutiny. The duping Alexander account suggests that neither Metternich nor Castlereagh feared European fallout from the Greek revolt and pushed Alexander in a purely hypocritical manner. But there is evidence that Castlereagh *did* suspect the Greek revolt came from the same cause as revolution elsewhere in Europe, or at least that its suc-

---

126. Schroeder 1994, 619–20.
127. Schroeder 1993, 49.
128. Schroeder 1993, 48.
129. Kagan 1997/98.
130. Kissinger 1957.
131. Lindley 2007, 74–75.

cess might have destabilizing repercussions.[132] This perhaps helps explain why he did not succumb to domestic pressures in this period to act on behalf of the Greeks.[133] As for Metternich, Greek success was at least as threatening to Austrian power as Neapolitan success would have been. Although he never publicly argued for a Troppau-based intervention to prop up the sovereign, Metternich hoped the sultan would quash it quickly.[134] In other words, all European established authority felt threatened by the liberal revolutions taking place in Europe, and the Greek revolt tapped into that common fear.

Additionally, by stressing that something kept Alexander from pursuing Russian self-interests, the duping Alexander account suggests that he would not otherwise have been dissuaded from aiding the Greeks. It suggests there was a singular, a priori, opportunistic Russian interest to grab the Balkans and destroy the Ottoman Empire. From here, what needs explanation is, what would motivate Alexander to forego this gain? The answer must be deception, paranoia, or moral commitment. But as shown above, the choice was not between law and opportunity, or Europe and opportunism. European public law supported both actions Russia was considering. Bilateral treaties of Bucharest and of Küçük Kaynarca were on Alexander's side, and the Balkans and Ottoman Empire were not part of the Vienna Settlement. Alexander could have remained a perfectly committed European sovereign and acted forcefully against the Ottoman Empire. The Hanover strategy narrowed the range of acceptable public actions, however, and on this basis Alexander drew back from a war posture. Instead of seeing great gain, Russia sought to avoid a great fear. But the choice does not imply self-sacrifice, and it was not an act of deception.

A second interpretation of Russia's action stresses collective identity, arguing that cultural bonds among the transnational elites made it possible for increased transparency among the great powers to cause collective self-restraint.[135] The European diplomatic corps was a transnational, "socioculturally homogenous" group, whose members often had more in

---

132. Webster 1925, 376–78.

133. The Greeks' seeming ancestral tie to Europe's first democrats had spurred a philhellenic movement throughout Europe since the mid-eighteenth century, and it was particularly strong in Britain. Castlereagh faced domestic pressures to respond. For histories of the movement, see Woodhouse 1998; Clogg 1986, 43–45, 55.

134. Schroeder 1962, 167–68, 173–74; Crawley 1973 (1930), 19.

135. Kupchan 2010, 198–99; Cronin 1999.

common with one another than with their own countrymen.[136] But the evidence suggests that as an interpretation of Alexander's restraint this perhaps goes too far. These are diplomats who easily could envision going to war with one another and had done so in the recent past, and whose allegiances shifted from conflict to conflict. Metternich and Castlereagh had an easy rapport, but Russia's decision is the focus here, and it is not clear what specific work their relationship did in producing Russia's restraint. Of course, some commonality among the five great powers was necessary. As I showed in chapter three, European diplomats shared a practice of commitment, a political language, and a set of institutions. Without these the Vienna commitment and forum could not have done the work they did. However, that is a different claim than the claim that friendship or culture made transparency possible, which caused restraint.

A third explanation is that Russia simply was satisfied with the Vienna Settlement and did not want to rock the boat. Its status quo interests account for the outcome.[137] On this account the balance of power functioned essentially as it had in the eighteenth century and forums were epiphenomenal. Stability prevailed simply because each great power, following its narrow self-interest, had nothing to gain from war. But this explanation also assumes monolithic interests—this time diametrically opposed to the Russian opportunism interpretation but no less monolithic. As noted above, however, evidence suggests that two competing and equally powerful interests paralyzed Alexander. One promised gain against a long-standing rival while the other posed an existential threat. Focusing on Russian self-interest alone does not yield a unique prediction. Interests were indeterminate.

Finally, there is no reason to think that the great powers' commitment and forums were superficial. The participants treated both as if they mattered. They did not have a similar commitment and public talk in the eighteenth century and were very often at war. They had both after 1815 and managed to avoid war.

The bottom line for any explanation of Russian self-restraint, in my view, is that there had to be something for Alexander to be "grouped" into. The ability of Metternich and Castlereagh to appeal consistently to Alexander's attachment to Europe and to make that stick in the face of

---

136. E.g., the Russian foreign minister, Nesselrode, did not even speak Russian fluently. Grimsted 1969, 14–15.

137. Slantchev 2005; Rendall 2000.

provocations and domestic opposition, and the ability of Alexander to choose to follow that interest, rely on the fact that this shared interest had a clear, concrete referent: the forum.

The fact that the great powers could successfully construct the Greek revolt as "European" in 1821–22 helps demonstrate that the notion of a "European interest" was not just something crafty diplomats would use to manipulate one another. The reality and salience of the collective interest was clear by the situation at the end of 1822, when Alexander shared the Greek revolt with his fellow great powers. Not only had war been averted, Russian policy reflected that this understanding was entrenched. Alexander had purged Greek sympathizers from his service and no longer spoke of the Greek situation as a possible cause of great power war.

## Conclusion

Between 1820 and 1822, the five powers that had charged themselves with guarding the Vienna Settlement began to act on that commitment, constituting themselves as a public power for Europe. It was by no means clear to the participants that their settlement would hold. The level of mistrust was high and the threat of war was close to the surface. They did agree on a few important premises, reflected in the Vienna Settlement: revolution is destabilizing, these territorial arrangements are stabilizing; and a threat to any subset of those arrangements threatens the whole settlement. But aligned interests do not necessarily produce mutually desired outcomes, and broad understandings do not necessarily translate to concrete behavioral recommendations in particular circumstances.

For that, the forum was necessary. The forum changed how the allies spoke, which affected their actions. Because the commitment to consult gave each the standing to call for a meeting, any crisis on the continent could potentially be vetted through the public frame. Was this a problem relevant to the commitment, or a bilateral, sphere-of-influence concern? If it was public, did it call for a collective response? All five Concert powers agreed that revolutions could qualify and in some cases warranted great power responses. But not all agreed that all revolutions required public attention, and some felt that collective attention could undermine rather than support the Vienna Settlement. Forum discussion in this time helped to resolve some of the uncertainty.

Metternich and Alexander, at different moments and in different ways, were trapped into doing things they otherwise might not have done: Metternich held a full dress Congress; Alexander disavowed his connection to the Greeks. Additionally, the five powers were able to contain their disagreements within the language of their commitment, an act of collective self-restraint that was unusual in this period. I have shown that their collective intention to keep the peace together made that restraint possible.

# Governing Together

*The Greek Revolt and the Eastern Question, 1823–32*

By the end of 1822 the great powers had absorbed the Greek revolt within the Vienna Settlement framework, which called for them to condemn the revolt and support the sovereign. Had the sultan put it down, the Greeks likely would have faded from great power attention. But by the end of 1822 Greek forces were in a strong position. They held several cities, including Athens, they had command of the sea, and they had proclaimed a constitution. Greek forces were not centralized and the government was not effective, but the rebels were holding their own.[1]

With Greek persistence the allied consensus broke down. Some form of action seemed necessary, not least because Greece abutted Europe and each of the great powers feared the spread of revolution on the continent. But it was not clear what to do. By treating the Greek revolt like a European liberal revolution, the powers had granted the sultan the sovereign right to govern and labeled the Greeks as rebels. But in the Greek case, the link from "European political instability" to "support the sovereign" was not as clear as it had been in the cases of Spain and Naples. These were Christian revolutionaries facing a Muslim sovereign, and none of the allies recommended overt military intervention to secure the sultan's throne. On the contrary, especially once reports came in of Ottoman massacres, European leaders and many civil society actors sympathized with the Greek plight.[2] Beginning in spring 1821, a relatively constant discus-

---

1. Dakin 1973a, 1973b; Crawley 1973 (1930); Schwartzberg 1988a, 1988b; Jelavich 1991, 67.
2. Penn 1936, 363–64, 647–49; Woodhouse 1969, 72–75; Cunningham 1978, 152–53, 158.

sion about Europe's responsibility to their Greek brethren kept the revolt on the allies' agenda. In other words, the great powers had incentives to intervene, albeit at cross-purposes. The Troppau/Laibach precedent called for supporting the sultan; Christian sympathy called for supporting the Greeks.

Further complicating matters, there were strong reasons that the Greek revolt did *not* warrant allied attention. First, as we have seen, it was not clear that their collective intention to maintain European stability had any relevance when it came to crises in the Ottoman Empire. Second, the great powers had not organized themselves to address this type of instability. Greek rebels were not making the same demand of constitutional reform as the European revolutionaries. The Phanariot Greeks of Constantinople already had substantial economic and governmental power, and the peasants of the Peloponnese were largely self-governing. Nor were the Greeks demanding religious protection. While Christians were second-class citizens in the Ottoman Empire, by and large they had freedom to worship. Rather, rebel demands were in the name of their identity as Greeks. This was a nationalist revolt. The argument was that a coherent political group should have political autonomy. In 1822 such demands were untested, and the great powers did not have a language for addressing the situation on its own terms. In other words, Greek persistence made salient both the Porte's ambivalent relationship to the great powers and the Greeks' ambiguous relationship to revolutionary causes elsewhere in Europe. Each of these counseled inaction.

As the decade wore on, it became increasingly clear that the Greek revolt was a symptom of a larger problem: the power vacuum on Europe's eastern border generated by the declining power of the Ottoman Empire. On this issue, which became known in the nineteenth century as the Eastern Question, the great powers shared the sense that *some* coordination was necessary in order to avoid great power war. But they could not agree on what to do. It was not clear that they could constitute Ottoman decline as a common European problem, much less resolve it together. In this ambiguous, uncertain context and through trial and error, from 1823 to 1832 the five great powers came to do just that. Like their cooperation earlier in the decade, in the late 1820s the great powers drew on the tools of joint commitment and forum consultation. But their governance here was framed specifically around the decline of Ottoman power and its impact on the European balance of power.

In this chapter I show how, by constituting the Greek revolt as a public, European problem, the great powers kept their own competition at bay.

Without their commitments and forums, it is hard to imagine that these intense rivals would have avoided war, much less worked together to do something they never had done before—namely, to jointly create a new state. This chapter is organized into three sections. First, I summarize the relationship between the Ottoman Empire and Europe from the eighteenth century to the early nineteenth to establish the Eastern Question as a distinct issue. Second, I return to the case and narrate the "Interlude" from 1823 to 1826, when consensus on the Greek revolt broke down as it became de-linked from the "liberal revolution" frame. This section ends with the signing of the Treaty of London, through which the Greek revolt once again became a shared problem.

The third section turns from chronology to analysis. In "Governing the Balkans" I trace great power diplomacy from 1827 to 1832, showing how the Treaty of London kept the Russo-Turkish War of 1828–29 limited, which allowed the London Conference on Grecian Affairs, a consultation mechanism established in that treaty, to hammer out the details of the new Greek state. This was no small accomplishment. The Greek revolt posed a new problem, and new problems create new uncertainty, heightening the security dilemma and raising the chance of war. However, in this case instead of war, the great powers established a new principle of public reason, "nations get states," which enabled them to avoid competition over the spoils of the Ottoman Empire. For some European problems, at least, the solution was not "support the legitimate sovereign" but rather "give the nation a state."

My goal in the analytic section is to show the plausibility and value of a collective intentionality lens for thinking about how states govern together. By working together the great powers accomplished more than they could have achieved separately, and commitments and forums played a crucial role. The main alternative account of this case in the IR literature is that of Matthew Rendall, who argues that the outcome—a contained, bilateral war and peaceful resolution of the Greek Question—can be explained by appealing to self-interest alone, particularly to Russia's defensive motives.[3] Rendall's explanation is bottom up, and relies on a particular, stable constellation of interests. In contrast, the explanation offered in this chapter is top-down, in that it does not rely on particular interests or motives among the actors. I do not disagree that self-interest "mattered" or that Russia was basically nonexpansionist in this period.

3. Rendall 2000; 2006; 2009.

But when analyzing particular decision situations, self-interest can be an elastic or moving target, and in any case defensive orientations do not preclude opportunistic actions. At many points in this period, what would have been in Russia's (or Britain's or France's) self-interest could be interpreted in various ways. Russia sought to preserve its sphere of influence but wanted to avoid great power war; Britain wanted to preserve its friendship with its Ottoman "ancient ally" but had humanitarian concerns and domestic pressure to support the Greeks and geopolitical concerns to restrain Russia; France had troops on the ground in the Peloponnese and an opportunity to advance. Amid these sometimes-conflicting and indeterminate interests, and in situations where each faced temptations to press their advantage and widen the war, I show a pattern of leaders relying on the Treaty of London and supporting the London Conference. My account suggests that these tools made a difference.

My argument also implies a counterfactual claim that without a public commitment the five powers could not have solved the problem and may have ended up at war. Since we cannot rerun history we will never know for sure, but it is instructive to compare this case to the Crimean War, a structurally similar case thirty years later. In the 1850s Russia and the Porte again faced a bilateral dispute that escalated to a Russo-Turkish War; France, Britain, and, to a slightly lesser extent, Austria, again were the most interested great powers. Each arguably favored their status quo regarding the Eastern Question, but was uncertain about the others' commitment to it. As I discuss in this chapter, in the 1820s there was a commitment and a forum, and in 1829 the great powers avoided war. In contrast, in the 1850s there was no commitment and in 1854 they fought the first great power war since the Vienna Settlement. I discuss the Crimean War case in chapter six. With this in mind, reading chapters five and six side by side helps illustrate the power of commitments and talk, and enhances the plausibility of my argument. Global governing is productively interpreted as a case of collective intentionality; collective intentions among states can shape behavior and outcomes.

## Context: The Eastern Question

The structural weakness of the Ottoman Empire and early Greek successes made clear a power vacuum was growing in the Balkans—a vacuum that was coming to be called the Eastern Question and that would continue to be a theme of great power politics until World War I. At the peak of its power, the Porte had controlled the entire Balkan Peninsula and even reached the gates of Vienna. But from the late seventeenth century on, the Islamic power was pushed back fairly steadily, with Austria and especially Russia taking most of the gains.

Ottoman decline had internal and external causes. Internally, the Ottoman system had depended on constant conquest and exploitation of the resources of conquered territories. After Europe had halted its advance, the Ottoman Empire was forced to attempt to expand its resource base without expanding the empire. European states faced a similar problem and responded by consolidating their states, hardening the inside-outside boundary, and centralizing power and authority.[4] But despite several attempts at reform, no sultan could consolidate even enough central control to reliably collect taxes, much less staff a reliable army. Farming reform increased the peasants' obligation to the state, but lack of central oversight meant money did not make it to the center. Tax revolts became common. Without a tax base the sultan could not afford to pay his elite fighting unit, the janissaries. In response, these units branched out into trade and crafts, joining guilds and developing into a powerful independent political force that increasingly was at odds with the sultan. This made them less effective as a military force for the empire.[5]

There also were external causes of decline. The Ottoman Empire was a major player in four wars in the eighteenth century (the Great Northern War of 1700–1721 and the Russo-Turkish Wars of 1735–39, 1768–74, and 1787–92), and the Balkans were a common theater. This meant that on top of internally generated tax revolts, throughout the century the land was subject to depopulation, refugee flows, and the destruction of cities and villages. Roving military groups kept the political situation chaotic. Although sultans sponsored local leaders, those leaders often had to hire private armies. Ottoman sovereignty was loosely structured and had enabled local identities to flourish. Now, local institutions and leaders gained the loyalty of many populations by providing protection, allowing these groups to become stronger and more detached from the Ottoman center.[6]

The causes of the eighteenth-century wars were mainly geostrategic—

---

4. Black 1999, 351–52; Spruyt 1994; Tilly 1992.

5. Jelavich 1983, 46–48; Stavrianos 2000, 119–120; Adanir 2005, 403; Davison 1999, chapter one.

6. Jelavich 1983, 60–61, 97; Stavrianos 2000, 120–23.

control of the Black Sea coastline and of the Turkish Straits. But the Eastern Question also had a religious dimension. The Porte had a large Christian population—over one-third—and it controlled the Christian holy sites of Bethlehem and Jerusalem, to which hundreds of thousands of Christians made pilgrimage each year. The presence of Christians gave all of the European great powers an additional interest in the Muslim empire as well as a pretext for intervention.

Because most Ottoman Christians were Orthodox,[7] Russia took a special interest. In the eighteenth century, Russian czars had openly negotiated with local leaders to incite rebellions. Peter the Great called on Balkan subjects to revolt in 1711; Catherine the Great encouraged a Greek rebellion in 1770 and distributed anti-Turkish manifestos to the Montenegrins. The crowning blow to Ottoman sovereignty was when Russia in 1774, through the Treaty of Küçük Kaynarca, took the broad rights to protect Orthodox Christians in the Ottoman Empire and to share in the governance of the Danubian Principalities.

In 1815, as the great powers reached the Vienna Settlement, the Ottoman Empire held sovereign authority over the bulk of what we today think of as the Balkans: Bosnia, Montenegro, Macedonia, Albania, Bulgaria, Romania, Greece, and most of Serbia.[8] But Ottoman sovereignty was already quite perforated by Europe, and especially, in the 1820s, by Russia.

Thus while the Ottoman power vacuum tantalized all the great powers, Russia was especially poised to take advantage, and the Greek revolt was a tempting trigger. As discussed in chapter four, Russia had a host of grievances arising from the Treaty of Bucharest (1812), and war often seemed on the horizon.[9] Add to this the special relationship with the Greeks as co-religionists and as reliable merchants and shippers, and Russian action against the Ottomans on behalf of the Greeks seemed unavoidable. The other great powers felt that Russia, if left unchecked, easily could destroy the Ottoman Empire, which would demolish the European balance of power. But the problem was that if the great powers worked to prevent Russian hegemony "the old way," by balancing, they risked an-

---

7. A small percentage of Catholics also resided in the empire. Gooch 1956, 35.

8. Magocsi 1993, 76–82. But Austria held what we know of as Croatia and much of the coast of the former Yugoslavia (Dalmatia), and Russia held Bessarabia and Bukovina, to the Pruth River, from 1812.

9. Kagan 1999, 2, 28ff.; Flockerzie 1992, 215, 218.

other continental war. The Ottoman Empire may have been outside the purview of the Vienna Settlement, but the continuing Greek revolt threatened the very object the settlement was designed to protect. The balance was tipped toward great power attention to the Greeks, but it was not clear exactly what the powers would do or whether they would act the old way (separately) or the new (together).

## Interlude: 1823–26

At the end of 1822, as the great powers left Verona, Greek forces were in a strong position vis-à-vis the Ottomans, and the great power consensus seemed to be on inaction. From 1823 on, as the conflict continued, inaction became less attractive, but the great powers could not agree on how the Greco-Turkish conflict mattered to Europe, much less on what to do. Support the legitimate sovereign, grant Russia its sphere of influence, mediate between the two "belligerents": none of these strategies was acceptable to all five allies. By the end of 1825, their consensus on Greece verged on disintegration, and the prospect of war loomed.

Collective great power responses are not necessarily better than unilateral responses. The fact that the powers ultimately decided to act together in regarding the Greek Question and not concurrent instabilities in the Spanish American colonies does not mean they mishandled America and triumphed regarding Greece.[10] The difference was that the Spanish American colonies did not threaten to spark a great power war on the European continent, while the Greek Question posed exactly the type of problem the Vienna Settlement was meant to address. Russia and Britain feared each other's intentions and they feared the destruction of the European balance. As fears grew, the two rival powers could have chosen familiar balancing practices. Instead they chose to experiment again with the innovation of 1815. An explicit goal of the Treaty of London, spearheaded by Britain and Russia but to which all five great powers were invited to sign, was to maintain the European balance especially through

10. The British foreign minister, George Canning, rejected the Spanish king's call for a congress on the issue in 1824, despite the fact that his own king favored one, as did Spain, France, and Austria. The Spanish American colonies declared independence with little European intervention, certainly without European management, and without great power war. Seton-Watson 1968, 85.

consulting together. In this section I narrate the unraveling of the collective definition of the Greek revolt and show how the continued threat of great power war led to a redefinition of the problem they faced and to a commitment to work together. This section is descriptive rather than causal and sets the stage for the analytic section that follows.

### Casting Themselves Adrift

In March 1823, Britain unilaterally recognized the Greeks as belligerents. From then on, it was difficult to sustain the definition of Greece as a branch of Europe's revolutionary epidemic. George Canning defended the policy shift as a self-interested move to safeguard British trade against Greek piracy in the Mediterranean. The Ottomans could not protect English shipping while the Greeks had "'a certain degree of force and stability' of self-government that permitted them to be held responsible."[11] Recognition need not have been an anti-Concert strategy, since it was consistent with Castlereagh's instructions for the 1822 Verona congress to inform the allies that such a move might be necessary. But Canning omitted even that semblance of consultation. Recognition was designed explicitly to bypass the allies, to solve the problem, as he put it, the old way.[12]

British recognition of the Greeks acted as a centrifugal force on the alliance. Alexander saw it as an attempt to infringe on Russia's sphere of influence. One year earlier Alexander had asked Britain to support Russia's special role toward the Greeks and found himself grouped. Now Britain was ignoring the allies and pursuing a unilateral strategy. The czar responded by attempting to recapture the initiative and make Greek international personality a European policy. Meeting at Czernowitz in October 1823, Alexander and the Austrian emperor, Francis I, determined to act through the alliance for Greece. Their vague plan did not specify either what they would do or the principle according to which they would justify invoking the alliance. Russia's grouping logic was not legitimist, as it had been a few years before, but quid pro quo: Austria was granted special rights in Naples, France was taking special rights in Spain, and now Russia should be granted special rights in the Balkans. The Russian sphere of influence was generally acknowledged to extend into the Danubian Principalities; Russia now put Greece in its sphere as well. After se-

11. Temperley 1966, 326.
12. Temperley 1966, 326.

curing Habsburg support for the policy if not necessarily the rationale, Russia called for a congress. In January 1824, Alexander proposed the formation of autonomous Greek principalities similar to those along the Danube, achieved through mediation between the great powers and the Porte and guaranteed by the five powers.[13]

The prospect of an allied conference to discuss the Russian proposal was more threatening to the allies than unilateral British recognition had been. It seemed to portend the explicit great power sanction of Russian tutelage of the entire Balkans and a Russian presence on the Mediterranean Sea. However, the alternative, of refusing Alexander's request for a meeting and letting Russia act on its own, was equally threatening. Either the powers would meet and try to constrain Russia by grouping, or they likely would have to attempt the same goal in the future, by balancing Russia's power and potentially going to war.

Representatives of the five powers met at Saint Petersburg in June 1824, but it was hardly a congress. Canning rebuked the British ambassador for attending and Austria and France did not give their Petersburg negotiators the power to commit the state.[14] In addition, the Paris *Constitutionelle* published the Russian proposal prior to the conference, which gave the Greeks and Ottomans enough information to make clear to the great powers that they would refuse Russia's terms. Alexander then suspended the conference until early 1825, admonishing the powers to empower their representatives.[15]

While each alliance member had done its part to scuttle to the conference, British actions were particularly significant in light of Canning's unilateral turn. In part this was because British civil society had mobilized around the Greek cause in the early 1820s, and several groups were actively working for the Greeks. British newspapers stressed Ottoman atrocities and portrayed the Greeks as descendants of the first democrats; British elites rallied for the Greeks. Canning permitted pro-Greek activity in the private sector,[16] and despite Ottoman protests he allowed Lord Byron to travel to Greece.[17] In the summer, after the Petersburg conference had broken up, the Greeks appealed to Britain for help achieving

13. Temperley 1966, 330; Seton-Watson 1968.
14. Temperley 1966, 332; Seton-Watson 1968, 101.
15. Schroeder 1994, 639; Woodhouse 1998, 142; Jelavich 1991, 70; Anderson 1966, 62.
16. Penn 1936, 648–49.
17. Penn 1936, 650, 658–59; Bass 2008, 76–87.

independence.[18] Canning proclaimed neutrality but promised to consult the Greeks on any settlement, and he offered British unilateral mediation if both the Greeks and Ottomans would agree.[19] Canning would not concert his policy with the allies and offered little explanation to them for his permissiveness on Greek activism. This combination increased allied (and Ottoman) mistrust. From a Russian perspective, Britain's pro-Greek actions and continued diplomatic distance revealed a clear intention to usurp Russia's influence in the Balkans.[20] As 1824 ended, Alexander instructed his ambassadors that Russia would no longer discuss the Eastern Question with Britain.

After a second failed Saint Petersburg conference in 1825, which Britain did not attend even as an observer,[21] prospects for great power conflict heightened as both Russia and Britain pulled further from each other and the other alliance partners. After Austria, Prussia, and France ignored the czar's proposal of an ultimatum to the sultan backed by force, Alexander withdrew from the allies, circulating a memo to Russian representatives in all European capitals ordering them not to discuss Russo-Turkish relations. Russia would "follow her own views exclusively and [would] be governed by her own interest."[22] Alexander left for the Crimea in November.[23] Meanwhile, prominent Greeks formally petitioned Britain in an "Act of Submission" to English protection. Canning rejected the appeal but promised that Britain would work toward a compromise between Greeks and Ottomans short of independence.[24] He also kept British strategy unilateral, rejecting Austrian and French requests in September for a joint approach.[25]

The intersubjective terrain of the Greek revolt had clearly shifted from the "support the sovereign" rationale prevailing in 1822. But while Russia and Britain each supported the Greeks, they did so for different reasons and did not trust each other's intentions. Rather than see the benefits of sharing the problem and avoiding great power war, it was looking

18. Temperley 1966, 333.

19. Temperley 1966, 333–34.

20. Schroeder 1994, 640; Temperley 1966, 335; Anderson 1966, 62; Phillips 1934b, 186.

21. Temperley 1966, 334; Nichols 1961, 65; Schroeder 1994, 640; Woodhouse 1998, 143–46; Phillips 1934b.

22. Anderson 1966, 63.

23. Temperley 1966, 350; Schroeder 1994, 641–42.

24. Seton-Watson 1968, 106; Temperley 1966, 340; Marriott 1940, 212.

25. Temperley 1966, 342.

as if isolated Russia and isolated Britain would use the Greek Question to compete for influence.

Two face-to-face conferences among the great powers had failed to tame the security dilemma, much less generate a commitment to address a shared problem. To some extent, meeting together reduced uncertainty: by the end of 1825 they knew that they could not assume interests were shared. This is consistent with Dan Lindley's argument that forums alone do not amount to a collective security system, that appearing together cannot itself cause states to act on their enlightened self-interest.[26] But Lindley goes further to argue that a few failed meetings mean that the Concert died in the early 1820s, and this would seem to overburden public talk. Face-to-face talk cannot create cooperation whole cloth, and forums without commitments risk being idle talk shops, particularly if, as with the Petersburg conference, the parties do not empower their representatives to commit the state. In this case, by 1825 the great powers had loosened the Greek revolt from its 1822 European frame. While Russia attempted to use the forum to create a common interest, Britain was working hard to keep it a private affair. What the meetings clarified and deepened was a gulf of mutual suspicion between Britain and Russia.

### (Re-)Grouping

At this point the situation could have gone either way, and what happened next was a surprise: Britain and Russia stepped back from the brink and adopted a European strategy based on the Vienna model. They committed to address the Greek Question together in an effort to prevent great power war. At first their initiatives seemed destined to remain bilateral. First to move was Alexander. In summer 1825, even as he instructed the Russian ambassadors not to discuss the Greek Question with the allies, Alexander asked Madame Lieven, the wife of the ambassador to London, to open a diplomatic window.[27] Lieven shared rumors about an Egyptian plan to slaughter or take as slaves the Greeks of the Peloponnese and to repopulate the region with Egyptians. Canning responded by sending Viscount Strangford (Percy Smythe) to Russia with instructions to pursue cooperation but avoid discussing a great power conference.[28] December 1825 brought another wrinkle, because Alexander had died the month

26. Lindley 2003/4, 2007.
27. Temperley 1966, 345.
28. Temperley 1966, 343, 348–50; Anderson 1966, 64.

before and there was a brief succession crisis before Nicholas I became czar. Unlike his romantic, internationalist brother Alexander, Nicholas was a pragmatist and uninterested in Concert diplomacy. In winter 1826 Canning sent the Duke of Wellington to Russia reiterating his offer of bilateral cooperation on the Greek Question. Britain promised no aggrandizement and made clear that it expected the same from Russia.[29]

In the course of the negotiations these two unilateralists decided to cooperate and to vet their bilateral cooperation through the alliance. The fact that the Greek Question would be handled on the Vienna model, as a shared, European problem, is evident in the wording of the resulting 1826 protocol, the subsequent Treaty of London, and in the defense of its initiative that Britain offered to the Prussians. In the protocol, while they reserved for themselves the right to mediate and approve any settlement, the two powers explicitly disavowed aggrandizement and invited the allies to join in the final arrangements on Greece and in a full Concert guarantee. In Article VI, Britain and Russia asked their allies to be parties to "definitive arrangements of which this Protocol contains the outline." Therefore they "will communicate this instrument confidentially to the Courts of Vienna, Paris, and Berlin, and will propose to them that they should in concert with the Emperor of Russia, guarantee the Treaty by which the reconciliation of Turks and Greeks shall be effected, as [Britain] cannot guarantee such a Treaty."[30] The clause bringing in the allies was vague—they were to join in a treaty for reconciling Greeks and Ottomans, but there was not yet a treaty, only an "outline," suggesting that the goal was to bring all five powers on board as full parties. Although the allies would have to accept Russian and British leadership, they were invited to negotiate on the arrangements for Greece and to guarantee the final outcome. Anglo-Russian cooperation was not a return to old balancing practices, and it seemed to be modeled on the new, concerted approach.

Britain courted the allies and by the end of the year France was willing to join as a full partner.[31] Austria refused, citing the Troppau Protocol, and Prussia followed its lead.[32] It had taken around four years to constitute the Greek Question as a European problem on its own terms, but now all five

29. He also sent his cousin, Stratford Canning, to Constantinople to offer the sultan a British mediation. Temperley 1966, 329.

30. Holland 1885, 6.

31. Anderson 1966, 66; Temperley 1966, 362.

32. Vinogradov 1981, 27–28; Phillips 1934b, 194.

powers at least offered tacit support (if only, in Metternich's case, by not threatening to form a countercoalition and preventing the treaty from moving forward). Despite much intrigue and even the fear of war, this re-definition of the Greek Question took place peacefully.

The 1827 Treaty of London called for a Greek state guaranteed by the signatories, but it circumscribed the authority the great powers gave themselves. First, it articulated precise reasons for their intervention. The preamble cited the material costs of the conflict. Anarchy in Greece "daily causes fresh impediments to the commerce of the states of Europe, and gives opportunity for acts of piracy" that hurt the contracting parties. Second, Britain and France "received from the Greeks an earnest invitation to interpose their mediation with Ottoman Porte."[33] Russia was similarly "animated with the desire of putting a stop to the effusion of blood ... [and t]hey have resolved to combine their efforts, and to regulate the operation thereof by formal treaty, for the object of re-establishing peace between the contending parties."[34] The great powers also pledged to include the "two contending parties" in the final negotiations.[35] Finally, the three great powers included a self-denying clause and outlined a preliminary agreement on the outcome: a Greek vassal state, guaranteed by whichever of the three powers wished to sign on to a guarantee.

In other words, the powers were not arrogating unlimited authority to dictate the outcome. This was not a Holy Alliance hammer like the Troppau Protocol had been. Canning distinguished this new cooperation by arguing that it better met the criteria of fairness and acting for the European common good, and was therefore a better extension of the role they had given themselves at Vienna 1815—not rulers of Europe, but the first among equals. Canning argued that the Greek mediation was legitimate because one of the belligerents had formally requested it, there was some bargaining space, the mediators had a clearly outlined goal and explicitly renounced expansionary aims, and the full alliance had been invited.[36] Russia and France also adopted the public language and signed on to the public commitment regarding the Greek Question.

There was one important sense in which the treaty was disingenuous

---

33. Although the Greeks did not request mediation officially until three weeks later. Crawley 1973 (1930), 59–60; Temperley 1966, 397ff.

34. Holland 1885, 7.

35. Holland 1885, 8.

36. Temperley 1966, 397ff.

in its stress on collective disinterested mediation. It had three secret additional articles that set conditions for the use of force. The public section of the treaty stated that the negotiations could begin only under the conditions of armistice. The secret articles made this an ultimatum. If the Ottoman Empire rejected mediation, the signatories vowed to take "immediate measures for forming a connection with the Greeks ... effected by establishing commercial relations ... and by sending to and receiving from them ... consular agents."[37] If both sides rejected the armistice, then the powers would "exert all the means which circumstances may suggest to their prudence, for the purpose of obtaining the immediate effects of the armistice which they desired the execution, by preventing, as far as possible, all collision between the contending parties.... [They would] jointly exert all their efforts to accomplish the object of such armistice, without, however, taking any part in the hostilities between the two contending parties."[38]

There also was a final secret provision stating that regardless of how the Greeks and Ottomans responded to the mediation offer, the contracting parties would "continue to pursue the work of pacification ... and, in consequence, they authorize, from the present moment, their representatives at London to discuss and determine the future measures which it may become necessary to employ."[39]

### Why Address the Greek Question Together?

The Treaty of London marks a clear turning point, where the great powers backed down from the brink of conflict and committed to treating the Greek Question as a European issue, linking its resolution to a forum. While it is beyond the scope of my framework to account for the causes of joint commitments, it is natural at this point to ask why Britain and Russia chose to work together rather than separately, and why they chose to invite the allies.

There are several candidate explanations, but most do not hold up to scrutiny. First, Greek strength on the battlefield cannot explain great power cooperation or the Treaty of London; there is an inverse relationship between the two. Greek forces had held their own through 1824, but

37. Holland 1885, 8.
38. Holland 1885, 9–10.
39. Holland 1885, 9–10.

by 1826, the sultan (with the help of Egypt, specifically Mehmet Ali's son Ibrahim) was on the verge of successfully quashing the revolt (Athens fell that year, followed by Missolonghi), while the Greeks, mired in near constant civil war, had no effective government. Things were no better on the ground for the Greeks in 1827. Yet Greek international standing only grew. From international invisibility in 1821 they achieved belligerent status in 1823. In 1824 the great powers specified borders and floated an autonomy plan, and Britain communicated formally with the Greeks. In 1825 the powers spoke of autonomy and mediation between belligerents rather than pacification by the sovereign.[40] In the 1826 Saint Petersburg Protocol, Greeks were mentioned in a formal diplomatic document as international actors with the right to request mediation. The Treaty of London took their stature further by adding a great power enforcement mechanism. It is hard to say that the Greeks forced their own way to freedom.

Second, domestic activist pressure did not seem to play a large role in the choice to work together. Philhellenism was a strong movement especially in Britain, but by 1826 Philhellenes were becoming disillusioned with the Greek cause. British loans were being poorly administered and the rebels were neither consolidating into a functioning political unit nor successfully policing piracy. As Virginia Penn points out in her study of the Philhellene movement, "practically nothing more was done in England to assist this country" after 1825, and the movement was dead by summer 1827, when the Treaty of London was signed.[41]

Third, humanitarian sympathy on the part of decision makers seems to have played some role, although more for Britain than Russia. In particular, Canning's opening seems spurred in part by the fear of what we today would call ethnic cleansing and the potential public outcry if Britain did nothing. His 1826 instructions to Wellington note that such rumors might serve as a rationalization for the joint protocol. For their part, the Russians were from the start eager to boost the status of the Greeks, citing both the humanitarian interest and their long-standing bilateral treaty rights of protection. But it seems that sympathy for the Greeks' shifting plight could have played little role for the czar, because Russia had little information on the course of the war. Russia had no consuls in the Balkans for most of this period and received little intelligence.[42]

---

40. Metternich continued to resist this interpretation and the elevation of the Greeks until around 1829. Woodhouse 1998 (1968): 142.

41. Penn 1936, 653–60; Seton-Watson 1968 (1937): 100.

42. Jelavich 1991, 72–73. Cf. Bass 2008, 131ff.

The most plausible explanation of the treaty commitment seems to be great power competition. While Britain and Russia sought a resolution of the Greek Question, their convergent interest was a thin layer over their rivalry. Russia explicitly sought to "one-up" Britain's belligerent recognition with its 1824 proposal and the Saint Petersburg conferences. Britain coveted the role of protector of Greek interests. From here, a common view of the negotiations resulting in the Treaty of London is that Russia won the competition. Britain went to Russia seeking permission for peaceful unilateral mediation but came home with an agreement that permitted Russia to use force and brought the full alliance on board. From here, several scholars argue that Nicholas "duped" Wellington into giving Russia the quid pro quo it had sought all along.[43] But it is important to point out that Russia did not win the right to act unilaterally. Canning's instructions to Wellington called for him to push for alliance participation, especially a five power guarantee of Greece, and this is exactly what we see in the Treaty of London.[44]

While the Treaty of London reflects the competition between Russia and Britain, it certainly was not an inevitable outgrowth of it. They could have chosen to pursue the Greek cause separately. Nor was it consistent with the great power consensus on how to respond to European revolts, in that it inverted the Holy Alliance principle of intervention to restore legitimate sovereigns and also rejected the nonintervention platform of Castlereagh's State Paper. Here the great powers agreed to intervene in a sovereign's internal affairs, to negotiate with rebels as equals, and to give and guarantee them national autonomy. But in one important sense it continued the project the great powers had begun in 1815. With the Treaty of London the great powers committed to pursue a shared goal to-

43. The historiography is nearly unanimous on this, building from Temperley. Cowles 1990 points out that Schwartzberg 1988a and 1988b is the sole historian who argues Wellington was not duped, although Vinogradov 1981 seems to support that interpretation.

44. Temperley 1966, 397ff. There is a debate over why Canning changed his mind. Conventional wisdom is that Canning was an adept diplomat, aiming to contain Russia. See Temperley 1966; Dakin 1973a and 1973b; and Vinogradov 1981. Schwartzberg 1988a and 1988b argues Canning was a Greek nationalist looking for an outlet to give Greeks international personality. Cunningham 1978 and Cowles 1990, 697ff., 712 argue that Canning had no clear Greek policy and was exploited by Russia. None of these explain why Canning chose to include all five powers. Cowles maintains Canning kept cooperation bilateral, which the evidence does not bear out. See Cowles 1990, 703, 711. On page 712, Cowles argues there is little reason to believe that Canning called for cooperation for domestic politics reasons. See also Jelavich 1991, 74–75; Crawley 1973, 66ff.

gether and linked that commitment to a forum for problem solving. This collective intention, I argue below, made it possible to govern the problem together and avoid great power war.

## 1827–32: Governing the Balkans

Between 1827 and 1832 the great powers governed the Greek Question together: they prevented a Russo-Turkish War from widening and midwifed the birth of a Greek state. This would not have been possible without the Treaty of London. That treaty commitment created a structure for seeing their common interest while the forums made that interest concrete. This section first shows how the Treaty of London restrained the great powers. It then develops the role of the London Conference on Grecian Affairs, showing that the conference operated outside the sphere of great power competition and effectively solved the problem it was set up to address. Certainly if each of the powers wanted great power war, no treaty commitment could have restrained them. But security dilemma logic tells us war can happen among status quo states. The evidence in this section, combined with consideration of a counterfactual scenario, shows that far from marking the fragility of the allied commitment, as some realists argue,[45] the period from 1827 to 1832 shows its resilience.

### Restraint

The prospect of great power war became especially salient after the Treaty of London. Three months after signing the treaty, in carrying out the treaty's "pacific blockade," the three allies decimated the Egyptian/Ottoman fleet in Navarino Bay, which is on the southwest coast of the Peloponnese, in the Ionian Sea. The sultan responded by closing the Straits to Russian ships and declaring a holy war against Russia.[46] At this point, the security dilemma among the great powers intensified, particu-

---

45. See Kagan 1997/98; Lindley 2007. Cf. Rendall 2000; 2006.

46. Specifically, the Ottoman Empire repudiated the 1826 Convention of Akkerman, through which Russia had taken broader rights in the Danubian Principalities, secured greater autonomy for Serbia, and had taken control of Bessarabia, at the mouth of the Danube. The Ottoman action was despite the fact that the commander of the squad that destroyed its fleet was British not Russian. Kagan 1999, 78. Cf. Bass 2008, 148–49.

larly when Russia declared war on the Ottoman Empire in the spring. The alliance teetered on the verge of collapse throughout the Russo-Turkish War, with pressure at various points to abandon the Treaty of London. Russia and France each considered widening the war; Britain and Austria toyed with a countercoalition to balance Russian power. By the logic of great power competition that these powers were familiar with, Russian aims should have expanded as the war progressed, a coalition should have formed to counter Russia, and European Turkey should have (at best) gone the way of Poland. This outcome seemed likely because there was a power vacuum in the Balkans, Russia wanted war, and other powers feared Russian hegemony in the Balkans.

But the Russo-Turkish War did not conform to such expectations. At every crucial decision point, the Treaty of London allies resisted efforts to balance or form countercoalitions. The Russian war remained limited and bilateral and the treaty to end it, the Treaty of Adrianople, preserved Turkish sovereignty and abjured any special Russian connection to Greece. Three years later the great powers acting together granted Greek independence under their guarantee. The equilibrium of power constructed at Vienna stayed intact. Three decision points show the role of the Treaty of London in the Russo-Turkish War: the outbreak of the war, decisions to keep the war limited, and the decision to end it through the moderate Treaty of Adrianople.

RESTRAINED DECLARATION.    After the sultan declared holy war, Nicholas pressed his treaty partners to allow Russia to occupy the Principalities on their behalf until the sultan agreed to mediation. France was amenable but Britain was opposed. The steps the alliance took instead were largely symbolic, that is, they signed a protocol reaffirming the Treaty of London and reiterating their promises of nonaggrandizement, and they withdrew their ambassadors from Constantinople.[47] But at least with respect to Britain these steps reflect a clear choice: the sultan had approached Britain suggesting separate cooperation and Britain refused.[48]

Russia continued to seek support for stronger coercion during the winter, informing France and Britain that it intended to declare war and suggesting that they join Russia and treat the war as enforcement of the

47. Dakin 1973b, 236; Phillips 1934b, 197; Crawley 1973, 96–97; Seton-Watson 1968 (1937), 123.

48. Phillips 1934b, 198–99; Seton-Watson 1968 (1937), 123; Crawley 1973, 97.

Treaty of London. Russia proposed that in addition to occupying the Principalities, France and Britain should allow Russia in the name of the alliance to block Greece and the Straits and to take Constantinople. With respect to Greece he proposed that the allies send consuls, remove Ibrahim from the Peloponnese, and convene a conference to determine the details of the Greek state.[49]

Despite changes in foreign policy leadership in both France and Britain, once again France supported Russia's suggestion while Britain opposed it. Wellington was the new British prime minister, and he was against British military involvement specifically and Russian coercion overall. Parliament was divided. The king, speaking to Parliament in late January 1828, referred to the Ottoman Empire as Britain's "ancient ally" and Navarino as an "untoward event." But the "ancient ally" claim was hotly contested in parliamentary debate and several voices defended British actions at Navarino.[50] When Wellington finally responded to the Russian proposal, he favored limited coercion—a blockade of Egypt but no French troops in the Peloponnese.[51] The sultan continued his attempts to pry Britain from its alliance partners, inviting the British ambassador alone to return to Constantinople. Wellington refused, citing the alliance commitment.[52] Although unwilling to expand the alliance mandate, Britain would not unilaterally to break the treaty.

At a conference convened in London in March, Russia pressed ahead. Lieven announced that Russia would declare war, defending its right to do so by referring to the clause of the protocol of 1826 in which Britain and Russia had pledged to pursue their joint goal of Greek autonomy "separately or in common." By the protocol, a Russian war on bilateral issues should not abrogate British-Russian cooperation on Greece. Since the treaty was no more than an extension of the protocol, by Russian logic it should be possible to maintain the treaty.[53] Russia then went a step further on the Greek Question. If Britain and France refused its proposal, Russia would execute the treaty and resolve the Greek Question on its own.

This was an ultimatum, and it went too far. Britain refused to acknowl-

---

49. Crawley 1973, 101; Phillips 1934b, 199.

50. Jelavich 1983, 226; Albrecht-Carrie 1968, 113; Seton-Watson 1968 (1937), 53; Crawley 1973, 100.

51. Crawley 1973, 102.

52. Marriott 1940, 221.

53. Phillips 1934b, 199–200.

edge it and suspended the conference. Wellington then attempted to pull Britain or expel Russia from the treaty, approaching France with an offer to make enforcement of the Treaty of London a two-power affair. Not that Wellington trusted France any more than he trusted Russia, but his goal was to send a clear signal that Britain would not sanction a Russian war over Greece. France refused, and even the British cabinet sided against Wellington, refusing to pull out of the treaty. Several members of Parliament still favored the Canning policy of cooperating with Russia to restrain Russia.[54] They argued that Russia had been restrained all decade on Ottoman issues and that the sultan was being intransigent. The combination of the protocol to which it was a part, French sympathy for Russia, and the Russian history of self-restraint made it difficult for Britain to stand up to Russia. The official British reply to Russia did not contest Russia's right to go to war but said that joint allied operations would not be possible. Britain would sanction, but not participate in, the fight against the sultan.

At about this time, when tensions were rising in London, Metternich floated a proposal that the allies should recognize a small Greek state, with or without the sultan's approval. This was roundly rejected. Nicholas argued that the Russo-Turkish War was about bilateral issues and stressed his intense hatred for the Greeks; Wellington disavowed the "liberal'" cause of an independent Greece.[55]

Russia declared war on the Porte on April 26, 1828. Nicholas himself crossed the Pruth River in May with 150,000 men and occupied the Principalities, while a Russian fleet entered the Dardanelles. But as promised, the Russian declaration of war invoked the protocol only, not the Treaty of London, and it did not mention the Greek Question. Russia's ultimatum that it would act alone on Greece if the allies did not support its declaration of war was now gone.[56]

In addition, Wellington backed down from his obstructionist position. All spring, despite opposition from both the alliance and his own cabinet, Wellington had opposed the Russian war, kept the London Conference suspended, and opposed any French occupation (threatening to declare war on France if it sent troops).[57] Finally, pro-Canning members of the cabinet resigned. This gave Wellington a free hand to pursue his anti–

---

54. Seton-Watson 1968 (1937), 128.
55. Crawley 1973, 104–5; Seton-Watson 1968 (1937), 127–28; Fleming 1970.
56. Dakin 1973b, 251; Jelavich 1983, 227; Daly 1991, 18–19.
57. Crawley 1973, 107.

Treaty of London agenda, and the Ottoman Empire was ready for separate cooperation. But instead of breaking free, Wellington began to "yield on every point which had been in dispute."[58] First, he sent Stratford Canning to the Aegean in late May, despite the fact that Canning was pro-Greek and favored sending French troops to the Peloponnese. Second, Wellington allowed the London Conference to resume. Third, when Russia announced at the first meeting of that conference that it was no longer a belligerent in the Mediterranean, Wellington in response agreed to send an ambassador to Russia (there had only been a chargé d'affaires or commercial representative since 1826). Treaty of London cooperation was alive again.

In November 1828 the reis effendi (the Ottoman equivalent of a foreign minister) reported that the sultan preferred a full congress to allied mediation on the Eastern Question and proposed that the European great powers collectively guarantee the Ottoman Empire.[59] France and Britain saw Metternich behind the suggestion—throughout the Greek revolt Austria had consistently (if not publicly) supported the Ottomans, and after Navarino Metternich was the central mediator between the alliance and the Porte. In December 1828 Wellington refused, arguing that the Treaty of London must be fulfilled before convening any such congress. In other words, the Greek Question must first be addressed by the signatories. The treaty might be "an evil" he acknowledged, but "it is an evil firmly established on which we must base our policy."[60]

At the end of 1828, there was an ongoing Russo-Turkish War, but the fact of a war does not signify the breakdown of the alliance. First, Russia approached the allies for support. Second, Britain did not balance its treaty partner. Even as it strongly opposed Russian actions Britain refused several Ottoman overtures. Third, Russia's declaration cited only bilateral issues and not the Greek Question, which, despite the waning European sympathy for the Greeks, was still treated by all as a European concern.

LIMITED WAR.    The first season of the war proved more difficult than the Russians had anticipated. The Ottomans were tough and determined, and the Russian army was wracked with recruitment and leadership problems, not to mention the plague. Nevertheless, to the extent that there were

58. Crawley 1973, 108.
59. Davison 1999, 335; Seton-Watson 1968 (1937), 131; Crawley 1973, 119.
60. Crawley 1973, 123.

limitations on Russia's prosecution of the war in theaters where it could expand, it is fair to say that these were due to the Russian commitment to the treaty. Russian self-restraint, staying on the verge of but not crossing the line into violating allied cooperation, enabled the London Conference to continue its work.

Events in Greece had little impact on Nicholas's war aims. He helped authorize French troops to the Peloponnese to stabilize the situation and remove the Egyptian troops. Greece factored in Nicholas's calculations only instrumentally: if an action in the Mediterranean Sea or in Greece might help compel the Ottomans on Treaty of Akkerman issues, Nicholas did not hold back. On September 18, 1828, Russia blockaded the Dardanelles in an effort to starve the Ottomans at Constantinople and hasten victory.[61] But beyond this, Russian moves in the Balkans remained small. This restraint was tested in February 1829. Britain had lifted its blockade of Crete in January and Russia stepped in, on Capodistrias's request (Capodistrias was now president of Greece), to blockade the island. After capturing some Egyptian ships, Russia requested that the allies jointly demand the Egyptian leader define his position. Wellington protested that this was not consistent with the Treaty of London and he called a conference. From here, Nesselrode saved the alliance by freezing the blockade, that is, nominally maintaining it but making clear that Russia would stop no more ships. Russia similarly froze the blockade in the Dardanelles in the spring of 1829. There was no western expansion of the war. For all intents and purposes the war was not taking place in the Mediterranean.[62]

Many voices in Britain still favored excluding Russia from the Greek Question. Wellington tried again to make good on this, suggesting a meeting in Constantinople of French and British ambassadors without Russia. The French refused.[63] But for a third time, when the sultan requested that Britain act alone and unilaterally send its ambassador back to Constantinople, Wellington declined, invoking his Treaty of London commitment to France and Russia.[64]

MODERATE PEACE.   In 1829, Ottoman fortunes fell. General Hans Karl Diebitsch took command of the Russian army and from here on the war

61. Daly 1991, 26.
62. Crawley 1973, 155–57; Seton-Watson 1968 (1937), 133; Phillips 1934b, 201.
63. Crawley 1973, 121.
64. Seton-Watson 1968 (1937), 130; Crawley 1973, 113–14.

belonged to Russia. On August 20, Russia occupied Adrianople, less than
150 miles from Constantinople, and the sultan's troops surrendered.[65] At
this point, it was not clear what would happen. Russia was close to Constantinople, France was occupying the Peloponnese, and Britain was paralyzed by its domestic situation.[66] There were rumors of a French plan to
carve up the Ottoman Empire. The French scheme[67] would overthrow the
Vienna Settlement through a secret agreement with Russia and the acquiescence of Prussia. The French king, Charles X, approved the plan, even
while recognizing that it might lead to great power war. Prussia, however,
refused.

Meanwhile, Ottoman diplomacy was conflating the two tracks of European diplomacy. As Russian troops approached Constantinople, the sultan offered concessions on Greece. First he offered to give amnesty to
the Greeks. Later in the summer he agreed to give Greece the same level
of autonomy and Russian influence as the Principalities.[68] By the time
the Ottomans surrendered, it was not clear what would happen at Adrianople. Russia was in a strong enough position to dictate the terms of the
settlement, and the sultan was offering essentially what the previous czar,
Alexander, had proposed for Greece in 1824.

But the Treaty of Adrianople between Russia and the Ottoman Empire, signed on September 14, 1829, was moderate and Greece was hardly
mentioned. The bulk of the treaty reaffirmed the 1826 Convention of Akkerman. Russia took the Danube Delta, Georgian territory, and other
areas in the Caucasus, an indemnity on the Ottoman Empire, and free
navigation on the Black Sea and in the Straits. The treaty also made the
Principalities and Serbia formal protectorates of Russia and expanded
their autonomy vis-à-vis the Ottoman Empire. In sharp contrast, when it
came to Greece, the treaty delegated authority to Europe. Article 10 stipulated that the Ottoman Empire accept the Treaty of London and the authority of London Conference decisions.[69] In other words, on the doorstep
of Constantinople, with the freedom to remake suzerainty relations in the
northern Balkans and an Ottoman opponent fixated on the Greek Ques-

65. Dakin 1973b, 273; Marriott 1940, 223; Seton-Watson 1968 (1937), 134.

66. Seton-Watson 1968 (1937), 135, 138–39.

67. Called the Polignac plan. Seton-Watson 1968 (1937), 138.

68. Seton-Watson 1968 (1937), 134; Holland 1885, 10.

69. Albrecht-Carrie 1968, 114; Jelavich 1983, 228; Woodhouse 1998, 150; Marriott 1940,
223; Dakin 1973b, 273; Holland 1885, 10.

tion, Russia did not resolve that question unilaterally but referred to the collective management process and explicitly declared that it wanted no more land in Europe. Considering the commanding position Russia held in August, such behavior in the treaty was very restrained.

While Diebitsch was negotiating the treaty at Adrianople, in Saint Petersburg Nicholas was convening a "Special Committee on Turkish Affairs" to discuss Russia's Ottoman policy. Since Catherine the Great, Russia's policy had been expansion. Now that Russia clearly could destroy the Ottoman Empire, the strategy needed to be reassessed. The committee decision was in sync with the moderation of Adrianople. It argued that Russia should work to keep the Ottoman Empire alive, and offered three reasons. First, if Russia unilaterally destroyed the empire there would be a European war. Second, it the tottering empire fell independently, an international congress would have to convene in Saint Petersburg to determine the status of its territories.[70] Such a congress might decide on partition, which was not in Russian interests. Any partition settled by the powers would put "dangerous enemies [rather than] indifferent Turks" in southern Europe, including Austria in the Balkans, and England and France in the islands and Egypt.[71] Third, even abstracting from complications with the European allies, it was not clear military victory over the Ottomans was desirable. Expelling the Ottomans from Europe would only send them to Asia, where they surely would threaten Russian possessions in the Caucasus. In his summary, Nesselrode noted that "any order of things which might be substituted [in Constantinople] would not balance for us the advantage of having for a neighbor a weak state, always menaced by the spirit of revolt which agitates its vassals, reduced by a successful war to submit to the law of the conqueror."[72] That is, at Adrianople and in Saint Petersburg, Russia made the same choice, to preserve Ottoman sovereignty and to uphold European commitments.

Rendall draws on the committee's decision to support his argument that Russia had defensive aims in the Russo-Turkish War and in the 1820s more broadly.[73] For Rendall, Russia's self-interest, not its commitment, accounts for its decisions. But while the Adrianople and the Russian committee decisions were mutually consistent and restrained, Rendall's argu-

---

70. Kerner 1937, 281. Also Kagan 1999, 82ff.
71. Kerner 1937, 284–85.
72. Kerner 1937, 281.
73. Rendall 2000; 2009.

ment needs to be qualified in two ways. First, the timing of the decisions suggests they were made independently, and Diebitsch was in a sufficiently strong negotiating position that he did not have to keep the Greek Question a European concern; he could have privatized it. The committee's recommendation was announced on September 16, and Nicholas accepted its findings three days later. He then sent word to Diebitsch. This suggests that Diebitsch negotiated the treaty without knowledge of the committee meetings or their decisions, and so the terms of the Treaty of Adrianople reflected the initial war aims and were not derived from the committee's findings. This seems significant because Diebitsch could have dictated harsher terms, both because of his location and because the sultan was facing internal threats and needed the war to end. It is true that Diebitsch's troops were at this point quite weak, and he concluded he could not have advanced on Constantinople even if Russia's goals had been expansionist. But Diebitsch was a skillful diplomat, acting as if he was willing to take Constantinople and threatening to advance even though he knew he could not, and compelling the sultan's forces to surrender.[74]

Second, the rationale for the committee's policy recommendation reflects Russia's commitments to its European allies. Supporting documents submitted with the decision reminded Nicholas of his repeated promises to the allies that despite the Russo-Turkish War he would act with them to achieve the Treaty of London goals. The documents reiterated the self-denying or disinterested clauses of the Treaty of London and December 1827. Russia would not seek conquest or exclusive advantages (January 1828); Russia had no expansionary aims in European Turkey and would not take Constantinople (April 1828). The fact that Nicholas rhetorically invoked treaty commitments does not rule out a balance of power interpretation, and the policy switch reflected his sense that overt expansion would be more likely to trigger great power war than covert influence. But Russian grand strategy was explicitly premised on its public commitments.[75] Only a few years later Russia sanctioned Greek independence through a joint allied guarantee. Russia still sought to control the neigh-

74. Moltke 1854, 412ff., 418, 437, 442. See, e.g., Daly 1991, 36; Jelavich (1991, 84ff.) argues Russia was restrained. Rendall 2006 argues that Nicholas had limited aims.

75. Kagan argues that despite the fact that the czarship was unconstrained by law, Nicholas respected legal commitments. For example, the succession crisis at Alexander's death was spurred because Nicholas would not accept the throne until his accession could be

borhood, but the first commitment was to the European allies, to keep the balance by working together.[76]

These qualifications seem to belie a strict self-interest, balance of power interpretation of the outcome in this period. Despite the Ottoman offer to grant Greece the status of the Principalities and despite the prospect of a fallen Constantinople, Russia fought and won the Russo-Turkish War as a limited war within its sphere of influence, while keeping the Greek Question separate. It therefore is reasonable to attribute to the Treaty of London a causal role in constraining the meaning of the Russo-Turkish War and keeping the Greek Question out.

Consider a counterfactual scenario where the Treaty of London and London Conference did not exist as Diebitsch negotiated and Nicholas's committee met. In the absence of a treaty, British intentions would have been more opaque. There would have been more incentive for Nicholas to push for Greece to have a status like that of Serbia and the Principalities: nominally within the Ottoman Empire but under Russian protection. That would ensure that in the event of another Russo-Turkish War, the Ottomans could not muster forces in the Balkans. From a European perspective that would amount to a continuation of the policy of the Hanover strategy eight years before, which allowed Russia to handle bilaterally relations with the Porte over the northern Balkans and in the east while demanding that it concert with the European allies regarding European Turkey. Indeed, the policy traces back to 1815, when the Treaty of Bucharest was allowed to remain bilateral while the other treaties ending the Napoleonic Wars came under the umbrella of the Vienna Final Act.

Keeping the Greek Question out of the Treaty of Adrianople was significant in another way. By preserving Ottoman sovereignty, Russia effectively acknowledged that there were limits to the Eastern Question as a problem in European diplomacy. The powers had decided at Vienna in 1815 and again in this period that they would not guarantee the Ottoman Empire, that its integrity would not be governed by Europe. Their collective attention was focused only on European Turkey, a region in the Balkans that at this point included Greece but not Serbia or the Danubian Principalities. While the boundaries of European Turkey would widen in the next fifty to seventy-five years, a tacit agreement remained

---

properly legally sanctioned. There is no evidence he treated commitments to his allies with any less respect. See Kagan 1999, 48–49.

76. Jelavich 1983, 227–28; Jelavich and Jelavich 1997, 49–50.

that Europe ends where Constantinople begins. The decision to keep the Greek Question distinct from Russo-Turkish issues and maintain a sphere in which the sultan remained sovereign set a hard boundary for Europe. The powers would govern the outcomes of violence in the Balkans, but the Porte would remain a factor in the balance of power.

Many analysts lament that the Treaty of London seemed to permit rather than prevent a Russo-Turkish war. But this section has shown how the treaty was, to a large extent, a *limitation*, a tool that enabled allied self-restraint that otherwise would not have been expected. As long as Russia kept its aims limited, it was fighting a war over issues considered to lie east of Europe and could defeat the Ottomans without fearing a counter-alliance. If war aims expanded to the west, it was clear that Russia would face an allied countercoalition. Limiting a war being waged by a stronger power with expansionist aims and sympathetic ties is no mean feat.

To sum up this period, in 1828 Russia declared war on the Ottoman Empire, and Russia, France, and Britain decided to maintain treaty cooperation and the London Conference. After Navarino, things could have gone several ways. The alliance could have pressed forward and further compelled the sultan; the pressure of the Ottoman reaction could have split the alliance, and Britain could have allied with the sultan and Austria to defend against the Russians. Indeed, one of Russia's motivations in proposing the immediate occupation in fall 1827 and winter 1828 was to keep Austria from occupying the Balkans.[77] Instead, although both options were considered, the allies continued their policy of keeping the Greek Question collective while allowing Russian treaty rights to be pursued bilaterally with the Ottomans. The Russian decision to go to war involved discussion with the allies; its choice to prosecute the war unilaterally and the allied reaction demonstrated a continued commitment to keep the Greek Question insulated. This meant that they committed to keep disputes between Russia and the Ottomans on the "two tracks" that had been operative since 1821. As long as Europe was involved in decisions on Greece, this part of the Ottoman Empire could not be among Russian spoils. *All* of Europe had to agree on the disposal of this territory.

### Governance

While the Treaty of London kept the Greek Question distinct from the Russo-Turkish War, it neither created Greece nor insured that an inde-

---

77. Fleming 1970; Anderson 1966, 85.

pendent state would be established. For this, what came to be called the London Conference on Grecian Affairs was crucial. Beginning in July 1827, the ambassadors of the three Treaty of London signatories met periodically; and in summer 1828, the Greek Question was put on the table. The London Conference also authorized subsidiary meetings at Poros and Constantinople. Records of all of these meetings were made public to the British Parliament and the great powers accepted all of its decisions. London Conference protocols became the anchors of the Greek state of 1832.

The authority of the conference's decisions was remarkable considering that this type of meeting was unprecedented. As Frederick Dunn[78] points out, the London Conference was fundamentally different from the great power congresses of the early 1820s. This conference was more regularized but involved only ambassadors, not sovereigns. It had no formal organization, not even a designated secretary. The negotiators did not have full powers to commit the state, so the results of the conference were not formally binding in the way the Treaty of London was binding.[79] Yet the conference made crucial decisions and states stood by them. These decisions were resolved through consultation. Proposals were put forward and debated out of the heat and light of high politics, and the minutes and final protocols were made public for the sovereigns. Three moments stand out: the authorization of French occupying troops; the establishment of boundaries for the new state at Poros; and the determination of Greek independence under great power guarantee, including selection of a mutually acceptable sovereign.

THE FRENCH OCCUPATION. In the summer of 1828, the London Conference accomplished two crucial tasks. It negotiated the stationing of French troops in the Peloponnese to keep the war out of Greece, and it delegated authority to representatives at Poros, who devised a scheme for a Greek vassal state. Wellington allowed French troops, suppressing his suspicion of France in order to focus on containing Russia. Britain and France feared Russian intentions and did not want Russia to act alone. They together determined that France should occupy the Peloponnese to expel the Egyptians and hold the land. If the Egyptians left Greece, Russia would have one fewer excuse to care about it. Britain did not want to act against its Ottoman ally and so did not contribute forces. The conference protocol stated that Britain and France together were acting in the

78. Dunn 1929.
79. Dunn 1929, 85–86.

European interest, not against the Ottoman Empire.[80] The French representative announced that they wanted to act with the allies but could do it
alone with allied acquiescence: "in such case, he would act in the name of
the three courts, and for the common interest, declaring, at the same time,
that so soon as the object of the expedition should be attained he would
recall his troops."[81]

France and Britain were containing Russia, but Russia was on board
and signed the protocol regarding the French troops in July. French troops
would divert the sultan's attention from Russian campaigns in the north.[82]
French forces landed in August. The French took over the major fortress
at Corinth with no resistance, although the lack of resistance was mainly
because the British already had negotiated with Egypt for the evacuation
of Greece and a prisoner exchange.[83] The French commander had been
eager for a military victory, however. With such an easy time at Corinth
he turned his attention to the idea of regaining Athens for the Greeks
and sought permission from the French war office to advance beyond
the Peloponnese onto the mainland. The war office vetoed the action.
France was concerned not to appear to the Russians or the Ottomans as
if it was seeking its own aggrandizement rather than acting for the alliance.[84] With French troops in place, Ibrahim started to leave in early October, and Greece became relatively stable. A November 1828 protocol
issued from the London Conference placed the Peloponnese and islands
under great power protection until agreement with the Porte could be
reached.[85]

Mutual suspicion was behind the stationing of French troops. Britain
feared French expansionist aims, and France was suspicious of British
intent to isolate Russia and would not take any action without Russian
sanction. For its part, Russia favored the presence of foreign troops to dis-
tract the Ottomans from the northern campaign.

THE CONFERENCE AT POROS.    The London Conference also authorized the
ambassadors to Constantinople to hold a conference at Poros in 1828, to

80. Dunn 1929, 85–86.
81. Albrecht-Carrie 1968, 113–14; Jelavich 1983, 227.
82. Phillips 1934b, 200.
83. Crawley 1973, 115–16.
84. Crawley 1973, 117–18.
85. Marriott 1940, 222.

devise recommendations on what to do with Greece.[86] The instructions stated that the conference would support Greek independence conditional on the sultan's approval. The Ottomans refused to send a representative, however, arguing again that it would not negotiate with rebels.[87] The Greeks were not invited but were requested to provide statistical information. Capodistrias's resulting memo provided detailed instructions on the boundaries Greece would accept and the sovereign Greece preferred.[88] Recommendations in the Poros report went beyond the London Conference's instructions and were sent to the great powers and to Capodistrias in December.[89] Greece's boundaries were larger, including even some districts that had not been in revolt. The principles behind the boundaries included both defensible frontiers and identity of the population. The ambassadors also specified such details as the form of nomination of governor and the tribute to be paid to the sultan.[90]

The Poros report reached London in January, and while its provisions suited Russia, Britain accepted it only with reluctance. Wellington argued that vassal states do not need defensible frontiers. The Earl of Aberdeen (George Hamilton-Gordon), who was now foreign minister, made clear that Britain would not treat the report as an ultimatum but would consider Ottoman objections. Britain then replaced its negotiator.[91] However, anticipating that rejecting the report would run the risk of a break with Russia and prompt Russia to expand its war aims, Britain allowed it to serve as the basis for negotiations at the next meeting of the London Conference.[92] The March 22, 1829, Protocol of the London Conference defined the boundaries and established the government of Greece; it also sanctioned the opening of negotiations with the sultan at Constantinople. Greece would be an autonomous tributary vassal state, under Ottoman suzerainty but governed by a Christian hereditary prince selected by the powers from outside the ruling families of the Treaty of London

86. Dakin 1973b, 157; Crawley 1973, 111–12.

87. Crawley 1973, 111–12. While the sultan would not attend the Conference at Poros, he invited the ambassadors to Constantinople to discuss the Greek Question. These discussions began in winter 1829. Crawley 1973, 116.

88. Crawley 1973, 143.

89. The Russian minister gave Capodistrias a copy of the Poros report. Crawley 1973, 151.

90. Crawley 1973, 145–48. The conference had worked from bad information. The statistics from Capodistrias were not reliable. Crawley 1973, 149–50.

91. Seton-Watson 1968 (1937), 132; Crawley 1973, 154.

92. Crawley 1973, 152.

signatories, and under great power guarantee.[93] Russia gave permission for the treaty partners to negotiate on its behalf, in the collective interest.[94]

GREEK INDEPENDENCE.  Britain then began to push for full Greek independence, particularly once Russia defeated the Ottomans. The fear was that if Greece became a tributary today it would soon follow its Balkan neighbors and become a Russian protectorate.[95] The question was whether independence provided any greater immunization against that outcome. In October, Aberdeen and Wellington suggested Greece be placed under the Vienna Settlement's guarantee.[96] Aberdeen argued that Greece should be a "solid power" that Britain could ally with and influence. But he linked this to the collective interest: "All Europe expects the independence of Greece."[97] Despite its grand strategy of using the Porte's weakening sovereignty to expand its own influence in the Balkans, Russia agreed.[98]

If not for the Treaty of London and the forum in which the signatories together discussed the shape of Greece, it is reasonable to believe that Russia would have treated Greece as it was treating the Principalities. After all, Nicholas had no special sympathy for the Greeks—certainly nothing like the romantic connection of the British philhellenes.[99]

But in the context of this agreement between the main competitors for Greek influence, Britain and Russia, Greek independence became more of a technical than a political matter. In February 1830 the London Conference signed three protocols effectively creating a Greek state. They reduced its boundaries and gave themselves the role of joint guar-

93. Albrecht-Carrie 1968, 114; Marriott 1940, 222; Crawley 1973, 153; Phillips 1934b, 202; Holland 1885, 10.

94. Dakin 1973b, 262.

95. Phillips 1934b, 203.

96. Phillips 1934b, 203; Seton-Watson 1968 (1937), 141.

97. Seton-Watson 1968 (1937), 140.

98. Seton-Watson 1968 (1937), 141.

99. Nicholas's correspondence with the Austrian ambassador, Count Zichy, in 1828 reflects this: "I detest, I abhor the Greeks, although they are my co-religionists. They have behaved in a shocking, blamable, even criminal manner; I look upon them as subjects in open revolt against their legitimate sovereign; I do not desire their enfranchisement; they do not deserve it, and it would be a very bad example for all other countries if they succeeded in establishing it." Kagan 1999, 78.

antors, and they designated a sovereign and a constitution proclaiming religious equality.[100] A few months later the final settlement created the Greek Kingdom, naming Otto, the seventeen-year-old son of King Ludwig of Bavaria, as king. The powers guaranteed a loan and they guaranteed the state.[101] The final step, in July 1832, brought in the Ottoman Empire. At Constantinople, the three powers negotiated the boundaries of Greece with two representatives sent by the sultan. The conferences were at this point declared over and the Greek Question was deemed "irrevocably settled."[102]

In sum, Greece was created as an independent state by the European great powers, acting through the London Conference, a body created by the Treaty of London. These technical aspects of state formation had not been taken on jointly before. The closest precedent was the Vienna congress in 1815, where the great powers relied on statistical committees and other devices to collect information as they reconstructed the European balance of power. In the Greek case, in contrast, statehood was negotiated out of the light and heat of high politics. The Treaty of London cordoned off the Greek Question from the bilateral dispute between Russia and the Ottoman Empire in Russia's sphere of influence. Throughout the conference negotiations, one party or another threatened to undermine the Treaty of London by expanding the war into Greece and pulling in all of the great powers. But negotiations continued as a second tier of great power cooperation. Having this second tier arguably strengthened the treaty's power to maintain the two separate tracks, because conference protocols became public documents and were regularly referred to by the great powers in their diplomacy during the Russo-Turkish War.

## Conclusion

In this chapter I have shown how the great power commitment and forum enabled them to avoid war over Balkan instability and to devise the innovative solution of a sovereign national state. Confronted with the persistence of the Greeks, the great power allies shifted their focus to face the

---

100. Holland 1881, 11–12; Seton-Watson 1968 (1937); Jelavich 1983, 228; Albrecht-Carrie 1968, 114.

101. Marriott 1940, 223; Woodhouse 1998, 155; Jelavich 1983, 228–29.

102. Holland 1885, 13–15.

Eastern Question head on, linking their commitment to work together to their earlier commitment at Vienna. This was not inevitable and it was not easy. Even if the Vienna Settlement held in Europe it is not necessarily the case that its principle of joint consultation regarding European problems could be extended to their relations in European Turkey. In those years of transition, the European allies shared the sense that the destruction of Ottoman authority would upset the European balance of power, which helped keep the Greek revolt on their radar screen. By 1832, Concert powers had managed the birth of Greece, organized around the principles of preserving some Ottoman sovereignty—Constantinople and the east—and recognizing (some) national groups. Great power management of the Greek revolt, in other words, did not mark a breakdown of Concert cooperation. On the contrary, once the powers acknowledged that the Greek Question posed a threat to the object of their collective management, the European balance of power, they applied the same principles: commitments, public language, and public forums. These together enabled the self-restraint and collective problem solving that characterize governing.

Without their commitment and forums it is reasonable to expect that the Russo-Turkish War of 1828 would have widened, and it is impossible to imagine Greek independence. Without the Treaty of London there would have been no London Conference; without the London Conference there would have been no Greek independence. Their forums gave a concrete reference point for the collective interest in upholding the Vienna commitment.

It can be tempting to attribute the outcomes of the 1820s to great power self-interest, but I have shown the limits of bottom-up, interest-based accounts for explaining the Treaty of London, the Treaty of Adrianople, and Greek independence. Certainly competition between Britain and Russia over influence in European Turkey helped ensure continued attention to the Greek Question. But their competition need not have led to a treaty or been channeled through the alliance, and competitive orientations toward one another do not predict the restraint of the Russo-Turkish War or the outcomes of the London Conference. For both of those, committing to act together and talking together about those commitments was crucial. This suggests the plausibility of my argument.

None of this suggests that Britain, Russia, or France sacrificed self-interests and became public minded. These were not collective-minded friends, and they were not altruistically acting on any principle of self-determination. Each great power had its separate interests and was at least as concerned with containing the other two as it was with ending the conflict on the ground. Nor am I suggesting that pieces of paper and face-to-face talking can compel actors to do things against their will. If states want war, neither their commitments nor forums can prevent it. But even when states do not want war, security dilemma logic tells us war can happen. In the Greek revolt case, the great powers were torn. No one wanted war but all had incentives at various points to balance each other. Cooperation and the management of Greek independence were messy and competitive, with a seemingly constant threat that great power cooperation would break down. Taking into account the personalities in charge, the situation on the ground, and the three years of increasing isolation among the allies, the Greek Question easily could have been solved eighteenth-century style. Instead, when it came to access to the Mediterranean and the Straits and to influence in Greece, they managed to concert their behavior, which enabled a positive outcome that would not otherwise have been possible.

Stepping back to link this chapter to chapter four, in both cases we see concerting for a common, European interest. There were commitments and forums on the one hand and great power restraint on the other. While in the case of Greek independence it is difficult to determine whether the particular micromechanisms associated with talking in a forum obtained each time state representatives sat down at a table, the narrative above shows that shared, public language and the ability to put issues into a public forum enabled these states to go one step further in generating cooperative shared outcomes than they had ever done. And they did so despite changes in leadership and varying levels of personal commitment to the Greek cause.

Generalizing from a single case requires caution. But the combination of the theoretical grounding and empirical evidence above suggests the plausibility of my argument. One way to increase confidence in my findings would be to make use of the method of difference: the Crimean War broke out in a context not too dissimilar from that of 1828. Notably absent in the 1850s was a joint commitment; notably present in 1854 was great power war. Chapter 6 develops the Crimean War case.

But I want to end this chapter by taking, for a moment, the perspective of the Greeks, because while the outcome might be remarkable from a great power politics perspective, from the standpoint of the Greeks the story of their independence is less praiseworthy. It is indeed ironic that the Greek War of Independence was the first successful effort at "national self-determination," because the Greeks had such a small say in the timing, terms, or boundaries of their state. From 1829 to 1832 the London Conference negotiated the sovereign and boundaries, and the decisions reflected great power competition, not local dynamics. For example, the logic of the frontiers in the initial independence protocol made no strategic sense. The Concert powers made Greece smaller as they granted independence, that is, the country was less defensible and yet more in need of defense against a strong neighbor. The initial borders also ignored strategic gains made by the Greeks under Capodistrias.[103] Then, in 1831 the Concert powers changed course and expanded Greece's boundaries. But the move was not a ratification of the capacity to self-govern. Indeed, Greece had been plunged into anarchy by the assassination of Capodistrias. It was, rather, an attempt to make governing Greece more attractive to a European royal. In other words, the great powers made their decisions with little input from Greeks and no regard for their military situation. Any choice Capodistrias had in the negotiations was due to his personal savvy at dealing with the powers rather than any European commitment to give voice to those affected by great power competition. The formerly sovereign Ottomans had little say in negotiations; the newly sovereign Greeks even less. There is an important sense in which sharing great power agency entailed suppressing the agency of less powerful and non-European others.

But the blatant hierarchy should not blind us to the substantial accomplishment. From the perspective of the nineteenth-century great power politics, the birth of Greece was an innovation on two dimensions: rivals cooperatively created a neutral state rather than dividing it as spoils among them, and this independent state was established according to a principle, "defensible boundaries for a coherent 'people,'" that was new to the system and jointly constructed and accepted. While it is generally acknowledged that the French Revolution marked the first national revolution, the Greek revolt marked the first example of national self-determination as an international principle.

103. Dakin 1973b, 284.

# CHAPTER SIX

# Things Fall Apart

*From a Russo-Turkish Dispute to the Crimean War, 1853–56*

An important factor keeping war at bay in the 1820s was that the great powers concerted their power for a common purpose. Despite mutual suspicion and temptations they intended to, and succeeded in, maintaining European stability together by keeping the Russo-Turkish War contained and jointly creating the state of Greece. But the great powers went to war thirty years later, and the Crimean War (1854–56) raises questions about how powerful great power collective intentions could possibly be. This war did not destroy the great powers' capacity to work together, and they continued to turn to joint commitments and public forums when faced with the crises or problems later in the nineteenth century.[1] Also, technically the war does not mark a failure of the 1815 commitment, since the Ottoman Empire had been excluded from the Vienna Settlement. Nonetheless, many of the central actors at the time expected their forums to prevent or at least contain war.

The Crimean War challenges the link between commitments and forums on the one hand, and their behavioral effects of self-restraint and commitment-consistent behavior on the other. This war began as a minor dispute, escalated into a Russo-Turkish War, and then, despite the near constant reliance on great power forums, pulled in the other great powers, notably Britain and France.[2] On its own terms the Crimean War is a case

---

1. E.g., the conferences at Berlin in 1875 and 1878.

2. It also pulled in Austria, which occupied the Danubian Principalities. Sardinia/Piedmont joined the war, too, on the side of the Western allies in 1855, and a British offer to

in which one would think the great powers could have avoided war. First, it began with the same major players[3] and even in some cases the same decision makers as the 1820s. Second, in the early 1850s none of the great powers intended to fight one another over the Ottoman Empire. Third, the great powers engaged in a steady stream of face-to-face, conference diplomacy, invoking the European order and the balance of power throughout. Fourth, and finally, they had the precedent from the Greek case of treating aspects of the Eastern Question as shared European concerns. Despite these similarities, in 1853 these states failed to make the Russo-Turkish War a common concern. As a result, the outcome in 1856 could not be more different than the outcome in the 1820s: great power war in the one case, jointly creating a new independent state in the other. My claim that states can execute collective intentions over time, therefore, must be able to speak to the failure of joint commitments and public forums in the Crimea case.

In this chapter I take up the challenge of the Crimean War and reflect on why these states could not work together in the 1850s as they had in the 1820s. After setting up the historical context between Europe and the Porte in the 1840s and 1850s, I trace the diplomacy, dividing it into two phases: the Russo-Turkish War, which broke out in October 1853, and the great power war, which broke out in March 1854. I show that at a key moment the diplomatic road forked, when the powers faced a choice between grouping—a public strategy—and the private strategy of balancing. They chose the latter, but it was a choice, and not inevitable. After summarizing how diplomacy and events did in fact unfold from November 1853 through the 1856 Treaty of Paris, I ask why the war widened—why did the great powers balance against rather than group with Russia?—and speculate on the difference a public commitment might have made. Of course, there are many causes of any war, but my approach highlights the lack of an important resource: a commitment to maintain the integrity of the Ottoman Empire. In the 1820s, Russia, Britain, and France publicly com-

---

Sweden was in the making. Finally, there was some talk of the United States joining, on Russia's side. See Badem 2010 and Baumgart 1999. Much Crimean War scholarship is focused on the question of how it could have broken out. Badem and especially Baumgart focus more on the puzzling fact that it did not widen into a world war. Baumgart argues that the diplomatic machinery set up in 1815 played a key role in preventing that.

3. Russia, Britain, France, the Ottoman Empire, and to a lesser extent Austria. Prussia was a quiet voice in both cases.

mitted to a version of this when they pledged nonaggrandizement in the Treaty of London. There was no such commitment in the 1850s.

Despite a great deal of conference diplomacy and the intentions of some key players to avoid great power war, other strong players had individual intentions explicitly to scuttle any approach other than balancing militarily. The Crimea case thus shows the limits of the mechanisms I have identified. But in another sense the case sheds light on their importance by showing the preconditions that must obtain for commitments to hold and have behavioral pull. Forum talk is not a silver bullet; there are scope conditions for governing together.

## Context

The dispute that slowly ignited the Crimean War was an outgrowth of the Eastern Question, which had become more pressing and more difficult to address in the decades after the Greek revolt. The Ottoman Empire continued to decline. Neither Mahmud II, sultan from 1808 to 1839, nor his son, Abdülmecid, could build a tax base. Corruption was rampant, and the economy overall was mismanaged. On top of this was the growing centrifugal force of nationalism, especially after the Greeks' success. The Serbs and Romanians also had gained some measure of autonomy from the empire.

Mahmud II tried to forestall decline and prevent secession. He went a long way toward integrating the Porte into the system of European diplomacy, expanding its permanent diplomatic presence to several European capitals and, in 1835, establishing a European-style foreign ministry. In this period, references to Islamic law in the Ottoman Empire's diplomatic discourse declined, while the language of equality and public law rose.[4] In 1840–41 the Porte was a signatory to two major multilateral treaties, the London Convention and the Straits Convention. Mahmud also laid the groundwork for the Tanzimat (reform) era, which began the year he died. That year, 1839, Abdülmecid issued a formal statute that outlined wide-ranging social, economic, and political reforms, for example, ending slavery and establishing formal equality, reorganizing the financial system and the tax codes, establishing secular education, and modernizing the civil and criminal codes. The publication of books and pamphlets ex-

4. Davison 1990, 23, 85; Hale 2000, 17–18.

panded, and the first nonofficial newspaper was founded. Abdülmecid was aided especially by Mustafa Reshid Pasha, who served in many key posts through the 1850s, from grand vizier (the most powerful role in the empire after the sultan), to ambassador to Paris and London, and reis effendi, or foreign minister.[5]

Integration to the European system was painful internally. Powerful conservative groups fought against the idea of equality, while the Christians it was designed to help did not fully embrace it. But perhaps the greatest internal challenge the Ottoman Empire faced in the 1830s was from Mehmet Ali of Egypt. In 1831 Ali made a move for control of the whole empire, taking Syria and threatening Constantinople. Egypt at this point had economic and military ties to France, and French forces were nearby, since France had taken Algiers the year before. Mahmud first turned to Britain for help. Lord Palmerston (Henry John Temple), the foreign minister at the time, declined, but Russia under Nicholas sent fourteen thousand troops to protect Constantinople and repel the advance. In exchange for Russian help, the Ottoman Empire signed the bilateral 1833 Treaty of Hünkâr İskelesi (Unkiar Skelessi), an eight-year agreement that rendered the Porte something of a Russian protectorate. Russia pledged to protect the empire if the sultan would guarantee to close the Straits to warships whenever Russia was at war. After this, the threat from Ali did not fully recede, and in 1839 Abdülmecid attempted to reverse Ali's gains in Syria. This attack did not go well for the Ottomans. This time, both Russia and Britain stepped in to help the sultan while France in 1840 switched sides. Ali finally was defeated. The latter crisis led to the Straits Convention of 1841, signed by all five European great powers.[6] It replaced Hünkâr İskelesi and forbade any warships from entering the Straits in peacetime. Internal challenges still did not disappear, however. In 1848, with the democratic revolutions in Europe, the Ottomans faced revolts in the Danubian Principalities. Once again the sultan turned first to Britain for help. After being turned down twice, the request went to Russia, which as usual agreed. Russia occupied the Principalities until 1852.[7]

In sum, the Ottoman Empire materially was in a worse position in 1853 than it had been in the 1820s. Increasingly the European powers saw its

5. Saab 1977, 6ff.; Jelavich 1983, 282.
6. France had been excluded from the London Convention of 1840 between the four great powers and the Ottoman Empire.
7. Saab 1977, 8.

demise as imminent. Nicholas was the first to characterize the Porte the sick man of Europe, but no one disputed that characterization. Its weakness did not make it an overt target of any of the great powers, but by 1850 the Ottoman Empire seemed to owe its continued independence merely to the fact that none of the great powers had concrete plans for how to handle its demise.

## Another Russo-Turkish War

In 1850 Louis Napoleon Bonaparte picked a fight with Russia by appealing to the sultan on behalf of the Catholics in Jerusalem. Napoleon had come to power in 1848 with the explicit goal of restoring glory to France and to the Bonaparte name. This meant, first, consolidating his power, which he did by declaring himself dictator and then emperor—Napoleon III, Emperor of the French. It also meant undermining the Vienna Settlement, which he found overly punitive, particularly since it forbade another Bonaparte from ruling France. Napoleon made clear to his European partners that he did not see the 1815 treaties as binding and that they would be "cancelled" in the event of a new European war.[8] His strategy for unraveling the settlement included forging an (unprecedented) alliance with Britain and breaking up the Holy Alliance connection between Russia, Austria, and Prussia.[9]

Napoleon's specific aim in 1850 was to restore Catholic rights at the holy sites in and near Jerusalem.[10] France had legal rights dating from 1740 to protect all European Catholics in the Ottoman Empire, which included rights regarding the holy sites. But Greek Orthodox Christians, a much larger group, had taken over those rights in practice, and Catherine the Great had secured them the legal right to do so in the 1774 Treaty of Küçük Kaynarca. Orthodox rights were reiterated in bilateral treaties between Russia and the Porte in 1812, 1826, 1829, and 1833. Napoleon's 1850 negotiations with the sultan continued until February 1852, when Abdülmecid attempted to please both sides by issuing two contra-

8. Chamberlain 1983, 472–73.

9. The relationship between the Holy Alliance powers had tightened in the 1830s. In the 1834 Treaty of Münchengrätz, the three autocratic powers agreed to cooperate to quash liberal revolts, and Russia helped Austria put down the democratic revolts of 1848.

10. Rich 1985, 21; Saab 1977, 11.

dictory *firmans*.[11] One was directed to France and granted the keys to the shrines to the Catholics; the other, to Russia, promised that Orthodox rights would remain unchanged.[12] Neither France nor Russia was satisfied. Several months later, under some duress from Napoleon, Abdülmecid reneged on Nicholas and granted primary rights to the Catholics.

Russia responded by sending a special negotiator, Prince Alexander Menshikov, to Constantinople in February 1853. The goal was to get the Orthodox rights back and to confirm Russia's special role as protector of the largest Christian sect in the Ottoman Empire. Over one-third of the empire's population (somewhere between twelve and thirteen million), and the bulk of the 12,000 Christians who made pilgrimage to Jerusalem each year, was Orthodox. The Catholic population was significantly smaller, and "less than a hundred" Catholics made an annual pilgrimage.[13] Menshikov, a military man with a style that was by all accounts more abrasive than that of Russia's foreign minister, Nesselrode, was slow to get started, and his mission dragged on until the end of May. By the time he left, the holy sites issue was resolved, peacefully, among the three interested parties—France, Russia, and the Ottoman Empire.

However, Menshikov also demanded that the sultan formally recognize Russia's broader rights with respect to Orthodox Christians in the Ottoman Empire. This intensified rather than resolved tensions. Specifically, Menshikov requested the right to "make representations on behalf of" Orthodox Christians and for the Orthodox church, clergy, possessions, and religious establishments to have "the privileges and immunities that were assured to it *ab antique*," that is, that had been granted "by the Imperial favor."[14] He claimed that these privileges were merely a restatement from the Treaty of Küçük Kaynarca. But that treaty had specified only "the new church of Constantinople . . . and its officiating ministers."[15] Menshikov's demands were for this right to be restated and expanded so that they would apply beyond Constantinople, and to all Orthodox Christians rather than merely to clergy. He demanded that this broadening of rights be recognized in a *sened*. A *sened* was a stronger commitment than a *firman* and had the force of a treaty.

11. A *firman* was a decree by the sultan and was considered binding.

12. Badem 2010, 65.

13. Gooch 1956, 35.

14. Quoted in Curtiss 1979, 141. Curtiss includes the full text of the *sened* Russia proposed in late April.

15. Curtiss 1979, 119; Chamberlain 1983, 480.

To put the Russian demand in context, religious groups were important politically in the Ottoman Empire. Organized in political units called *millets*, they were responsible for their own courts, prisons, schools, hospitals, tax collection, and such. The patriarch at Constantinople headed the Orthodox millet and spoke on its behalf to the sultan. However, there was no Catholic millet. Because historically the Catholic population had been so small, if Catholics as a group had grievances then France would speak for them rather than a Catholic patriarch. Disputes between the Ottoman Empire and its Catholics were negotiated at the interstate level and resolved through treaties. The Orthodox, however, being more numerous and more politically powerful, did not have the same right. They were required to appeal to the sultan first.[16] Russia was asking for this same right of appeal on behalf of the Orthodox population. Needless to say, if recognized legally, such a right would be far more threatening to Ottoman sovereignty than in the French case. If one-third of its population could appeal to Russia first rather than the sultan, for all intents and purposes the sultan would no longer be sovereign over that portion of its own population. Russia already had been taking for itself this protector role, but the demand to legalize it put in sharp relief the implications for Ottoman sovereignty at a time when consolidating sovereignty was the sultan's central concern.

When the Ottomans steadily refused, offering Russia instead only "spiritual rights," Menshikov progressively toned down his demands, from a treaty or *sened* to a diplomatic note (not even a *firman*). He assured the sultan that Russia's goal was simply to reiterate already-existing rights and not to create new ones.[17] But he linked the demand for this diplomatic note to an ultimatum: the sultan must accept it or else Russia would occupy the Danubian Principalities. The Principalities were already under Russian influence, with the most recent Russian occupation ending in 1852. Russia described the ultimatum to the Ottoman foreign minister, Reshid Pasha, as a "material guarantee" until Russia received the sultan's signed note.[18] When Menshikov left Constantinople at the end of May, the ultimatum hung in the air.

Although the Menshikov mission was bilateral, France and Britain had become heavily involved. Menshikov's instructions were leaked the month before he began to talk to the Ottoman foreign minister, and in

16. Rich 1985, 19; Saab 1977, 11–13.
17. Curtiss 1979, 143.
18. Curtiss 1979, 147.

April the European powers each took a key step: the British ambassador, Stratford Canning, who had become Lord Redcliffe in 1852 (hereafter, Redcliffe), arrived in Constantinople, and he had the ear of Ottoman decision makers;[19] and France moved a fleet east, from Toulon to Salamis (near Athens, on the west side of the Aegean Sea).[20] France asked Britain to send a ship as well, but the government, now headed by the Earl of Aberdeen, refused. Two months later when Menshikov left Constantinople, Britain and France each moved warships from west to east, that is, to Besika Bay, which is near the Dardanelles. They gave a precautionary rationale—namely, that the ships should serve as a signal that Russian expansion would be unacceptable.[21] At this point, with friendly great power ships in the bay, the Porte rejected the Russian ultimatum. In early July Russia responded by occupying the Principalities.[22]

With a Russian army of fifty thousand[23] just north of the Danube and British and French warships near the mouth of the Straits, the situation was heating up. In the summer of 1853 European diplomacy intensified. At the same time as Menshikov issued the May ultimatum, Nicholas had sent separate notes to France and Austria asking for help in getting the Ottomans to accede to what he saw as now-limited Russian demands. He reassured the European sovereigns of Russia's benign intentions and defensive approach: he would not attack unless the Porte struck first.[24] Nesselrode's circular to the Russian diplomats reiterated that defensive intent. They should stress in their communications that Russia asked only for confirmation of old rights. He acknowledged that this may well amount to a religious protectorate, but averred that if so, "Russia has at all times exercised [one] in the East." Therefore, since Russia already had shown since the Treaty of Adrianople (1829) it could do this without harming Ottoman sovereignty, there was no reason to believe Russian behavior would change.[25] The Russian general, Mikhail Gorchakov, even took the unusual step of writing directly to Reshid Pasha, in charge of foreign affairs for the sultan, informing of his troop movements and restating Russia's defensive aims. He promised not to fight unless the sultan's troops

19. Rich 1985, 44; Schroeder 1972, 12; Saab 1977, 4; Badem 2010, 39.
20. Rich 1985, 42–43.
21. Saab 1977, 54.
22. Schroeder 1972, 45; Rich 1985, 70.
23. Schroeder 1972, 44.
24. Rich 1985, 67–69; Schroeder 1972, 44–45; Curtiss 1979, 149–50.
25. Curtiss 1979, 148.

crossed the Danube, and if the Russians were massively outnumbered he would withdraw rather than maintain the occupation. He gave these same instructions to his troops.[26]

Despite Russian insistence in its private diplomacy that its aims were defensive, there also is some evidence that Nicholas at least flirted with larger aims. In December 1852, when Nicholas first heard of the sultan's decision in favor of France, he had a different idea in mind than Menshikov's mission. He mobilized two corps in southern Russia and alerted his Black Sea forces, and he also discussed partition with Nesselrode.[27] Then, stepping back from this aggressive stance in January and February, as the idea of the Menshikov mission gelled, in conversations with the British ambassador to Saint Petersburg, Sir Hamilton Seymour, Nicholas broached the subject of the Ottoman Empire's imminent demise and talked about his vision of a partition. Their conversation echoed an earlier, informal conversation in 1844, between Nicholas and Aberdeen (who was not prime minister at the time). In May 1853 the czar acknowledged to Austria's Emperor Franz Joseph that if Ottoman intransigence continued Russia would step up its coercive tactics. He outlined three stages, of which the occupation of the Principalities was the first. Continued Ottoman intransigence would lead Russia to blockade the Bosporus (and he expressed the desire for Austria to enter Serbia and Herzegovina to demonstrate support), and then a threat to declare independence for the Principalities.[28] Nicholas had no reason to anticipate that Austria would protest. They had recently worked together handling unrest in Montenegro, and before that Russia had helped the Habsburgs put down the 1848 Hungarian revolt and had supported Austrian demands to extradite Hungarians who had fled to the Ottoman Empire. To Nicholas, there was no daylight between Russian and Austrian policy stances toward the Porte. None of the czar's European interlocutors communicated concern about Russian intentions.

Europe's response to the Russo-Turkish crisis was a remarkable back and forth of diplomatic initiatives throughout the summer, all aimed at mediation: the Turkish Ultimatum, the Vienna Note, the Turkish Amendments, the Violent Interpretation, the Olmütz Proposal. The first diplomatic effort was the Turkish Ultimatum.[29] An informal conference of the Constanti-

26. Curtiss 1979, 149–50.

27. Rich 1985, 22.

28. Saab 1977, 52; Badem 2010, 79–80.

29. In some accounts this is called the Constantinople Note. Rich 1985, 70; Badem 2010, 82–83.

nople ambassadors of the four neutral powers—Britain, France, Austria, and Prussia—in close consultation with Ottoman foreign minister Reshid Pasha and working from his draft, resulted in a joint memo. What became known as the Turkish Ultimatum consisted of three documents: a note from the sultan protesting Russia's occupation; the sultan's formal, negative response to Menshikov; and "the text of the latest Turkish government decrees confirming the spiritual (but no other) privileges of the non-Moslem subjects of the Sultan."[30] The Turkish Ultimatum basically reiterated the sultan's position. Reshid Pasha's intention was that it should be sent directly to Russia as the sultan's response to Menshikov's May ultimatum.

The Turkish Ultimatum went first to Vienna,[31] however, where it intersected with another diplomatic effort, a more formal conference of the ambassadors, which was a French and Austrian initiative. The French foreign minister, Édouard Drouyn de Lhuys, had written a note intended to resolve the dispute by offering an interpretation of the Menshikov demands, and the governments of Britain and Austria, and then the czar, approved it.[32] Building from Drouyn's text, the ambassadors at Vienna of the four neutral powers devised the Vienna Note in a conference officiated by the Austrian foreign minister, Count Karl von Buol-Schauenstein (hereafter, Buol). The Vienna Note reiterated the sultan's promise to respect the rights and immunities of the Orthodox Church based on the already-existing treaties between Russia and the Porte.[33] The note also generalized the claim to protect Christians, calling for international protection of all Christians in the Ottoman Empire rather than simply noting Russian protection of the Orthodox, and it made provisions to scale back the crisis in a way for all to save face. The Vienna Note was written as if it came from the sultan, but no Ottoman voices were involved in the drafting. Russian and Ottoman representatives were in Vienna, but it is not clear whether the latter were kept informed.[34] Insofar as it both reaffirmed the existing treaties and legitimated Russia's special position vis-à-vis the Ortho-

---

30. Rich 1985, 72.

31. Vienna was the closest European capital to Constantinople that had telegraph links to all of the other capitals. Constantinople was not yet linked to the telegraph system. On the history of the telegraph in the Ottoman Empire, see Davison 1990, 133–65.

32. Rich 1985, 73.

33. Curtiss 1979, 567–68.

34. Schroeder 1972, 57; Curtiss 1979, 158. Even if the Ottoman representative was there, he may not have spoken French and so would have been excluded from the diplomacy. See Badem 2010, 404. Cf. Chamberlain 1983, 484, who claims the Ottoman Empire was not invited to Vienna.

dox, this note differed from the Turkish Ultimatum, and insofar as it called for all of Europe (not just Russia) to care about all Christians, it differed from Menshikov's initial note. To Nicholas, then, this was a concession. But from the sultan's perspective the violation to sovereignty was no less.

The four neutral powers already had agreed to adopt the Vienna Note as the basis of their mediation effort when the Turkish Ultimatum arrived. Since the ultimatum's tone, particularly the protest by the sultan, was harsher, Buol chose not to even officially acknowledge its receipt, much less append it to the Vienna Note.[35] Instead, Nicholas received the Vienna Note only—and quickly accepted it. The next step was for the ambassadors of the four neutral powers to persuade the Ottomans to accept the Vienna Note, which would end this diplomatic crisis by giving Russia just enough of its initial demands to remove its troops without losing face. The Europeans were cautiously optimistic that they had resolved the crisis.[36]

But Russia's acceptance of the Vienna Note was conditional on the Porte accepting it in full, without any changes. Instead, insulted by not having been consulted on the language of the note, and concerned, as always, about European encroachments on its sovereignty, the sultan sent what came to be known as the Turkish Amendments. These noted that several passages in the Vienna Note violated Turkish sovereignty and gave Russia sufficient pretext for treating the entire empire as a protectorate. The language of the Vienna Note was ambiguous regarding the right to intervene, admitting both a broad and a narrow interpretation. The sultan's amendments sought to nail down precisely what rights Russia would have. The sultan articulated an interpretation of the Treaty of Küçük Kaynarca that denied Russia any special rights regarding Ottoman Christians. It divided the Christian issue, as discussed in the treaty, into two separate statements: the Russian *spiritual* connection to Orthodox Christians in the empire, and the sultan's exclusive *sovereign right to govern* his subjects. In doing so, what it specifically excluded was any Russian (or European, for that matter) legal right to hear Christian grievances. Christians with grievances against the Ottoman sultan must directly address the sultan and not to some external power. The amendments also called for a European great power guarantee of nonintervention in the Principalities once Russia left.[37]

35. Rich 1985, 73–74.
36. Schroeder 1972, 60; Bartlett 1996, 59; Saab 1972, 66.
37. Curtiss 1979, 161–62. The Treaty of Küçük Kaynarca was an ambiguous text, partly because it was written in three languages, Ottoman Turkish, Russian, and Italian, and the texts

Russia refused to accept the amendments. Nicholas and Nesselrode saw their own demands as status quo, that is, reaffirmations of old rights, and they saw the sultan's amendments as revisionist, that is, an attempt to reduce or remove already-existing Russian rights. Accepting the amendments would be the very opposite of the outcome the Menshikov mission intended.[38] Nesselrode therefore instructed the Russian diplomats in Europe to reiterate Russia's demand that the Vienna Note stand without modifications and to ask the neutral powers to pressure the Ottomans to back down. He also included a separate document "prepared by his chancellery officials analyzing the modifications of the Vienna Note desired by the Porte, with instructions to communicate it to the governments of the four powers."[39] The note reiterated Russian rights to protect Christians, speaking of Russia's "active solicitude for her co-religionists in Turkey."[40]

This latter document became problematic. Nesselrode's analysis of the amendments was translated and became widely known because a Berlin newspaper published it. Before reading Nesselrode's analysis, the great powers had determined that their energies should be put to getting the Ottomans to sign on to the Vienna Note. On reading the analysis, Buol was unmoved and simply renewed instructions to the Austrian diplomats to get the Porte to sign the Vienna Note.[41] However, France and especially Britain did not receive Nesselrode's analysis well. It came to be known as a Violent Interpretation of the Vienna Note, which went too far and read as if a claim for a protectorate.[42] Until then it had been the Ottoman Empire that the powers, by and large, had considered intransigent. Austria, Prussia, Britain, and France all had supported the Vienna Note and found the Turkish Amendments to be overboard. But the Violent Interpretation was a key turning point. From here on, Russia was treated as the aggressor and the Porte as the victim. Britain and France stopped pressuring the sultan to accept the Vienna Note.[43] Even Aberdeen, long a supporter

---

do not fully match. However, its meaning in practice had been the Russian interpretation, so any attempt to settle on a common meaning would effectively limit Russian practices. See Davison 1990, 29–50.

38. Curtiss 1979, 165.
39. Rich 1985, 79.
40. Chamberlain 1983, 485.
41. Curtiss 1979, 164–66; Rich 1985, 81.
42. Chamberlain 1983, 485.
43. Curtiss 1979, 164. Schroeder 1972, 64–65 argues that the violent interpretation was a consequence rather than a cause of Britain's policy switch.

of Russia, at this point changed his rhetoric and complained of Russian "double dealing." He expressed worry that Nesselrode's note unmasked Russia's true intentions to destroy the Ottoman Empire bit by bit.[44] The Earl of Clarendon, the British foreign minister, noted that against the Russian conniving giant, "however foolish the Turks may be we cannot abandon Turkey."[45]

At this point, the sultan requested that Britain and France bring their fleets closer to Constantinople. This was not in response to the Violent Interpretation, which had not yet reached Constantinople, but was a request for help responding to rising domestic unrest. Anti-Russian opinion in Constantinople had reached a boiling point.[46] Britain and France answered in the affirmative. This is a key moment. To get the western ships to Constantinople from Besika Bay would require passing through the Straits. This would violate the terms of the 1841 Straits Convention, which prohibited the passage of warships in peacetime. Aberdeen's instructions to Clarendon specify that he should make clear to Russia the defensive aims of this move. The intention was to protect British interests and "the person of the Sultan"; this was not a hostile action against Russia, and thus did not violate the convention.[47]

With Britain and France seeming to lean toward supporting the Ottomans, Russia initiated another round of diplomacy aimed at ending the crisis, which culminated in the Olmütz Proposal.[48] Nicholas and Nesselrode went to Olmütz, in Austria, and met with Franz Joseph, Buol, and representatives from each of the other neutral governments. A conciliatory Nicholas offered to meet "every legitimate wish" of those governments and asked only to maintain existing treaties and the status quo when it came to religion.[49] With Austrian help the czar then drew up a plan to resend the Vienna Note to the sultan, along with an additional document: an unambiguous interpretation of the note signed by all of the European powers and including a guarantee to enforce the interpretation. Once the sultan signed, Russia would evacuate the Principalities.[50]

---

44. Chamberlain 1983, 486.
45. Schroeder 1972, 63.
46. Saab 1977, 84–87; Baumgart 1999, 14. Badem 2010, 94–95.
47. Rich 1985, 84; Saab 1977, 85, 97. Cf. Schroeder 1972, 73–74.
48. Also known as the Buol Project.
49. Rich 1985, 84; Chamberlain 1983, 486.
50. Rich 1985, 85.

Nicholas was explicitly backing down from the Violent Interpretation. France favored accepting the proposal, but Britain did not. The British cabinet did not even debate the proposal, dismissing it as a deception.[51]

Finally, the sultan declared war in early October. While the British and French ships formally were coming for domestic politics reasons, they seem to have given the sultan confidence to stand up to Russia. Shortly after the ships entered the Straits, the Porte gave Russia a fifteen-day ultimatum, which is considered its war declaration: evacuate the Principalities or face hostilities.[52] Russia equivocated long enough, and the Ottomans initiated hostilities. Russia waited a few weeks before issuing its own war declaration, and when it did, the czar included language in the declaration intended to reassure the other powers that Russia would act only defensively.[53] For his part, Aberdeen claimed a defensive posture as well, assuring Russia in bilateral communication that Britain would do nothing as long as Russia did not take the offensive.[54] As for France, Napoleon told the British ambassador, Lord Cowley (Henry Wellesley), that "he would not send a single soldier to the Ottoman Empire, and he had not increased his army as late as November 1853."[55] The overall strategy of each of the European powers seemed to be to avoid fighting as much as possible and solve the problem through negotiations in the winter.[56] But at no point did the three powers, much less the five, discuss, much less commit, to a defensive strategy or a common interpretation of the function of the western ships.

By late October 1853, then, Russia and the Porte were at war over Russia's presence in the Principalities and Russia's relationship to Orthodox Christians in the Ottoman Empire. France and Britain had ships in the Straits. Russia and Britain both claimed in bilateral diplomacy that they had defensive aims. Fighting between Ottoman troops and Russians began in late October, with the Ottomans attacking and defeating the Russians in a few relatively small battles in the Balkans and Caucasus.

---

51. Rich 1985, 85.

52. Rich 1985, 86; Saab 1977, 95–96; Badem 2010, 99–100, 111.

53. Rich 1985, 88; Curtiss 1979, 185, 203.

54. Rich 1985, 93.

55. Gooch 1956, 46. Gooch argues that Cowley's papers show that Napoleon was not pressing for war and was focused on relations with Britain. Rich 1985, 99 provides this quote: "When we sent our fleet to Salamis, we had only one wish, to draw a cool and hesitant England into an alliance with ourselves."

56. Saab 1977, 95, 115 calls this a preference for a "phony war."

## A Fork in the Road

Some scholarship on the Crimean War considers it inevitable at this point that the great powers would be drawn into the conflict. But the diplomacy could have gone two very different ways. Few European decision makers wanted a wider war, but there was enough uncertainty about Russian intentions that protecting the Ottoman Empire was a shared goal. The question was whether that was best accomplished by grouping Russia or by balancing against it. I will lay out the logic of each approach, and what it might have meant behaviorally, to show that a grouping strategy was plausible. The purpose of this section is not to explain why the war widened or to pass judgment on the fact that it did. Rather, I want to point out that given the problem the great powers faced, they had a choice. Great power war was not inevitable. For now, I will bracket the intentions of the other great powers, because the issue in 1853 was their perception of Russian intentions.

### The Road Not Taken

Despite the tense situation, key players still felt that the conflict could be resolved. For example, the French ambassador to Vienna was still "convinced that the diplomatic systems that had served Europe so well since 1815 would again prevent war."[57] There was a constituency for a concerted approach and there were discursive resources—the language and the practice of grouping through commitments and public talk. What would this have looked like? The other great powers could have approached the situation as they had in the 1820s, walling off the bilateral problem between Russia and the Porte from the humanitarian concerns of Russia's fellow Christian, European powers. The template for how to handle such an issue was their own. In the 1820s, when Czar Alexander I invoked the Treaty of Küçük Kaynarca, Castlereagh and Metternich ignored the reference and did not refer to that treaty in the Hanover strategy.

The Vienna Notes similarly generalized Russia's claim regarding the Orthodox into a European claim regarding all Christians. They did not refer to any particular treaty, but, in Redcliffe's words, "associate[d Russia] . . . with [Britain's] disinterested and constant efforts in behalf of the

57. Saab, Knapp, and de Bourqueney Knapp 1986, 484.

Christians, drawn from the principles of humanity."[58] By specifying the interest as spiritual rather than as a legal right, they rationalized diplomatic efforts on behalf of Christians without justifying material intervention. In other words, the great powers in the 1820s did not denounce or overrule Russia's special claim. What they did was to demote it; it was not acceptable as a basis for European military action.

But there the similarity between the two cases ends. What the powers did not do—and what they could have done—was treat the 1853 occupation of the Principalities as a matter within Russia's sphere of influence. Since 1815 the European powers had accepted spheres of influence on the continent, not only in the revolts of the 1820s but also in the silence after Russia crushed the Polish revolt in 1830 and after Austria annexed Kraków in 1846.[59] And the other powers had, until this point, treated the Principalities as de facto in Russia's sphere of influence, particularly by leaving the bilateral 1812 Treaty of Bucharest outside the 1815 Vienna Final Act's umbrella. By 1822 the Principalities had local Orthodox Christian rulers. In the 1820s, first at Akkerman (1826) and then at Adrianople (1829), the sultan formally recognized the Principalities as under Russian protection.[60] Russia occupied the Principalities from 1829 to 1834 and then again from 1848 to 1851. None of these actions resulted in great power protest. All were treated as matters within Russia's sphere of influence.[61]

That the Russian czar saw the Principalities as a bilateral issue, outside of the scope of European concern, is evident in his response to the French ambassador.[62] When France sent its fleet to Salamis and the French minister in Brussels threatened to invade if Austria and Russia defeated the sultan,[63] Nicholas protested that this was a mistaken analogy. Belgian independence was a great power, European issue, while the Principalities and agreements pertaining to them were purely bilateral, between Russia and the Ottomans.[64] Some prominent voices in Britain also treated

---

58. Curtiss 1979, 122–24.

59. Heydemann 2002, 202.

60. The Porte retained a relationship of suzerainty, but this was limited to an annual tribute.

61. The parties most opposed to Russian occupations were the locals (Romanians). Jelavich 1983, 272–74. Schroeder 1972, 14 discusses the Principalities.

62. The 1853 occupation did not violate any specific agreement, and Russia had treaty rights to intervene in the principalities. Gooch 1956, 41.

63. Curtiss 1979, 111–12; Schroeder 1972, 31.

64. Schroeder 1972, 76.

the issue as bilateral in spring 1853. In cabinet debates, Lord John Russell noted that the better the sultan treated his subjects the less the czar would find it necessary to protect Christians, a protection that is "no doubt prescribed by duty and sanctioned by treaty."[65] Aberdeen referred to Russia as a "civilized Christian power" facing the "barbarous Mahommedan.'"[66]

In other words, there were precedents of Concert powers granting one another limited freedom within their spheres of influence and precedents of treating the Principalities as part of Russia's sphere. Grouping Russia in this case would have entailed cordoning off the conflict with the Ottomans and ensuring that it did not spill over. The strategy would have acknowledged and contained Russia's possible ambitions, producing restraint by filtering Russian intentions through the collective European intention. This is the approach that, according to Paul Schroeder, guided Austria's policy: "avert war and check Russia by restraining her within the established Concert and compelling her to deal with Turkey through it, thereby preserving the existing treaties and boundaries in Europe."[67] A grouping strategy would not have required that Russian intentions were prosocial, or that Russia was altruistic. Rather, the strategy builds from the premise that regardless of Russian intentions toward the Ottoman Empire, its intentions toward the European balance of power were status quo. If those could be made salient then Russia would act in ways that would not undermine the status quo.

In autumn 1853, when Russia occupied the Principalities, its intentions suddenly were in question. By sending their ships into the Straits, British and French intentions were in question. There are at least two "grouping" strategies that would have mitigated the uncertainty. First, Britain, France, and Russia could have jointly committed to defensive intentions and nonaggrandizement. As noted, they did so in their private diplomacy, with Britain, France, and Russia each stating defensive intentions to one another. But they did not coordinate their actions in order to seem as if acting together—this was not a Hanover strategy. In the absence of a joint commitment, bilateral assurances easily could be treated as cheap talk. They did not reduce uncertainty and could not be made salient for behavior. A second possible strategy would have been to call for a conference among signatories of the Straits Convention to manage Britain's

65. Quoted in Curtiss 1979, 113.
66. Aberdeen, quoted in Chamberlain 1983, 480–81.
67. Schroeder 1972, xii.

and France's perceived need to protect the sultan from domestic unrest. Britain and the Ottoman Empire, at least, referred to the Straits Convention in their diplomacy. In June, Russia's ambassador at London "reported that the British did not agree with the French that the treaty of 1841 bound them to defend the Ottoman territory and integrity."[68] But this is precisely what the Western powers were doing in September 1853, and, as Reshid Pasha pointed out, the preamble to that convention could be read as if it called on the powers to protect the Ottoman Empire.[69] If the presence of Britain and France in the Straits raised the issue of the Straits Convention, a convention whose goal mirrored that of the Vienna Settlement, that is, of maintaining European stability, then the signatories should be able to call a meeting to discuss it.

Both of these would have been public, grouping strategies that could possibly have stemmed the tide toward war. Either would have provided a shared interpretation of actions that would have made behavior less ambiguous. It is true that the war party was gaining power in Britain and that Napoleon was following Britain's lead, so a public strategy may not have worked. But given the structural similarity between the 1820s and the 1850s and the power of the public commitments in the earlier case, it is plausible that a commitment, or meetings regarding an already-existing commitment, could have contained the drift to war. In their absence, actions were untethered and signals ambiguous. In this context, despite the presence of some statesmen who sought a negotiated outcome, the great powers continued to drift toward war.

### The Road Taken

The road taken was the balance of power approach. Since it is more familiar it can be summarized relatively quickly. It begins with the assumption that Russia's intentions were aggressive and Russia therefore needed to be deterred or defeated. There was evidence that Russia had long-standing revisionist intentions. Since Catherine the Great, Russia had made steady gains in the Black Sea region, adding not just the Crimea but also a large swath of the shoreline to the east and west. More recently, there were the 1844 conversations between Nicholas and Aberdeen mentioned above, in which Nicholas raised the possibility of partitioning the Ottoman Empire, and, of course the Seymour conversations and the note to Franz Joseph in

68. Gooch 1956, 56.
69. Saab 1977, 92.

1853. Thus it was plausible to argue that Russia was using the holy places dispute as a pretext to begin grabbing the Ottoman Empire.

Nonetheless, even a balance of power approach would not necessarily have meant great power war. Balancing Mehmet Ali in 1839 had entailed balancing France. But the European great powers kept their focus on Ali,[70] and French troops never came in contact with troops of the European allies.[71] Not that they sought out the earlier near miss: balancing made great power war more likely not less, and their overall goal was still to avoid war. Moreover, in the current case balancing might be an overreaction. Whatever Russia's ultimate designs, since Catherine's reign its czars generally had not acted on them. Russian czars had been talking of special rights regarding Orthodox Christians in the empire since 1774, yet repeatedly had acted with restraint. In 1828 Russia stopped short of Constantinople, and it did not annex the Principalities, and the 1830s interventions were in fact to defend the sultan. Then there were Russia's concessions in 1853, downgrading its demands from treaty to diplomatic note, then accepting the great powers' Vienna Note and showing restraint in its declaration of war.

The key difference between a balancing and a grouping strategy was that the latter required embracing the ambiguity of Russian intentions and working to channel them toward a common goal, while a balance of power approach meant downplaying or overlooking ambiguity. The balance of power approach rested on certainty not uncertainty about Russia's intentions; it amounted to overcoming the security dilemma rather than managing it.

## Great Power War

A summer's worth of diplomacy could not prevent war, which began in October 1853. But this was, still, only a Russo-Turkish war. The Concert powers had shown in the 1820s that they could work together to contain Russo-Turkish conflict. Unfortunately, they were unable to replicate that in this case, and within a few months, by March 1854, France and Britain entered the war against their Vienna Settlement ally; Austria joined them in December of that year.

The slide to great power war accelerated in November, when Rus-

---

70. Russia proposed resurrecting the Quadruple Alliance to intimidate France, but Britain refused. Chamberlain 1983.

71. Hale 2000, 23–25.

sia destroyed an Ottoman fleet in Sinop, a Black Sea harbor. This was a decisive victory for the Russians. Their superior fleet sank all but one of the Turkish ships and destroyed the city as well; some four thousand Ottomans died.[72] The Sinop attack was a legitimate act of war. It followed Ottoman land attacks of October and November, and the Turkish ship fired first, which suggests that technically the Russians were not breaking their pledge to fight only defensively.[73] Nonetheless, because it so blatantly demonstrated Russian superiority, it seemed to contradict Nicholas's pledges to remain on the defensive. Coverage of the attack in the British press mobilized an already Russophobic British public, and it quickly became known as the "Sinop massacre."[74] As a prominent British statesman colorfully put it, Sinop showed that "the eye-tooth of the Bear [is now] drawn; and till his fleet and naval arsenal in the Black Sea are destroyed, there is no safety for Constantinople—no security for the peace of Europe."[75] Shortly after Sinop, France and Britain ordered their warships in the Straits to take the significant step of entering the Black Sea. They demanded that Russian ships stay in port at Sevastopol, warning that any Russian ship that left the harbor would be attacked.

Austria's diplomatic efforts to avoid pulling Britain and France into the war continued through much of the fall and winter. Buol convened yet another ambassadorial conference in Vienna, which resulted in a Collective Note to send to Russia.[76] Meanwhile, the Constantinople ambassadors came up with their own note in consultation with the Ottomans. This time Vienna accepted the latter as a substitute and sent it to Russia. Nicholas had his own strategy. He sent separate personal letters to Queen Victoria, Emperor Franz Joseph of Austria, and Napoleon, reiterating his peaceful, status quo intentions.[77] Nicholas then sent Prince Alexey Orlov to Vienna, with two goals. First, he requested that Austria remain neutral (Austria refused); second, he formally responded to the first Collective

72. The precise number of deaths is disputed. Jelavich 1983, 283; Rich 1985, 97. Cf. Badem 2010, 109ff. Badem 2010, 143 notes that unlike the Europeans, especially the British, the Ottoman Empire did not treat Sinop as a massacre but as a regular wartime defeat.

73. Saab 1977, 115–17; Badem 2010, 115–17.

74. Some, such as Rich 1985, 97, argue that the sultan instigated the attack. Others point a finger at the British and French. The Ottoman ships had warned the Western fleets that Russians were near and asked for reinforcements, but the Western fleets did not respond. Kinross 1977, 494; Badem 2010, 116–17.

75. Graham, quoted in Rich 1985, 99.

76. Chamberlain 1983, 489; Rich 1985, 96.

77. Gooch 1956, 54.

Note (the four ambassadors jointly rejected this Russian response). Buol tried once more, asking Russia to modify its stance yet further (basically, to surrender). Nicholas's response did not go far enough,[78] and the four powers rejected it as well.[79]

In a separate track, in late January Napoleon sent a personal letter to Nicholas calling for Russia to evacuate the Principalities, and offering in exchange that Britain and France would leave the Black Sea. Russia would then negotiate a treaty with the Ottoman Empire, which the four other great powers would review at a conference. Napoleon warned that if the czar—who was responsible for the war, according to Napoleon— refused his note then France and Britain would have to resort to war to force Russia out of the Principalities.[80] Although a personal note, Napoleon upped the ante by making it public before Nicholas responded.[81] In early February, Nicholas responded by severing diplomatic ties with both Western powers. Britain and France then issued an ultimatum demanding Russian withdrawal. Russia did not, and in March 1854, Britain and France officially declared war on Russia. The Western powers allied with the Porte, declaring themselves "fully persuaded that the existence of the Ottoman Empire in its present Limits is essential to the maintenance of the Balance of Power among the States of Europe."[82] Article 5 of the treaty invited all states in Europe to join the alliance.[83] Russia declared war on Britain and France two weeks later, and its troops crossed the Danube into Bulgaria, which was Ottoman territory, to face Ottoman forces.[84] British and French troops landed in Gallipoli and Scutari in March and most went to Varna to counter the anticipated Russian offensive. At this point, Austria remained officially neutral[85] but signed a treaty with the Porte promising to be a stabilizing force in the Principalities for the remainder of war.[86] Austria pledged to occupy the Principalities once the Russians left, to stay through the end of the war, and to intervene

78. Rich 1985, 101–3.

79. Rich 1985, 105–6.

80. Rich 1985, 103.

81. Rich 1985, 103.

82. Quoted in Rich 1985, 106.

83. Baumgart 1999, 16.

84. Ottoman forces had improved since the 1820s. Since the 1826 destruction of the janissary corps, money and training had been channeled toward a general force for the empire. But the Ottomans relied on weapons from others and had financial difficulties. Hale 2000, 17.

85. Austria and Prussia signed a neutrality pact in 1854.

86. Hale 2000, 27.

in the event of revolts in Bosnia, Albania, or Montenegro.[87] Finally, Austria issued an ultimatum to Russia to leave the Principalities in the spring. Having lost Austrian support, in August 1854, with British and French troops on their way to the Danube, Russia vacated the Principalities.[88]

Russia's withdrawal was a substantial concession, and with it the original aim of the war was achieved. There had been no serious military engagement between Russia and the other great powers, and the great powers could have declared the crisis over. Instead the two Western powers pressed their advantage. Together with Austria, they settled on what became known as the Four Points: (1) Russia must give up the Principalities to a great power guarantee; (2) Russia must yield its control of the mouth of the Danube and allow free navigation; (3) the Straits Convention must be revised to permit warships to enter the Straits even in peacetime, if determined to be "in the interest of the balance of power"; (4) Russia must give up its special rights to protect the Orthodox Christians; the treatment of Christians in the Ottoman Empire would be a collective European concern.[89]

The powers demanded that Russia accept these as the bases for a negotiated peace. In late November 1854 it did.[90] A few days later, however, on December 2, Austria formally entered the war, signing a limited defensive alliance with Britain and France that called for a peace conference with Russia to discuss the Four Points. If Russia refused to accept a final ultimatum based on their shared understanding of the Four Points, then Austria promised to enter the war militarily, fighting for the allies, in the spring.[91] Meanwhile, fighting between Russia and the Western powers had begun. The battle of Sevastopol started in September 1854 and continued through a difficult winter where both sides suffered great losses (both from battle and illness).

The Vienna Peace Conference began in March 1855, between Britain, France, Austria, the Ottoman Empire, and Russia.[92] This was a peace con-

87. Arnold 2002, 13; Schroeder 1972, 206.

88. Schroeder 1972, 200.

89. Baumgart 1999, 17.

90. Schroeder 1972, 226. Schroeder 1972, 220 points out that Austria had ordered a general mobilization in late October to pressure Russia on the four points.

91. Schroeder 1972, 224.

92. Much happened between December and March. In Britain, the Aberdeen government fell and Palmerston took over as prime minister. He opposed the peace conference but was forced to support it in order to put together a domestic governing coalition. In France,

ference in name only. Britain and France were more focused on pulling Austria into the war than in settling on peace terms with Russia, and to this end had a secret agreement to keep the third point as harsh as possible or add a fifth point that Russian naval capability must be destroyed. Either of these would ensure Russia would reject the Four Points, which would force Austria to fight in the spring.[93] Meanwhile, Austria had its own secret understanding with Russia not to allow any agreement that would humiliate Russia. Needless to say, these secret agreements were incompatible. From here, historians disagree over which state was at fault for the failure of the conference. Winfried Baumgart blames the Russo-Austrian agreement,[94] while Paul Schroeder points the finger at Britain.[95]

But what's interesting is that despite the fact that the conference seemed doomed, the negotiators on the ground had some significant success on the most difficult issue: Russian naval strength and presence in the Black Sea. First, they fairly quickly resolved points one and two. Russia agreed to a great power guarantee of the Principalities and to end its exclusive control of the mouth of the Danube. More significantly, the negotiators for Britain, France, and Austria came to agreement on the third point. Russell, negotiating for Britain, and Drouyn, the French foreign minister, who each began negotiations with the position that the Black Sea must be neutralized or the Russian fleet significantly reduced, came around to the Austrian idea that it was possible to protect the Ottoman Empire without humiliating Russia.[96] Since the real goal was to increase the empire's security, they agreed that the five great powers should together explicitly guarantee its territorial integrity, and they should manage Russia's potential ambitions through a system of what they called "counterpoise." By this, they had in mind a system of checks and balances that would keep power balanced on the Black Sea. For example, Rus-

---

Napoleon announced plans to take over leading his troops in the Crimea, which strengthened Drouyn's support of the peace conference since he did not want Napoleon to go. In Russia, Nicholas died and was replaced by his son, Alexander II, who kept to the same policy. Schroeder 1972, 232–55; Chamberlain 1983, 363–81.

93. Schroeder 1972, 222. Britain and France aimed to destroy Sebastopol, limit the Russian fleet to four ships in the Black Sea, and place British and French observers in Russian ports. Schroeder 1972, 232.

94. Baumgart 1999, 19.

95. Schroeder 1972, 227.

96. This is noteworthy especially because Russell had been an early advocate of war; he was sent to the Vienna conference in 1855 as a special negotiator.

sia was entitled to a set number of warships, but if it exceeded that number then the outside powers had the right to enter the Straits. They also agreed to a three-power alliance to defend the Ottoman Empire in the event of a Russian attack or even a credible threat of Russian revisionist aims.[97] This way of specifying the third point was known as the Austrian Ultimatum. But the problem was that its premise was at odds with the instructions from the two governments. The negotiators had overreached and both governments rejected these terms as too easy on Russia.[98] After being "disavowed," Drouyn and Russell each resigned.[99] Thus, although the Austrian Ultimatum represented a genuine negotiated compromise among the major parties, it ultimately was meaningless and was not formally presented to Russia.[100]

The battle of Sevastopol continued until September 1855, when the allies defeated Russia, who sank its own fleet and left the city. The fall of Sevastopol did not immediately end the war, however. While Austria and France were ready, Britain had to be persuaded. Palmerston had been prime minister since 1855, and he sought a more decisive curbing of Russian ambitions, even a potential Russian partition. To this end he considered opening up a northern front, which would have drawn in Sweden.[101] But his allies persuaded him to come to the table. Russia took one more Ottoman fort, Kars, but then it, too, accepted the Four Points as the bases for a peace conference. Plans for the Congress at Paris began.

The Paris Peace Conference met in February and March 1856 and resulted in the Treaty of Paris. This treaty, signed by the five powers, the Ottoman Empire, and Sardinia/Piedmont (which had entered the war on the allies' side in January 1855), made good on the Four Points, and then some. (1) It granted autonomy to the Principalities under a great power guarantee, diluting Russia's relationship. (2) It returned parts of Bessarabia that had been held by Russia and put the Danube Delta fully back in Ottoman control. (3) It made treatment of Christians in the Ottoman Empire a collective concern of all signatories, including the Ottomans. (4) It

---

97. Schroeder 1972, 256–70.

98. When the British negotiator watered it down, Britain agreed conditional on French acceptance; Napoleon then rejected it. Schroeder 1972, 276–77.

99. Baumgart 1999, 20. Although the Palmerston government persuaded him not to resign.

100. Saab, Knapp, and de Bourqueney Knapp 1986, 488–91; Curtiss 1979, 382–407; Schroeder 1972.

101. Baumgart 1999, 28–29; Badem 2010, 3, 284–87.

admitted the Ottoman Empire formally to the Concert, inviting it "to participate in the public law and concert of Europe." The signatories agreed not to interfere "either collectively or separately" in Ottoman internal affairs,[102] which officially delegitimated Russia's special claims to protect the Ottoman Orthodox. The treaty also demanded an end to the Russian fleet in the Black Sea, so Russia was not permitted to rebuild Sevastopol. Finally, the treaty included a collective guarantee, by Britain, France, and Austria, of Ottoman territorial integrity.

The Treaty of Paris rectified a key failing of the 1815 Vienna Settlement by bringing the Ottoman Empire under its purview, guaranteeing its territorial integrity, and formally granting the sultan the right of nonintervention (conditional on continued internal reforms to give Christians equal rights). At the same time, the treaty undermined perhaps the very premise of the settlement in that the Concert powers certainly had not managed the Russo-Turkish conflict together. In 1856, Russia was neither grouped as in 1822 nor granted a sphere of influence as in 1828; it was balanced against and then defeated by its 1815 allies.

## The Missing Commitment

What caused the great powers to "superimpose"[103] themselves on this Russo-Turkish dispute? For a long time the conventional wisdom was that the Crimean War was accidental or inadvertent, caused by bungling decision makers. That argument has receded and others have taken its place, including arguments that the 1848 revolutions made it inevitable or that particular individuals were committed to scuttling all attempts to forestall or limit the war. My argument drawing out the power of joint commitments and public forum talk does not necessarily contradict any of these. But it brings to light something that was lacking in this case that other scholarship has not considered. Had the great powers committed to manage the conflict together and linked it to public, forum talk, that is, had they constituted the problem as a public problem the war quite possibly would not have widened.

In the 1850s discursive resources were available for a grouping strat-

---

102. Jelavich 1983, 284. Nonintervention was with awareness of the Hatti Humayun of February 1856, which expanded Christian rights.

103. Saab 1977, 155.

egy, and it may have made a difference. Thirty years earlier, the commitment to 1815 treaties and to cordoning off Russo-Turkish disputes and the Ottoman Empire more generally kept that war from widening. In 1826, Britain, France, and Russia had signed the Treaty of London, which explicitly pledged that they would not seek gains against the Ottoman Empire. When Russia declared war in 1828, the declaration was limited to bilateral concerns and did not mention the Greek case. The British expressed disapproval but refused the invitation by the Ottomans to restore diplomatic ties unilaterally. France did not oppose the war, but demonstrated its limited aims when it had troops on the ground in the Peloponnese and chose not to advance on Athens. The great powers certainly were suspicious of one another and eager to contain Russian and French ambitions. But the Treaty of London contained the war to a shared interpretation. Without the treaty and forums, I argue (counterfactually), it does not seem they would have been able to keep the Russo-Turkish War limited. That argument piggybacked on the chapter four argument that the public Hanover strategy made a difference for holding Nicholas's predecessor, Alexander, in check. Bilateral and private diplomacy failed; the same messages worked when linked to their commitment and to a forum.

Even once Britain and France had joined the Crimean War, there were two missed opportunities for ending it, but only one seems to have been a case in which public talk could have made a difference. First, when Russia evacuated the Principalities in summer 1854 it would have been possible to end the war, but France and especially Britain chose instead to expand their war aims. All of the public commitments in the world cannot contain actors who are committed to revisionist aims, and my argument only holds when aims are uncertain and mixed. However, second, the negotiations at the Vienna peace talks of 1855 are especially tragic because there is some evidence that appearing in public to talk about common problems made a difference. Talking together, face to face, enabled the negotiators to come to an agreement on the difficult issue of Russian naval presence in the Straits. Clearly, at these peace talks Britain and France sought to make Russia an offer it could only refuse. Their goal, cemented in a secret agreement, was to defeat Russia on the battlefield. But even in this context of being severely constrained by their governments' instructions, the negotiators on the ground in Vienna found a creative solution. By switching to a principle of counterpoise rather than punishment and adding a guarantee of the empire, the Russian threat could potentially have been neutralized without humiliating their fellow great power.[104] But this burst of creativity—unlike that of the London Conference in the 1820s, for example—was futile. Rather than allow the agreements on the ground to limit the war, Britain and France disavowed the negotiators. There certainly was a lot of diplomacy at all phases of the Crimean War. But the war widened and persisted because the Western powers simply would not be convinced of Russia's limited aims—not even after costly signals like troop withdrawals and deep concessions.

## Why No Public Commitment?

### The View from Europe

Charles Kupchan[105] argues that the Crimean War was largely a consequence of the revolutions of 1848, which had destroyed the Concert of Europe. Domestic political and social forces had finally become strong enough that Western elites' narratives of strategic restraint toward autocrats, narratives that were crucial to sustain Concert cooperation, had lost currency to home audiences. "Stable peace eroded from the inside out: political and social pressures at the domestic level induced elites to back away from the Concert's norms and practices."[106] The Holy Alliance rulers, Russia, Austria, and Prussia, held power the old way, autocratically and without constitutions, while the revolutions made clear there was a widening desire for constitutional power and self-government. It was easy after 1848 to be suspicious of an autocrat, and more difficult for the Western powers to justify cooperating with the autocratic regimes.[107] Kupchan points out that during the height of the Concert a dispute as minor as that over the holy sites "would never have escalated (to great power war); it would have been readily resolved, or at least fenced off and set aside." Once the Concert was gone, however, it was only a matter of time before the great powers fought one another. The security dilemma reemerged, snowballing a minor crisis into a full-blown war.

104. Schroeder 1972, 258–59 notes that the Austrians entered the peace talks with this strategy in mind, i.e., it did not emerge through brainstorming. Still, it was framed as in the interest of European peace and abided by the principle of not humiliating a great power.

105. Kupchan 2010.

106. Kupchan 2010, 237.

107. Kupchan 2010, 237–38.

Kupchan is certainly right that 1848 had a tremendous impact and that there were not thick societal roots among the five powers to fall back on. But ideology had not been the sole cause of war in the decades since Napoleon or the sole rationale for working together. Other rivalries among the powers that were salient had nothing to do with ideology, and great power responses to political events did not always reflect the ideological divide. For example, ideological differences did not prevent a cooperative solution to the Belgian crisis or cooperation between Britain and Russia in the second Syrian crisis of the late 1830s, and ideological similarity did not prevent British intense distrust of France in the 1840s. In addition, the great powers did not use the opportunity of the 1848 revolutions to go after one another or take advantage of weakness. When Russia invaded Hungary, Palmerston supported it because of the importance of the Habsburg Empire to European stability.[108] When Hungarian refugees then fled to the Ottoman Empire and Austria and Russia pressured the sultan to extradite, Britain and France sent warships to the neighborhood of the Straits. But the British ships were more bluster than real threat. Ann Saab notes that "the British fleet did eventually enter the Dardanelles, [but] it was never clear whether this was a calculated move in aid of the Ottoman Empire or a nonpolitical attempt to escape bad weather." Moreover, afterward Palmerston "formally apologized to the Russian government for the breach of the Straits Convention."[109] Certainly the national and democratic revolutions strained great power relations. But all political authorities feared revolution and all feared their own publics. In sum, as F. H. Hinsley puts it, the Concert was never merely "the three and the two."[110] Thus there is no reason to think they could not have resolved the 1853 crisis short of war, or that ideological homogeneity would have prevented it.

Indeed, in one sense the great powers *were* homogenous: both the Western and the Holy Alliance powers were Christian states while the Ottoman Empire was Muslim. Particularly when it came to the Eastern Question, religion and not regime type was the relevant divide. It may have been easier to be suspicious of an autocrat after 1848, but it was easier still to be suspicious of a Muslim. Thus while Britain in particular deepened its ties to the Porte in the 1830s and '40s, it still kept the sultan

108. Saab 1977, 8.
109. Saab 1977, 9.
110. Hinsley 1963, 216.

at arms' length. Not only did Britain turn down requests to intervene militarily when the sultan faced internal threats, it also turned down requests for loans to help stabilize the economy.[111] Even during the Crimean War, when Britain finally offered its Islamic ally a loan, it offered market or above par rates—a far cry from the subsidies it had offered the allies of the Final Coalition against Napoleon.

The relevant cleavage in the Crimean War case is less liberalism-autocracy than Christian-Muslim, and so the puzzle is, why did Britain forsake its fellow Christians to forge an alliance with Muslims? In my view the revolutions of 1848 do not shed nearly as much light on this question as does the plain old balance of power. Russia and Britain were competing for influence in the Ottoman Empire. Russia's focus was on rights to protect the Orthodox because given Russia's role as protector such rights would increase Russian influence. Britain focused on internal, domestic legal reform to give all Christians rights and strengthen the center, perhaps because the Ottoman Empire had virtually no Protestant population.[112] Britain wanted influence in Constantinople to keep the Straits open to maintain access to the Black Sea and because bilateral trade was expanding. With the help of an 1838 commercial treaty giving Britain special tariff concessions throughout the empire, British exports to the Ottoman Empire steadily rose, nearly tripling from 1840 to 1851.[113] The British economic relationship with the Porte was to some extent at the expense of Britain's relationship with Russia. Candan Badem notes that "while in 1827 British exports to Russia were three times more than the exports to the Ottoman Empire, this ratio had changed significantly by 1849, when the Ottoman Empire ... bought far more British goods than Russia. The principalities alone imported more goods from Britain than Russia did."[114] While 1848 was a watershed in European politics, the causes of the Crimean War were not solely internal to the European powers, and the issues cut differently. From the perspective of my argument, the resources to forestall great power war were in international society not domestic society, and it's not just liberal or nationalist states that are invested in international society.

---

111. Saab 1977, 3–4; Badem 2010, 59, 293–94, 308–9.

112. Gooch 1956, 35.

113. Badem 2010, 58–59. Under the Treaty of Adrianople, the Principalities were freed from the duty to send all grain to Constantinople and began a trade relationship with Britain.

114. Badem 2010, 3.

If 1848 is granted a lot of causal power, the Crimean War seems a foregone conclusion. Put in its proper balance of power context, however, the war is a lot more surprising and the diplomatic failure more profound. The great powers came very close to avoiding war. There were several points at which it looked like the war would be averted or would end, but each time something, or someone, got in the way. Indeed, the historiography distributes blame pretty widely, with different historians stressing different personalities. There seems to be evidence that can exonerate many of the key players and often as much evidence to justify holding responsible each of those same leaders. In Harold Temperley's words, "the web of this vast tragedy was ... woven from various and many-colored strands."[115] Waves of scholarship have focused on Napoleon, or on Redcliffe, or on Nicholas.[116] Schroeder's influential account points the finger at Britain, arguing that "the main reason war was not averted ... was that the Western powers, especially Britain, frustrated every hopeful effort at a diplomatic solution, primarily because no such solution could bring the defeat for Russia and the victory for Britain and her principles that Palmerston and liberal opinion demanded."[117]

Among IR scholars, Joseph Gochal and Jack Levy[118] generally concur that it was the statesmen themselves, not the structure of the situation or bungling and misperception that caused the war. Against their initial hypothesis that the structure of the situation (the security dilemma) constrained choices and produced a war no one wanted, they point to "numerous instances where state leaders could have settled their disputes short of war, if they had the desire to do so." They conclude that "most state leaders in the Crimean crisis behaved reasonably rationally in pursuit of their interests but ... their interests were fundamentally irreconcilable and ... some leaders were consciously willing to take the risks of securing their interest through force."[119] This was no security dilemma, they argue, it was a conflict of interests in which influential decision makers wanted war.

It is difficult to disagree that key individuals scuttled every effort to keep the conflict between Russia and the Ottoman Empire contained.

---

115. Quoted in Gooch 1956, 58; Rich 1985, 4.
116. Gooch 1956 reviews some of the literature.
117. Schroeder 1972, xii.
118. Gochal and Levy 2004.
119. Gochal and Levy 2004, 333.

And it is difficult not to single out the Western powers, France and especially Britain. French actions are perhaps more ambiguous. On the one hand, Napoleon had a revisionist attitude toward the Vienna Settlement, and the specifics of the holy sites dispute could be interpreted as revisionist, a strategy to drive a religious wedge between the Holy Alliance partners of Catholic Austria and Orthodox Russia. But on the other hand, even if true,[120] these do not mean Napoleon was bent on war in this case. France did not act unambiguously as a revisionist—Drouyn was actively involved in the Vienna Note seeking a compromise solution, and in the fall of 1853 France had made no preparations for war.[121] Moreover, some evidence shows that Napoleon had no consistent approach to the conflict. He left major decisions to his ministers and, apparently, was strongly influenced by the British ambassador to Paris.[122]

As for Britain, however, revisionism once it took root only deepened. From the start there were solidly anti-Russian voices in the government, most notably Palmerston (who in 1853 was home secretary),[123] and by the end of the summer of 1853, such voices dominated political discourse and war began to be seen as a viable option. Many in Britain found the Vienna Note to be "probably a useful diplomatic prelude to some form of Western action against Russia."[124] In November, Palmerston wrote to Aberdeen that "we must help Turkey out of her difficulties by negotiation if possible; and ... if negotiation fails, we must, by force of arms, carry her safely through her dangers."[125] Then, once Britain had declared war the government had little interest in the conference table, particularly once Palmerston took over as prime minister in January 1855. The instructions given to Russell for the Vienna Peace Conference were to stall in order to give the allies a chance to defeat Russia. Schroeder points out[126] that Palmerston had a vision of partitioning Russia, and he also had a plan, once the war started, for expanding the war to draw in Sweden. And the tactics of the British and the French in the run-up to the 1855 conference,

120. The latter is disputed. See Rich 1985, 21.
121. Saab, Knapp, and de Bourqueney Knapp 1986.
122. Saab, Knapp, and de Bourqueney Knapp 1986.
123. Palmerston initially called for a Mediterranean fleet to join the French in mid-March 1853, but was outvoted. After the Menshikov mission he favored military aid to the Ottomans. Peterson 1993, 119; Gochal and Levy 2004, 329.
124. Schroeder 1972, 51.
125. Rich 1985, 92.
126. Schroeder 1972.

with the expanding war aims and secret fifth point, clearly show that they had no interest in reaching a settlement with Russia.

At the same time, however, neither Palmerston nor Redcliffe wanted to destroy the European order. Both wanted to preserve it. Only as the crisis progressed did they come to think that war was their sole option, and then, further, "once involved in the war, they decided that the only goal which could justify waging it would be the permanent elimination of the Russian menace."[127] The idea that these leaders were swept away by the events gains credence on looking back at British policy up until summer 1854. Norman Rich points out that Britain did not take an active interest in protecting the Ottoman Empire and did not feel the Russian threat was urgent in the early 1850s.[128] Even the Seymour conversations, which later were seen as a smoking gun revealing Nicholas's rapacious intentions, at the time were not seen as manifesting aggressive intent. Seymour's report to Russell, who at the time was secretary of state for foreign affairs, asserted that "a noble triumph would be obtained by the civilization of the 19th century if the void left by the extinction of Mohammedan rule in Europe could be filled up without an interruption of the general peace, in consequence of the precautions adopted by the two principal governments of the most interested in the destinies of Turkey."[129] All of this is to say that it seems that a commitment in fall 1853 could have made a difference. It could have strengthened the Aberdeen position. The country only rallied around the idea of fighting after Sinop. Before that enough policy uncertainty remained that it is plausible to argue that a public commitment could have made a difference. A commitment to agreed-upon European interests and to preserving the peace, combined with forums, could potentially have served as a lodestar and pulled individual behavior, as the Treaty of London had done thirty years earlier.

Pulling these together, there were key moments in the diplomacy of the Crimean War when things could have gone another way. It is admittedly odd to say that what was needed was more talking and conference diplomacy, since the Crimean War was full of diplomacy and is even sometimes referred to as diplomacy punctuated by war. But the diplomacy was not in the context of a shared commitment to keep the peace. Collective intentions require a collective moment—actors must commit to do

---

127. Rich 1985, 9–10.
128. Rich 1985, 7.
129. Quoted in Badem 2010, 69.

something together. This constitutes them as a "team" for the purposes of working toward that goal. Here, the great powers did not invoke the Vienna Settlement or the Straits Convention, and they did not commit to defensive actions. Thus the forums were relegated to talk shops. This is not to say that great power war could have been avoided forever. But even after Crimea, conflict and war in Europe did not always break down ideologically, and in the 1870s congresses were able to solve problems among the powers without ideology standing in the way. Before 1848 and after, some conflict was ideologically driven and some was not.

### Reversing the Gaze

From a European standpoint, not only was the Crimean War a product of European forces, it also had primarily European effects: Austria's diplomatic isolation, France's diplomatic prestige, and Russia's retrenchment and then revisionism. It also was widely seen as useless, as having accomplished nothing that could not have been achieved through diplomacy, and therefore as having caused needless loss of life. The tragedy of the Crimean War is perhaps best exemplified by the famous charge of the light brigade, where bungled communication in the Battle of Balaclava caused British commanders to lead a misguided charge in which nearly all of them were killed. Widening the lens, bungled diplomacy starting in 1853 caused great power diplomats to unnecessarily intensify a dispute that in hindsight all felt could have been resolved diplomatically.

But when we reverse the gaze and consider the Crimean War from the Ottoman perspective, it does not look as tragic. At least it looks no more tragic than any other state-on-state conflict. Comparing the 1820s to the 1850s from the perspective of the Ottoman Empire, the 1828 Russo-Turkish War was the misfortune while the 1853 Russo-Turkish War was a success. The 1829 Treaty of Adrianople gave Russia control of the mouth of the Danube and reaffirmed and expanded Russian rights to protect Ottoman subjects in the Principalities. The 1856 Treaty of Paris took from Russia the mouth of the Danube and all semblance of unique legal rights, not to mention the naval capability, to protect any Ottoman subjects. Moreover, the Treaty of Paris admitted the Ottoman Empire into the Concert of Europe, and granted it the sovereign right of nonintervention and a great power guarantee of its territorial integrity. As icing on the cake, in the course of the war Britain had laid hundreds of miles of telegraph cable, materially integrating the Porte into the European system of communication. If public talk among the European powers had held back war in the summer of 1853—for example, if the great powers had persuaded the sultan to sign on to the Vienna Note—it is reasonable to conclude that the outcome would not have been nearly as good for the Ottoman Empire.

With this in mind, the intentions of the Ottoman Empire from 1853 on cannot be overlooked. The sultan made choices in 1853 that the European powers did not expect and did not always know how to respond to—for example, refusing the Vienna Note, declaring war, drawing Russian ships into battle at Sinop. He stood up to Russia at a time when he could be certain that the Western powers, especially Britain, would lend support. This was the one time when the Porte successfully played the European rivalries off each other. Once the sultan suspected that Russia wanted or was willing to go to war, his interest was in bringing the British in on its side. Bilateral conflicts with Russia always meant Ottoman losses; only by making sure that Britain's instrumental interests in its relationship with the Ottoman Empire remained the most salient could the Porte hope to gain from the conflict. The Ottoman Empire was a key force repeatedly blocking a negotiated settlement, taking advantage of Britain's fear of losing influence at Constantinople and its suddenly ascendant Russophobia. It was not obvious that this gamble would work. Britain had more of a stake in the Ottoman Empire in the 1850s than it had in the 1820s, but had demonstrated repeatedly that it was not willing to suffer costs for supporting the Porte. By no means was it a sure thing that Britain would rise to the sultan's bait. Indeed, when the Ottoman ships sighted Russian warships in their vicinity in fall 1853, the British and French minimized the threat and refused to act.[130] The result was Sinop. This and other moments in the crises lead Saab to discuss the war-widening as an Ottoman success: the Porte's "highly subtle, limited yet responsive diplomacy" turned this particular Russo-Turkish war into a European great power war.[131] In sum, by successfully widening the war in 1854, the Ottoman Empire literally fought its way into the Concert and secured a seat at the table with the Western powers that were eager to capture its spoils. It earned a voice in its own future. After 1856, the Eastern Question receded in European

---

130. Badem 2010, 115–16; Saab 1977, 115–17.

131. Saab 1977, 24. Rich 1985 agrees with Saab that this was a conscious Ottoman policy; Badem 2010 argues that Ottoman policy often was driven by personal rivalries and grievances rather than political ones.

diplomacy for decades. Despite the losses the Ottomans suffered, then, in many ways this war was a substantial success.

## Conclusion

I have claimed that states govern together, or concert their power for public interests, when they commit to do something together and link it to forums, which enable the commitment to have behavioral pull. In such cases, publicity dampens the effect of individual intentions—filtered through a collective intention, individual intentions come to matter less. But as the Crimea case shows, the power of public talk is not infinite. If strong parties aim to undermine or destroy a commitment, public talk alone cannot preserve it. In the 1820s the great powers stretched their Vienna commitment to cover the instability in the Ottoman Empire and to contain the Russo-Turkish War. In the 1850s, the Eastern Question had its own diplomacy and the Vienna commitment had little pull. The diplomacy from 1853 to 1856 shows that what the great powers lacked was a commitment to guarantee the Ottoman Empire. Now, perhaps a single commitment would not have prevented great power war. But in this case each great power had expressed the individual intention to permit the empire to die a natural death rather than exploit its weakness; what they doubted was the others' commitment to that goal. Given the similarities between the 1820s and the 1850s cases, it is not too far-fetched to propose the counterfactual that a public commitment among the powers not to seek individual advantage at the expense of the empire would have made a difference, perhaps working as the 1826 Treaty of London had done to keep that earlier Russo-Turkish War contained.

The scope conditions of my argument would seem to be that "governance works when parties want it and fails when they do not." The latter half of the claim is obviously true, but the former is not nearly as obvious. Wanting the same thing is different from doing something together, and the gap can be insurmountable. Particularly in situations where parties have mixed motives, sharing a goal is not enough, and outcomes can go many ways. These are the situations in which commitments and forums can make a difference.

# CHAPTER SEVEN

# Conclusion

My claim in this book is that states, acting in concert, can constitute an international public power, a locus of authoritative decision on matters seen to be in a shared public interest. Public power is worth highlighting and cultivating in today's globalized, interdependent world where there is a sense that the state has lost the capacity, acting individually, to provide for its population's basic needs. Scholars and practitioners increasingly argue that even minimal conditions for human well-being can no longer be reliably secured at the national level and that what's needed is a systemic approach to global governance that better links national to global well-being.[1] Visualizing how public power could be possible beyond the state is an important step toward regaining a sense of political control.

Because public power is associated with the state, it can seem as if international public power would require a world state. My argument that states can form an international public power therefore depends on a claim at the analytic level that states can concert their power, acting on collective intentions with other states, without losing their independent capacity and authority to act for their own populations. This claim is controversial for two reasons. First, collective intentionality implies purposiveness at the macro- rather than microlevel. When actors engage in joint action, their behavior can be pulled by their commitments to one another, rather than merely pushed by their individual interests and intentions. From the perspective of mainstream IR scholarship, where agency in world politics is in the units (usually states), the idea that a group of states can act with collective intentionality seems suspicious, conjuring up

---

1. This is articulated in the literature on global public goods. See Carbone 2007, 181–82; Kaul, Grunberg, and Stern 1999.

the image of a supranational group mind into which individual state preferences and desires are subsumed. Second, collective intentions are inherently normative, constituted by states' commitments to one another, which create obligations. In contrast, mainstream IR scholarship does not treat states' commitments to one another in normative terms. Unless commitments are incentive compatible, in the absence of reliable enforcement for the most part they do not matter.

I have countered that skepticism analytically by developing a framework for understanding collective intentionality among states, and shown that my claim is plausible empirically by telling the story of the origins of global governance. The Concert of Europe came about in 1815 when the five most powerful European states committed to work together to maintain continental stability. While enabled by a deepening of international society in the previous century and then precipitated by the shock of the Napoleonic Wars, what marks the Concert as the first case of international public power was its institutional innovation of meeting together, face-to-face, in forums. Talking together in public kept salient their obligation as they addressed problems, which enabled outcomes that otherwise would not have been possible. The great powers interacted in a markedly different manner from how they had acted in the eighteenth century or before, and judged by an important standard—the ability to avoid great power war—by acting together they accomplished outcomes far better than what would otherwise have been expected.

Many historians and IR scholars acknowledge the Concert's accomplishments, and the Concert continues to influence scholars and policy makers today. With great power rivalries significantly tamed compared with much of the twentieth century, the contemporary great power system seems to share some of the premises of the Concert. Since the end of the Cold War, the Concert frequently has been invoked as a model for European security cooperation and for great power relations more broadly.[2] I have shown that the concerting of nineteenth-century Europe can be interpreted as not "just" cooperation based on overlapping individual preferences and in the pursuit of self-interested goals, but as a purposive political project articulated and pursued together.

This chapter reviews my empirical findings and suggests some implications of the theoretical framework for how we approach global governance today. It can seem old fashioned to focus on states in an era of

2. E.g., Langhorne 1990; Kupchan and Kupchan 1991; Ikenberry 2001; Kupchan 2010.

globalization and jarring to posit continuities between practices that helped nineteenth-century monarchs hold back liberalism and practices of liberal great powers promulgating liberal values today. With this in mind, a goal of this chapter, like the book overall, is to suggest that steering the global social order is a long-standing state practice that transcends today's liberal ideology and is of continuing importance.

## Taking Stock

The main hypothesis that follows from my framework is that states' joint commitments can be authoritative in practice when there also is the expectation of regular public, forum talk. The mechanisms are the forum effects: face-to-face talk causes ways of talking and habits of speech that lead actors to follow through on commitments. Once actors know they will see one another again, they will tend to talk in certain ways, and their talk and the expectation of having to justify their actions makes it more likely they will act in ways consistent with their commitment. This can be true even in the face of mixed motives and without centralized decision making or enforcement, and it can be true even among corporate actors such as states. In the Concert case, the terms of the Vienna Settlement gave each great power the standing to call for a meeting, which meant that any crisis on the continent potentially could be a shared problem. If one of the Concert powers suggested they consult on a given crisis, the five together had to come to agreement on whether that crisis posed a European problem. The provision to meet together therefore helped to fix a common meaning of events, which made it possible to contain their actions. Behaviors had to be justifiable by reference to their commitment.

Through process tracing in chapters four and five, I showed that conferences in the 1820s enabled the great powers to manage several threats to European stability that in an earlier era might readily have led to war. In chapter four the Hanover strategy of using the same rationales and linking their actions to a great power meeting made it possible for the Russian czar, Alexander, to "see" Europe's collective interest in the Greek revolt and therefore to not intervene unilaterally. Without the European frame, it is likely that Alexander would not have acted with restraint. Moreover, the same rhetorical strategy, of placing Greece in Europe and defining the revolt in the frame of other European revolts, did not work when pursued privately but only when pursued together and linked to a forum. Similarly, in chapter five I showed that the combination of treaty and forum is what successfully created a European public interest in the Greek revolt. Relying on the Treaty of London and treating London Conference decisions as authoritative helped the great powers avoid war. It is reasonable to conclude that without their public resources, the great powers could not have kept the 1828 Russo-Turkish War contained. If these resources seem a slim reed, in chapter six I suggested just how sturdy they could be by showing how easily the security dilemma spiraled out of control among these powers without them. Because the Concert powers did not commit to act together in 1854, despite evidence that many of these leaders wanted to avoid war and despite plenty of talking, the Crimean War case adds plausibility to my argument that states' collective intentions can make a difference.

To what extent do these findings illustrate the framework developed in chapter two? There I argued that talk in interstate forums is the microlevel mechanism for pulling state behavior toward joint commitments. Of the four specific forum effects, three occur inside a given forum: generalized interest claims and impartial arguments, a norm of publicity, and public reason. The fourth refers to action outside the forum: self-restraint and commitment-consistent behavior. The findings of the empirical chapters show some support for all four, but with respect to the "inside the forum" effects the findings are merely suggestive. While Metternich's use of public rationales trapped him into holding a meeting, the rationale of "supporting legitimate sovereigns" was not necessarily produced inside the great power forum but was articulated in anticipation of it. Metternich's tight control over information meant that the early conferences were not cases of leaders actually sitting around a table addressing the problem and giving reasons for their positions. But the Troppau Protocol and Castlereagh's State Paper responding to it can be interpreted in these terms, as a competition between two public frames for the conflicts. Precisely because they had held these meetings, each side was compelled to articulate reasons acceptable to all. In the Greek case, the London Conference was an unambiguous instance of cooperative problem solving in the name of shared, European interests, and its presence arguably helped keep the Russo-Turkish War limited. Thus I have shown that decision makers in this period treated meeting together as something significant, and that they took their commitments to one another more seriously when they were linked to forums. My findings suggest one might want to further open up the black box of the interstate conversations (to the extent that this is possible) in order to gain confidence in the forum effects.

The evidence presented in those chapters supports the claim that the prospect of meeting together—the public setting for discussion—enabled great power commitments to have pull. But in the Concert case, what I called the ontic dimension of the forum, that is, the fact that it existed as a concrete referent for their shared intention, was as important as the epistemic one, that is, the fact that the great powers could learn about one another's intentions. Forums made it possible for the great powers to "see" Europe, which provided reassurance that a sphere of common concerns actually existed. This reminded the great powers of their commitment in a way that made it more possible to act on it than if they had merely invoked "Europe" without linking it to any practice of meeting. The resulting self-restraint and commitment-consistent behavior were due not necessarily to the great powers having more information about one another's true individual intentions, but because of their collective intention to maintain the peace.

The empirical chapters show that forums were crucial to the success of the Concert, something that realist interpretations of the Concert overlook. The specific argument for how forums were important adds insight to institutionalist-informed work on the Concert. At the same time, the empirical chapters show that forums could not work miracles. This was clear in the Crimean War case, when the great powers met together repeatedly but lacked the will to approach that crisis "in concert." Simply meeting face-to-face did not amount to concerting power for public interests. A moment of commitment in which a set of actors constitutes themselves as a "we" who will do something together is equally as important. Without it, even if intentions overlap or are in sync, it can be difficult to produce outcomes all actors recognize as consistent with their shared intention.

It also becomes clear in the empirical chapters that a focus on power as the capacity to do something together brackets the dark side of power, that is, power as domination. In the Concert case, stability among the great powers was produced by restraining liberalism and democracy, which means it was produced at the expense of the political aspirations of European revolutionaries and to some extent of the Ottoman Empire. These groups were deeply affected by the Concert's public power, and yet their voices played no role in either constituting or steering it. By largely bracketing great power domination I do not mean to sanction it. But I do mean to suggest that even where there clearly is "power over" it also is possible to constitute a public oriented "power to." After all, great power war itself was a kind of domination from which all of Europe suffered, and concerting held it at bay. Moreover, concerting their power made the practice of domination more visible in an era where the audience for state actions was expanding, which can be seen as a necessary condition for resistance or, ultimately, accountability.


## Then and Now

In today's globalized world, it can be easy to think that the thin institution I have focused on would be less relevant than it was in the nineteenth century. Then it was novel for states to talk together; now it goes without saying that they would do so. Interstate commitments and talk are far more prevalent than they were two hundred years ago. Today's world is "thick with [international] institutions,"[3] many of them highly legalized and some with third-party adjudication mechanisms. For many scholars and practitioners, these institutions create a "viscous"[4] decision-making environment for states, which translates to more rule-based behavior. Some go so far as to see an emerging global rule of law, arguing that the sphere of sovereign prerogative is shrinking and that even great powers can now be held accountable for some of their behavior. From this perspective, economic globalization and/or institutional density and rule proliferation sustain states' intentions and keep violence off the table. Particular commitments and forums are mainly incidental.

But it is not clear that having more rules translates to more constrained state behavior. International rules are not like domestic rules— they do not exist in a hierarchy of institutions with a final arbiter to determine which rules are authoritative in a given instance. Without such hierarchy, far from adding more discipline and restraint, creating more rules can even have the opposite effect of creating more freedom for great powers to maneuver. Especially since the end of the Cold War, in many issues more than one set of international legal rules applies. Robert Keohane notes that many international regimes are less "coherent," lacking an "overall architecture or hierarchy."[5] Daniel Drezner makes a similar point, invoking the idea of a "tragedy of the [global institutional] commons." In anarchy, the main mechanisms enabling cooperation—es-

---

3. Drezner 2008, 5; Keohane 2012, 128.
4. Drezner 2008.
5. Keohane 2012, 129; Drezner 2008, 11.

pecially focal points, clear rules delineating what behaviors count as cooperation versus defection, and behavioral transparency—tend to work best in a thinly institutionalized environment. Having too many focal points dilutes the ability of any one to truly focus behavior; too many rules for action make monitoring overly complex and signaling intentions more difficult. The proliferation of institutions and rules therefore diminishes the potency of their main mechanisms. Paradoxically enough, then, institutional proliferation can translate to outcomes that are more rather than less power based. Rather than be slowed down by institutions, states can more easily use them strategically to pursue narrow interests unfettered.[6]

With these arguments in mind, the current situation of rule proliferation might make the practices I stress, of states committing to address particular problems and talking, more important not less. With no preset hierarchy, for any particular problem the global governors themselves must resolve which rules apply. As they problem solve together their behavior is recognized by one another as consistent with commitments, and this is determined publicly, through talking to one another. Keohane draws a similar conclusion. Situating the decline of regime coherence in a larger trend of power diffusion away from the liberal core, he argues that placing too much stress on the quantity and formality of international institutions and rules problematically limits the system's ability to adapt. Rather than proliferate institutions that promulgate liberal values, in a time of transition, he argues, the most valuable institution is multilateralism.[7]

A second phenomenon that on first glance seems to mute the power states created by governing together is the spread of democracy. Democratic leaders are generally less insulated from domestic pressures than autocratic ones, and it is tempting to assume that democratic publics can steer state decisions in all domains, even foreign policy. It also can be tempting to assume that domestic publics systematically steer states toward advancing local, domestic concerns and away from keeping their international commitments. Paul Schroeder speculated along these lines that the ability of state leaders to think in systemic terms and prioritize international commitments, which developed over the course of the Napoleonic Wars and was crucial to the Concert's success, then declined with the rise of nationalism and democracy.[8] A strain of literature on public opinion and American foreign policy echoes this view, arguing that pub-

6. Drezner 2008, 9, 21.

7. Keohane 2012.

8. Schroeder 1993, 68.

lics are volatile and easily swayed, and public opinion drives democratic leaders to make decisions they would not otherwise make. New communications technologies and the twenty-four-hour news cycle, which enable real-time coverage of worldwide events, exacerbate the problem.[9]

Two premises of such arguments are that publics are parochial and democratic leaders are not insulated from publics when it comes to foreign affairs. For better or for worse, this does not appear to be the case. First, it is not clear that greater accountability to domestic publics makes leaders any more jealous of their domestic prerogatives or less able to think systemically than nineteenth-century autocrats, several of whom had nearly unchecked power. It even seems ironic to assume that nineteenth-century autocrats valued their obligations to other states more than today's liberal, interdependent leaders do. Second, as Matthew Baum and Philip Potter point out, the conventional wisdom in research on public opinion and American foreign policy long has been that publics are "fundamentally incidental" when it comes to foreign policy.[10] What is called the "Almond Lippmann consensus" is that once elected, leaders ignore publics. This is supported by recent arguments that publics do not tend to demand accountability on most foreign policy issues; they are more likely to rally around the flag.[11] It also is supported by research showing that real-time news coverage has not had a large impact on foreign policy choices. Far from media and emotive publics driving policy, this research finds that administrations and elites often "manufacture consent," that media often serve as mouthpiece—or "lapdog"[12]—for the government, publicizing the official interpretation of events.[13] The ability of democratic administrations to insulate themselves from public scrutiny also is an assumption in work concerned about the so-called democratic deficit[14] of global governance. The idea here is that the more states work together to man-

9. Baum and Potter 2008, 44; Aldrich et al. 2006, 491; Holsti 1996; Robinson 1999. Drezner 2008 sees a contemporary version of this in criticisms of the CNN effect, such as Nye 1999, and in the realist complaint that Americans are hostile to the idea of putting national security first.

10. Baum and Potter 2008, 44.

11. Holsti 1996; Mueller 1973; Dahl 1999. Since the end of the Cold War the consensus that publics follow leaders has fractured, but no definitive statement of the relationship between leaders and publics regarding foreign policy has taken its place. Baum and Potter 2008, 44; Aldrich et al. 2006, 496.

12. Baum and Potter 2008, 54.

13. Baum and Potter 2008, 50.

14. E.g., Dahl 1999; Wolf 1999; Keohane 2001. Cf. Moravcsik 2004.

age problems, the less voice their citizens have in self-governance, since states must answer to a second constituency of fellow sovereigns and international organizations (IOs).[15] Putting these together, even in an age of democracy, there is no reason to assume that domestic political commitments systematically trump international ones, and no reason to assume that interstate mechanisms are drowned out by local voices pressing for local interests.

A final difference between then and now that might potentially mute the power of states' collective intentions is the rise of nonstate transnational actors and networks. Some argue that this trend has transformed the global political space in a "post-Westphalian" direction. Two types of arguments are made for how private actors are gaining power at the expense of states. First, many argue that transnational nonstate actors advocating specific interests increasingly are able to pressure states to change policies.[16] Here the dynamic is states versus private interests, and as private interests increasingly "win," then the state is seen as in decline. By implication, commitments among states have less power to affect behavior in a world where transnational actors can get states to do what they otherwise would not do. From this perspective, states are still special sites of political authority, but they increasingly can be manipulated and disciplined by civil societies to support particular actions or policy goals. This work generally treats the post-Westphalian trend in positive terms, arguing that private actors are well positioned in civil society to identify problems and usually more flexible and adaptive than state bureaucracies in addressing them. Private actors also represent the voices of those affected by state power, and empowering those voices is crucial to good governance.

A more radical state decline argument focuses not on nonstate versus state authority but on emerging spheres of transnational authority into which state-like authority is disaggregating. As Anne-Marie Slaughter puts it, the unitary state always has been a fiction, but it is less of a useful fiction today than ever before.[17] Certainly it is less useful in today's globalized, democratized world than it was in the early nineteenth century. Slaughter focuses on issue-specific networks in which state and nonstate authorities problem-solve together. While state representatives play a role,

15. Dahl 1999.
16. E.g., Risse, Ropp, and Sikkink 1999; Avant, Finnemore, and Sell 2010a, 2010b.
17. Slaughter 2004.

they do not have special authority in these functionally defined networks. Along these lines, John Ruggie notes the emergence of a global public domain in which several different actors work together to address common problems. States occupy a transnational or global political space in which they play a role alongside other, equally important actors, such as corporations, stakeholder groups, and international organizations.[18] Both Slaughter's and Ruggie's arguments pick up on the earlier insights of James Rosenau, who argued in the 1990s that the relevant intentionalities of global governance increasingly are those of transnational networks, nonstate actors, and even individuals.[19] In place of state authority we see transnational functional authorities where states are one among several "private" or particularistic actors negotiating and problem solving together. For Rosenau, the state does not play a distinctive or privileged role.

The increased visibility and voice of nonstate actors and mixed policy networks certainly is an important phenomenon. But it does not necessarily mean that the world is now "post" Westphalia. While there are new actors on the world stage and states are more deeply integrated than ever before, from an empirical perspective it is not clear that the state is headed into oblivion. Documenting the rise of private and nonstate actors captures only half the story. A crowded field need not imply a "crowding out" of the state. Indeed, we can hardly know what the rise of nonstate actors portends unless we can place it in the context of trends among states, where arguably there is an equally strong trend toward deeper collective self-regulation. The latter dynamic is not nearly as well understood as the former.[20] From a normative perspective the interstate dynamic is important. After all, by definition private actors' interests are particular and not general. They focus on causes that matter to their members and not necessarily to any general public, which means that it is not the case that all problems relevant to all people will be articulated much less addressed.[21] And private actors are not responsible when needs are not met. The state, in contrast, is universally considered responsible for meeting basic needs, and it suffers legitimacy costs when needs are not met. No private actor has this default, care-taking responsibility.

In sum, while trends like globalization, the spread of international in-

18. Ruggie 2004.
19. Rosenau 1994, 1995.
20. Wight 2001.
21. Steffek 2008.

stitutions, the triumph of democracy, and the rise of nonstate and transnational actors occupy more of the headlines and grab more scholarly attention, great powers still govern together. Their commitments and their talk still affect international political outcomes. To be sure, a cacophony of voices talking about their commitments might be as easy for a global governor to ignore as the proliferation of rules. Commitments can conflict; publics are noisy; speakers can lie. But at the end of the day global governors must decide what to do. They must exercise their judgment and take action. It is politically important that decisions about what constitutes a shared problem and how to address it are made against the backdrop of public interest and are not hijacked by private interests. In global governance, that requires the practice of states governing together.

## Theoretical Implications

In closing I would like to suggest four main theoretical contributions of the book. First, my argument shows that states can be important governors empirically and normatively. The Westphalian system with its old-fashioned principles of state sovereignty and nonintervention is often seen as a "problem" in world politics that needs to be overcome. While not denying its problematic aspects, my argument points toward a more balanced assessment of the system's normative value. In particular, I argued in chapter three that the development of international society, with its mutual recognition of sovereignty and respect for difference, was an institutional precondition for the subsequent emergence of the ability to manage the problem of interstate violence together. This power of states to keep violence off the table makes the rest of global governance possible in the first place. That does not mean that states are the only important actors on the world stage, and it does not mean that interstate commitments do or ought to trump national-level ones. As public powers, states are primarily responsible for meeting the basic needs of their own, domestic publics. But the argument is meant to highlight that meeting the needs of domestic populations requires some attention to the international sphere. Clearly, when states are at war no population's needs are being met. This simple fact translates to a second set of responsibilities, state to state, to govern the use of violence. A collective intentionality approach to global governance offers a way to define the relationship among public powers as itself a relationship of responsibility or obligation to one another, and by extension a relationship of responsibility or obligation to a transnational or global public.

Second, the collective intentionality framework I have developed provides one way to conceptualize collective agency in international politics in the absence of a unitary agent. While there are potentially many applications of this idea, I applied it to global governance. A collective intentionality approach gives us a vocabulary for seeing global governing as purposive and intentional rather than as purely reactive or as functional responses to anonymous, behind-the-back processes. This is not to deny that there also is a great deal of nonintentional or impersonal power as well in global governance. Indeed, an international public power might constitute a kind of structural power that publics would rightly worry about. But those are separate issues from the question of whether there can be collective intentional power in the first place, which has not been obvious.[22] Before publics can worry about public power it has to exist in the first place, and collective intentionality is a framework for "seeing" the capacity that is there.

Being able to see collective agency among states is important because where there is agency, there also is responsibility. The model of collective intentional agency developed in chapter two highlights two normative moments, each implying a distinct responsibility: the moment when agents exercise sovereignty over their desires and beliefs and commit to a joint action, and the moment when agents execute those intentions. The analytic focus of this book has been on the latter. The question I have addressed is, once states have made a joint commitment, can those commitments meaningfully pull behavior, especially over time? That is, can states execute their joint intentions? The moment is normatively important, first, because following through helps to stabilize the social order and reproduce society. It also is normatively important to follow through when we act together, because when we commit to joint action we make ourselves necessary to the agency of others, and "weak will" or reneging on our part undermines their agency. Moreover, demonstrating that states can follow through on commitments is important because if they cannot then the production of those commitments is not very interesting in the first place.

Since the empirical chapters above have shown that states can indeed follow through, an implication of the book is to invite our attention to the

---

22. On intentional versus nonintentional power, see, e.g., Guzzini 2005.

prior moment. This is the moment when actors, alone or together, exercise sovereignty over their desires and intend to do something. A complete theory of international public power in global governance would want to understand the politics of those commitments, which raise both causal and normative questions.

From a causal perspective, in the book I established necessary but not sufficient conditions for states to govern together. I argued in chapter two (when conceptualizing collective intentions and scaling up to anarchy) that there are social preconditions for collective intentions among states, and I showed in chapter three that these conditions evolved in the European states system. More questions remain, such as how do states, who are, after all, primarily responsible to their own populations and not to one another, come to enter into joint commitments in the first places? Under what conditions and in what issues is this more likely to happen? This is the domain of much of the IR literature on cooperation, and a collective intentionality framework supplements this work.

The more distinctive value-added of a collective intentionality approach is on the normative side, in that it brings into focus new questions about global governance. If states can be treated as responsible for following through on commitments, it certainly is reasonable that they could be considered responsible for making commitments in the first place. In the Concert, the great powers saw themselves as having a duty to govern the European balance of power and acted as if obligated to do so. Can this be generalized? Do states—especially great powers—have a duty to identify and address global-level problems? Leslie Green has distinguished a "duty to govern" as an aspect of political authority that should be treated separately from legitimacy and compliance.[23] Drawing on the work of John Finnis, Green argues that the duty to govern arises from the premise that setting rules for and guiding a society is a "morally necessary task."[24] If no authoritative rules exist for a society, someone must make them. The duty falls upon those who can—those with the social power to "effectively settle coordination problems."[25] That is, at least when it comes to the basic tasks in a society such as safety, capacity implies responsibility. Of course, this does not mean that the problems recognized by those with the duty to govern are the "right" problems, nor does it negate the

23. Green 2007.
24. Green 2007, 167.
25. Green 2007, 168.

fact that the powerful might act in their idiosyncratic interests, and duty does not necessarily translate to any action at all. Still, once a duty is articulated, it becomes possible to talk about who ought to act and who is responsible for inaction; we also can debate which problems call for governing.

Scaling up Green's idea of a duty to govern raises the question of whether international public power is a type of collective agency that can be held responsible, both for the problems that it chooses to address and perhaps for problems it does not identify or act upon? After all, intending to do one thing entails intending not to do something else, and as long as actors could have decided otherwise, they can be considered responsible for their nonchoices. At the domestic level, at least in democracies, we hold states responsible if they do not act on important public problems. How might such an accountability translate upward? Pulling this together, the fact that states can execute their collective intentions opens up a range of questions about the politics of commitment and the possibility of a global duty to govern.

Third, my argument highlights talk in interstate forums as the mechanism for pulling state behavior toward common goals and realizing collective intentions. This is a different way of thinking about the power of talk than is found in much rationalist and constructivist work. Rationalists tend to treat talk as cheap and focus more on behavioral signaling; constructivists tend to treat talk as a means of persuasion, socialization, and preference change. The role of talk I have developed is between these two poles. The main effect of talk is to enable states to constitute and follow through on their commitments.

When combined with forums, commitments have a distinctive behavioral pull at both the micro- and macrolevels.[26] At the microlevel of state interaction, forum talk helps states manage the gap between their commitments and their actions. Consider that global governing intentions, like all intentions, influence but do not determine actors' behavior. At the individual level, we manage the gap through an internal dialogue as we execute our intentions. Collective intentions externalize this conversation and as such are elaborated dynamically, as social products.[27] In international politics, the forum is where participants manage the gap between intentions and action by talking the talk of commitment. Through public

26. On the distinction between micro- and macrostructure, see Wendt 1999, 145–65.
27. Gibbs 2001 makes this argument about individual intentions.

communicative practices, states translate plans into joint action and give meaning to one another's actions as part of (or not) their collective intention.[28] Talking together helps them stay on track.

At the macrostructural level where the focus is on patterns of outcomes over time, forum talk helps sustain collective intentions into the future, thereby making it more likely that actors can keep their commitments. Talking in a forum tends to produce public reason, principles for action relevant to the commitment that apply to the group as a whole. Once a collective intention is supported by a structure of public reason, public reason can condition social outcomes somewhat independently of the motives and intentions of the actors involved. Of course, actors must keep talking together, and cannot be committed to scuttling the collective intention. But the point is that different constellations of preferences at the microlevel are consistent with the macrolevel state of maintaining a collective intention.[29] This macrolevel of behavioral pull has not been thematized in IR scholarship.

Fourth, and finally, my argument speaks to the question of how much solidarity is necessary to sustain global governing. The Concert case showed that great powers, anchored by the relatively thin political ties of international society and their explicit commitments, could address important problems over a long period of time. These days the conventional wisdom about global governance privileges thicker ties. The idea is that the spread of liberalism has created a deeper solidarity, a community based on liberal values, reflected, for example, in the rise of the human rights regime and international criminal law. Shared liberal ideology has made it possible for global governors to aspire to much more than the level of cooperation achieved in the Concert period.[30] Such thick ties would seem to solve some of the key difficulties that plagued Concert governing. Global governors who share values would be more likely to agree on which situations are shared problems that ought to be addressed together. Global governors who share values might also better trust one another and thus be more able to contain disagreements within arguments rather than allowing them to spiral toward violence.

But there are reasons to be cautious about embracing liberal soli-

---

28. Cf. the epistemic function of forums as one form of centralization, in Koremenos et al. 2001, 787–91.

29. Wendt 1999, 151–52.

30. Ellis 2009.

darity in particular and the standard of communal solidarity more generally when thinking about the basis of global governance. Empirically,
today's liberal consensus is not as thick as it was in the early post–Cold
War days of the 1990s. The United States remains the hegemon in the
sense that its liberal values ground and its material power underwrites the
existing order. But the ideological consensus behind many international
institutions seems to be fracturing and new powers are on the horizon.
Charles Kupchan is not alone in seeing the future as one not dominated
by Western states, much less the United States, and more like "No One's
World."[31] These trends suggest that concerting, which rests on thin bonds
of international society rather than thick bonds of shared political ideology, is an important practice and international public power a crucial
capacity to keep in mind.

Normatively, as Craig Calhoun[32] and others have argued, communal
standards of solidarity are not necessarily appropriate for large-scale
political groups. Those communal standards tend to originate in small,
intimate groups and to reflect a homogeneity that is impossible to replicate in a large group. As groups get larger, seeking homogeneity only
privileges those who already are dominant, while making it more difficult for the collectivity to handle difference. As Calhoun puts it, "when we
think that unity must be founded on sameness, then difference immediately arouses anxiety."[33] Calhoun is focused on the domestic context, but
his distinction between public and community is instructive in an international context as well. In a world of nearly two hundred states, difference
is unavoidable. Recalling Jens Steffek's apt phrase, governing together on
a global scale will always be about building bridges across states rather
than closing gaps between them.[34] This suggests that too narrow a focus
on creating international community and forging a consensus on values
can occlude or potentially undermine important governance resources we
already have in international society.

This book was framed as a critique of global liberal governance, and
it has offered a contrasting model—international public power. But the
argument is not meant as a rejection of liberalism. I have argued that
global governing has parallels to domestic governing in the modern lib-

31. Kupchan 2012; also Keohane 2012, 134.
32. Calhoun 1998.
33. Calhoun 1998, 28.
34. Steffek 2005; Sunstein 1995

eral state in that it is about commitments that enable mutual self-restraint among the powerful in the name of a common project, accepting pluralism and publicity, and talking instead of fighting. Moreover, international society requires that members accept something like liberal premises for interacting with one another, insofar as these institutions are premised on toleration of difference. And identifying and communicating political problems to leaders requires some level of openness and allowing of civil society. An implication is that the global spread of liberalism has been double edged: it has been part of the problem in the way we think about global governance, but it also is a crucial aspect of the solution.

Pulling this together, the key lesson of the book is that we should not forget how to concert state power. While this ability is crucially important in world politics today, it has not been obvious what it means or how precisely to do it. I have argued that states governing together is not just bargaining or sharing information, and it is not just attempting to win an argument or change someone's mind. Governing in anarchy is states concerting their power to solve public problems. In international as in domestic politics, this requires committing to a common project, in public, with your peers, and working across lines of difference rather than erasing them. This power is fragile in the absence of a world state, but it is possible. The nineteenth-century Concert was the first time it was tried, and it was messy and conflictual and plagued by uncertainty, but it also had substantial accomplishments. It was a normative improvement on the anarchy before it, and as we look forward to ideologically diverse global governing today it is a lesson worth keeping in mind.

# References

Abbott, Kenneth, and Duncan Snidal. 1998. "Why States Act through Formal International Organizations." *Journal of Conflict Resolution* 42 (1): 3–32.

Abbott, Kenneth, Robert Keohane, Andrew Moravcsik, Anne-Marie Slaughter, and Duncan Snidal, eds. 2000. "Special Issue: Legalization in World Politics." *International Organization* 54 (3).

Adanir, Fikret. 2005. "Turkey's Entry into the Concert of Europe." *European Review* 13 (3): 395–417.

Adler, Emanuel, and Michael Barnett, eds. 1998. *Security Communities*. Cambridge: Cambridge University Press.

Adler, Emanuel, and Vincent Pouliot. 2011. "International Practices." *International Theory* 3 (1): 1–36.

Albrecht-Carrie, Rene. 1968. *The Concert of Europe*. New York: Harper and Row.

Aldrich, John H., Christopher Gelpi, Peter Feaver, Jason Reifler, and Kristin Thompson Sharp. 2006. "Foreign Policy and the Electoral Connection." *Annual Review of Political Science* 9: 477–502.

Alvarez, José. 2001. "Do Liberal States Behave Better? A Critique of Slaughter's Liberal Theory." *European Journal of International Law* 12: 183–246.

Anderson, Kenneth. 2005. "Squaring the Circle? Reconciling Sovereignty and Global Governance through Global Government Networks." *Harvard Law Review* 118: 1255–312.

Anderson, M. S. 1966. *The Eastern Question, 1774–1923: A Study in International Relations*. New York: St. Martin's Press.

———. 1993. *The Rise of Modern Diplomacy, 1450–1919*. New York: Longman Group.

Anderson, Sheldon. 2007. "Metternich, Bismarck, and the Myth of the Long Peace, 1815–1914." *Peace and Change* 32 (3): 301–28.

Archibugi, Daniel. 2008. *The Global Commonwealth of Citizens*. Princeton, NJ: Princeton University Press.

Arendt, Hannah. 1958. *The Human Condition*. Chicago: University of Chicago Press.

Arnold, Guy. 2002. *Historical Dictionary of the Crimean War*. Lanham, MD: Scarecrow Press.

Avant, Deborah, Martha Finnemore, and Susan Sell. 2010a. "Conclusion: Authority, Legitimacy and Accountability in Global Politics" In *Who Governs the Globe?*, edited by Deborah Avant, Martha Finnemore, and Susan Sell, 356–70. Cambridge: Cambridge University Press.

———. 2010b. "Who Governs the Globe?" In *Who Governs the Globe?*, edited by Deborah Avant, Martha Finnemore, and Susan Sell, 1–31. Cambridge: Cambridge University Press.

Badem, Candan. 2010. *The Ottoman Crimean War (1853–1856)*. Leiden: Brill.

Baldwin, David A. 1993. "Neoliberalism, Neorealism, and World Politics." In *Neorealism and Neoliberalism: The Contemporary Debate*, edited by David A. Baldwin, 3–25. New York: Columbia University Press.

Barnett, Michael. 2009. "Evolution without Progress? Humanitarianism in a World of Hurt." *International Organization* 63 (4): 621–63.

Barnett, Michael, and Raymond Duvall, eds. 2004. *Power in Global Governance*. Cambridge: Cambridge University Press.

———. 2005. "Power in International Politics." *International Organization* 59: 39–75.

Barnett, Michael, and Martha Finnemore. 2004. *Rules for the World: International Organizations in World Politics*. Ithaca, NY: Cornell University Press.

Bartlett, C. J. 1996. *Peace, War, and the European Powers, 1815–1914*. New York: Palgrave Macmillan.

Bass, Gary Jonathan. 2008. *Freedom's Battle: The Origins of Humanitarian Intervention*. New York: Alfred A. Knopf.

Baum, Matthew A., and Philip B. K. Potter. 2008. "The Relationships between Mass Media, Public Opinion, and Foreign Policy: A Synthesis." *Annual Review of Political Science* 11: 39–65.

Baumgart, Winfried. 1999. *The Crimean War: 1853–1856*. New York: Oxford University Press.

Bennett, Andrew, and Colin Elman. 2007. "Case Study Methods in the International Relations Subfield." *Comparative Political Studies* 40 (2): 170–95.

Bjola, Corneliu. 2009. *Legitimising the Use of Force in World Politics: Kosovo, Iraq, and the Ethics of Intervention*. London: Routledge.

Bjola, Corneliu, and Markus Kronprobst. 2011. "Introduction: The Argumentative Deontology of Global Governance." In *Arguing Global Governance: Agency, Lifeworld, and Shared Reasoning*, edited by Corneliu Bjola and Markus Kornprobst, 1–16. Oxford: Routledge.

Black, Jeremy. 1994. *European Warfare, 1660–1815*. New Haven, CT: Yale University Press.

———. 1999. *Eighteenth-Century Europe*. 2nd ed. New York: St. Martin's Press.

Bohman, James. 1994. "Complexity, Pluralism, and the Constitutional State: On Habermas' *Faktizitat und Geltung*." *Law and Society Review* 28 (4): 897–930.

———. 1995. "Public Reason and Cultural Pluralism: Political Liberalism and the Problem of Moral Conflict." *Political Theory* 23 (2): 253–79.

———. 1996. *Public Deliberation: Pluralism, Complexity, and Democracy.* Cambridge, MA: MIT Press.

———. 1997. "The Public Spheres of the World Citizen." In *Perpetual Peace: Essays on Kant's Cosmopolitan Ideal*, edited by James Bohman and Matthias Lutz-Bachmann, 179–200. Cambridge, MA: MIT Press.

Bratman, Michael. 1999. *Intention, Plans, and Practical Reason.* Stanford, CA: Center for the Study of Language and Information.

Bridge, Roy. 1979. "Allied Diplomacy in Peacetime: The Failure of the Congress 'System,' 1815–23." In *Europe's Balance of Power, 1815–1848*, edited by Alan Sked, 34–53. London: Macmillan.

Brooks, Stephen. 2005. "Hard Times for Soft Balancing." *International Security* 30 (1): 72–108.

Brunnée, Jutta, and Stephen Toope. 2010. *Legitimacy and Legality in International Law: An Interactional Account.* Cambridge: Cambridge University Press.

Bruun, Geoffrey. 1965. "The Balance of Power during the Wars, 1793–1814." In *The New Cambridge Modern History.* Vol. 9, *War and Peace in an Age of Upheaval, 1793–1830*, edited by C. W. Crawley, 250–74. Cambridge: Cambridge University Press.

Bukovansky, Mlada. 2002. *Legitimacy and Power Politics: The American and French Revolutions.* Princeton, NJ: Princeton University Press.

Bull, Hedley. 1977. *The Anarchical Society.* New York: Columbia University Press.

Büthe, Tim. 2004. "Governance through Private Authority: Non-State Actors in World Politics." *Journal of International Affairs* 58 (1): 281–90.

Buzan, Barry. 2004. *From International to World Society? English School Theory and the Social Structure of Globalization.* Cambridge: Cambridge University Press.

Caldwell, Robert Granville. 1918. "The Peace Conferences of the 19th Century." Rice Institute Pamphlet, Rice University, vol. 5, no. 2.

Calhoun, Craig. 1998. "The Public Good as a Social and Cultural Project." In *Private Action and the Public Good*, edited by Walter W. Powell and Elisabeth S. Clemens, 20–35. New Haven, CT: Yale University Press.

Calvert, Randall. 1995. "Rational Actors, Equilibrium, and Social Institutions." In *Explaining Social Institutions*, edited by Jack Knight and Itai Sened, 57–94. Ann Arbor, MI: University of Michigan Press.

Camic, Charles. 1986. "The Matter of Habit." *American Journal of Sociology* 91 (5): 1039–87.

Carbone, Maurizio. 2007. "Supporting or Resisting Global Public Goods? The Policy Dimension of a Contested Concept." *Global Governance* 13: 179–98.

Chamberlain, Muriel E. 1983. *Lord Aberdeen: A Political Biography.* New York: Longman.

Chambers, Simone. 2004. "Behind Closed Doors: Publicity, Secrecy, and the Quality of Deliberation." *Journal of Political Philosophy* 12 (4): 389–410.

Chant, Sara Rachel, and Zachary Ernst. 2007. "Group Intentions as Equilibria." *Philosophical Studies* 133: 95–109.

Chayes, Abram, and Antonia Handler Chayes. 1995. *The New Sovereignty: Compliance with International Regulatory Agreements.* Cambridge, MA: Harvard University Press.

Checkel, Jeffrey. 1998. "The Constructivist Turn in International Relations Theory." *World Politics* 50 (2): 324–48.

———. 2001. "Why Comply? Social Learning and European Identity Change." *International Organization* 55 (3): 553–88.

Cialdini, Robert. 2009. "Commitment and Consistency." In *Influence: Science and Practice.* 5th ed., 552–96. New York: Allyn and Bacon.

Claude, Inis L. 1962. *Power and International Relations.* New York: Random House.

Clogg, Richard. 1986. *A Short History of Modern Greece.* 2nd ed. Cambridge: Cambridge University Press.

Cowles, Loyal. 1990. "The Failure to Restrain Russia: Canning, Nesselrode, and the Greek Question, 1825–1827." *International History Review* 13 (4): 688–720.

Craig, Gordon, and Alexander George. 1995. *Force and Statecraft: Diplomatic Problems of Our Time.* New York: Oxford University Press.

Crawford, Neta. 2002. *Argument and Change in World Politics: Ethics, Decolonization, and Humanitarian Intervention.* Cambridge: Cambridge University Press.

Crawley, C. W. 1965. "International Relations, 1815–1830." In *The New Cambridge Modern History.* Vol. 9, *War and Peace in an Age of Upheaval, 1793–1830,* edited by C. W. Crawley, 668–90. Cambridge: Cambridge University Press.

———. 1973 (1930). *The Question of Greek Independence: A Study of British Policy in the Near East, 1821–1833.* New York: Howard Fertig.

Cronin, Bruce. 1999. *Community under Anarchy.* New York: Columbia University Press.

Croxton, Derek. 1999. "The Peace of Westphalia of 1648 and the Origins of Sovereignty." *International History Review* 21 (3): 569–91.

Cunningham, Allan. 1978. "The Philhellenes, Canning, and Greek Independence." *Middle Eastern Studies* 14 (2): 151–81.

Curtiss, John Shelton. 1979. *Russia's Crimean War.* Durham, NC: Duke University Press.

Daalder, Ivo, and James Lindsay. 2007. "Democracies of the World Unite." *Public Policy Research* 14 (1): 47–58.

Dahl, Robert. 1957. "The Concept of Power." *Behavioral Science* 2 (3): 201–15.

———. 1999. "Can International Organizations Be Democratic? A Skeptic's View." In *Democracy's Edges,* edited by I. Shapiro and C. Hacker-Cordon, 19–36. Cambridge: Cambridge University Press.

Dakin, Douglas. 1955. *British and American Philhellenes during the War of Greek Independence, 1821–1833.* Thessaloniki.

————. 1973a. "The Formation of the Greek State, 1821–1833." In *The Struggle for Greek Independence*, edited by Richard Clogg, 156–81. Hamden, CT: Archon Books.

————. 1973b. *The Greek Struggle for Independence, 1821–1833.* Berkeley: University of California Press.

————. 1979. "The Congress of Vienna, 1814–15, and Its Antecedents." In *Europe's Balance of Power, 1815–1848*, edited by Alan Sked, 14–33. London: Macmillan.

Daly, John. 1991. *Russian Seapower and "The Eastern Question," 1827–41.* Annapolis, MD: Naval Institute Press.

Daugherty, William. 1993. "System Management and the Endurance of the Concert of Europe." In *Coping with Complexity in the International System*, edited by Jack Snyder and Robert Jervis, 71–105. Boulder, CO: Westview Press.

Davison, Roderic H. 1990. *Essays in Ottoman and Turkish History, 1774–1923: The Impact of the West.* Austin: University of Texas Press.

————. 1999. *Nineteenth Century Ottoman Diplomacy and Reforms.* Istanbul: Isis Press.

Dean, Mitchell. 2010. *Governmentality: Power and Rule in Modern Society.* 2nd ed. Thousand Oaks, CA: Sage.

Deitelhoff, Nicole. 2009. "The Discursive Process of Legalization: Charting Islands of Persuasion in the ICC Case." *International Organization* 63 (1): 33–65.

Deitelhoff, Nicole, and Harald Müller. 2005. "Theoretical Paradise—Empirically Lost? Arguing with Habermas." *Review of International Studies* 31 (1): 167–79.

Delfiner, Henry A. 2003. "Alexander I, the Holy Alliance, and Clemens Metternich: A Reappraisal." *East European Quarterly* 37 (2): 127–50.

Del Mar, Maksymilian. 2011. "Concerted Practices and the Presence of Obligations: Joint Action in Competition Law and Social Philosophy." *Law and Philosophy* 30: 105–40.

Diez, Thomas, and Jill Steans. 2005. "A Useful Dialogue? Habermas and International Relations." *Review of International Studies* 31 (1): 127–40.

Downs, George W., David M. Rocke, and Peter N. Barsoom. 1996. "Is the Good News about Compliance Good News about Cooperation?" *International Organization* 50 (3): 379–406.

Doyle, Michael. 1986. "Liberalism and World Politics." *American Political Science Review* 80 (4): 1151–69.

Doyle, William. 1992. *The Old European Order, 1660–1800.* 2nd ed. New York: Oxford University Press.

Drezner, Daniel. 2008. "The Realist Tradition in American Public Opinion." *Perspectives on Politics* 6 (1): 51–70.

Duchhardt, Heinz. 2000. "War and International Law in Europe Sixteenth to Eighteenth Centuries." In *War and Competition between States*, edited by Philippe Contamine, 279–99. Oxford: Clarendon Press.

Dunn, Frederick. 1929. *The Practice and Procedure of International Conferences.* Baltimore, MD: Johns Hopkins Press.

Dwyer, Philip. 2008. "Self-Interest versus Common Cause: Austria, Prussia, and Russia against Napoleon." *Journal of Strategic Studies* 31 (4): 605–32.

Eliasoph, Nina. 1998. *Avoiding Politics: How Americans Produce Apathy in Everyday Life.* Cambridge: Cambridge University Press.

Ellis, David C. 2009. "On the Possibility of International Community." *International Studies Review* 11 (1): 1–26.

Elrod, Richard. 1976. "The Concert of Europe: A Fresh Look at an International System." *World Politics* 28 (2): 159–74.

Elster, Jon. 1983. *Explaining Technical Change: A Case Study in the Philosophy of Science.* Cambridge: Cambridge University Press.

———. 1986. "The Market and the Forum: Three Varieties of Political Theory." In *Foundations of Social Choice Theory*, edited by Jon Elster and Aanund Hylland, 103–32. Cambridge: Cambridge University Press.

———. 1995. "Strategic Uses of Argument." In *Barriers to Conflict Resolution*, edited by Kenneth Arrow, Robert H. Mnookin, and Amos Tversky, 236–57. New York: W. W. Norton.

———. 1998. "Deliberation and Constitution-Making." In *Deliberative Democracy*, edited by Jon Elster, 97–122. Cambridge: Cambridge University Press.

Fearon, James. 1994. "Domestic Political Audiences and the Escalation of International Disputes." *American Political Science Review* 88 (3): 577–92.

———. 1995. "Rationalist Explanations for War." *International Organization* 49 (3): 379–414.

———. 1998. "Deliberation as Discussion." In *Deliberative Democracy*, edited by Jon Elster, 44–68. Cambridge: Cambridge University Press.

Fearon, James, and Alexander Wendt. 2002. "Rationalism v. Constructivism: A Skeptical View." In *Handbook of International Relations*, edited by Walter Carlsnaes, Thomas Risse, and Beth Simmons, 52–72. London: Sage.

Festinger, Leon. 1957. *A Theory of Cognitive Dissonance.* Evanston, IL: Row, Peterson.

Finel, Bernard I., and Kristin M. Lord. 1999. "The Surprising Logic of Transparency." *International Studies Quarterly* 43 (2): 325–39.

Finlay, George. 1887. *A History of Greece from Its Conquest by the Romans to the Present Time.* Vol. 6, *The Greek Revolution, Part I, 1821–1827.* Oxford: Clarendon Press.

Finnemore, Martha. 1996. "Norms, Culture, and World Politics: Insights from Sociology's Institutionalism." *International Organization* 50 (2): 325–47.

———. 2000. "Are Legal Norms Distinctive?" *New York University Journal of International Law and Politics* 32: 699–705.

———. 2003. *The Purpose of Intervention.* Ithaca, NY: Cornell University Press.

Finnemore, Martha, and Stephen Toope. 2001. "Alternatives to 'Legalization': Richer Views of Law and Politics." *International Organization* 55 (3): 743–58.

Fleming, D. C. 1970. *John Capodistrias and the Conference of London, 1828–1831*. Thessaloniki: Institute for Balkan Studies.

Flockerzie, Lawrence. 1992. "The Eastern Question and the European States System: Linkage from a Small Power Perspective." In *Labyrinth of Nationalism, Complexities of Diplomacy: Essays in Honor of Charles and Barbara Jelavich*, edited by Richard Frucht, 214–33. Bloomington, IN: Slavica Publishers.

Florini, Ann. 1996. "The Evolution of International Norms." *International Studies Quarterly* 40: 363–89.

Fraser, Nancy. 1992. "Rethinking the Public Sphere: A Contribution to the Critique of Actually Existing Democracy." In *Habermas and the Public Sphere*, edited by Craig Calhoun, 109–42. Cambridge, MA: MIT Press.

———. 2007. "Transnationalizing the Public Sphere: On the Legitimacy and Efficacy of Public Opinion in a Post-Westphalian World." *Theory, Culture, and Society* 24 (4): 1–24.

Galston, William A. 2010. "Realism in Political Theory." *European Journal of Political Theory* 9 (4): 385–411.

Gestrich, Andreas. 2006. "The Public Sphere and the Habermas Debate." *German History* 24 (3): 413–30.

Gibbs, Raymond. 2001. "Intentions as Emergent Products of Social Interactions." In *Intentions and Intentionality: Foundations of Social Cognition*, edited by Bertram Malle, Louis Moses, and Dare Baldwin, 105–22. Cambridge, MA: MIT Press.

Gilbert, Felix. 1951. "The 'New Diplomacy' of the Eighteenth Century." *World Politics* 4 (1): 1–38.

Gilbert, Margaret. 1992. *On Social Facts*. Princeton, NJ: Princeton University Press.

———. 2000. *Sociality and Responsibility: New Essays in Plural Subject Theory*. Lanham, MD: Rowman and Littlefield.

———. 2003a. "Agreement, Coercion, and Obligation." *Ethics* 105: 679–706.

———. 2003b. "The Structure of the Social Atom." In *Socializing Metaphysics: The Nature of Social Reality*, edited by Frederick Schmitt, 39–64. Lanham, MD: Rowman and Littlefield.

———. 2006a. "Rationality in Collective Action." *Philosophy of the Social Sciences* 36 (1): 3–17.

———. 2006b. *A Theory of Political Obligation*. Oxford: Clarendon Press.

Gilpin, Robert. 1981. *War and Change in World Politics*. New York: Cambridge University Press.

Gochal, Joseph R., and Jack S. Levy. 2004. "Crisis Management or Conflict of Interests? A Case Study of the Origins of the Crimean War." In *Multiple Paths to Knowledge in International Relations*, edited by Zeev Maoz, Alex Mintz, T. Clifton Morgan, Glenn Palmer, and Richard J. Stoll, 309–42. New York: Lexington Books.

Goddard, Stacie. 2008/9. "When Right Makes Might: How Prussia Overturned the European Balance of Power." *International Security* 33 (3): 110–42.

Goldsmith, Jack, and Eric Posner. 2005. *The Limits of International Law*. Oxford: Oxford University Press.

Goldstein, Robert. 1983. *Political Repression in 19th Century Europe*. Totowa, NJ: Barnes and Noble Books.

Gooch, Brison D. 1956. "A Century of Historiography on the Origins of the Crimean War." *American Historical Review* 62 (1): 33–58.

Green, Leslie. 2007. "The Duty to Govern." *Legal Theory* 13 (3–4): 165–85.

Grigorescu, Alexandru. 2007. "Transparency of Intergovernmental Organizations: The Roles of Member States, International Bureaucracies, and Nongovernmental Organizations." *International Studies Quarterly* 51 (3): 625–48.

Grimsted, Patricia. 1969. *The Foreign Ministers of Alexander I*. Berkeley: University of California Press.

Gruber, Lloyd. 2000. *Ruling the World: Power Politics and the Rise of Supranational Institutions*. Princeton, NJ: Princeton University Press.

Gulick, E. V. 1955. *Europe's Classical Balance of Power*. New York: W. W. Norton.

———. 1965. "The Final Coalition and the Congress of Vienna, 1813–1815." In *The New Cambridge Modern History*. Vol. 9, *War and Peace in an Age of Upheaval, 1793–1830*, edited by C. W. Crawley, 639–67. Cambridge: Cambridge University Press.

Guzzini, Stefano. 2005. "The Concept of Power: A Constructivist Analysis." *Millennium* 33 (3): 495–521.

Haas, Ernst. 1990. *When Knowledge Is Power*. Berkeley: University of California Press.

Haas, Mark. 2005. *The Ideological Origins of Great Power Politics, 1789–1989*. Ithaca, NY: Cornell University Press.

Habermas, Jürgen. 1984. *Theory of Communicative Action*. Vol. 2. Boston: Beacon Press.

———. 1989. *The Structural Transformation of the Public Sphere: An Inquiry into a Category of Bourgeois Society*. Translated by Thomas Burger, with the assistance of Frederick Lawrence. Cambridge, MA: MIT Press.

———. 1996. *Between Facts and Norms*. Cambridge, MA: MIT Press.

Hale, William. 2000. *Turkish Foreign Policy, 1774–2000*. Portland, OR: Frank Cass.

Hall, Rodney Bruce. 1999. *National Collective Identity: Social Constructs and International Systems*. New York: Columbia University Press.

Hatton, Ragnhild. 1980. "Nijmegen and the European Powers." In *The Peace of Nijmegen, 1676–1678/79*, edited by J. A. H. Bots, 1–17. Amsterdam: Holland Universiteits Pers.

Hazen, Charles. 1917. "The Congress of Vienna." In *Three Peace Congresses of the Nineteenth Century*, edited by Charles Hazen, 3–19. Cambridge, MA: Harvard University Press.

Headlam-Morley, J. W. 1927. "Treaties of Guarantee." *Cambridge Historical Journal* 2 (2): 151–70.

Hertslet, Edward. 1875. *The Map of Europe by Treaty Showing the Various Political and Territorial Changes Which Have Taken Place since the General Peace of 1814.* Vols. 1 and 2. London: Butterworths.

Heydemann, Gunther. 2002. "The Vienna System between 1815 and 1848 and the Disputed Antirevolutionary Strategy: Repression, Reforms, or Constitutions?" In *"The Transformation of European Politics, 1763–1848": Episode or Model in Modern History?*, edited by Peter Kruger and Paul Schroeder, 187–203. New York: Palgrave.

Hinsley, F. H. 1963. *Power and the Pursuit of Peace.* Cambridge: Cambridge University Press.

Holland, T. E., ed. 1885. *The European Concert in the Eastern Question: A Collection of Treaties and Other Public Acts.* Oxford: Clarendon Press.

Holmes, Marcus. 2011. "The Force of Face-to-Face Diplomacy in International Politics." PhD diss., Ohio State University.

Holsti, K. J. 1991. *Peace and War: Armed Conflicts and International Order, 1648–1989.* Cambridge: Cambridge University Press.

———. 1992. "Governance without Government: Polyarchy in Nineteenth-Century European International Politics." In *Governance without Government: Order and Change in World Politics*, edited by James Rosenau and Ernst-Otto Czempiel, 30–57. Cambridge: Cambridge University Press.

———. 2004. *Public Opinion and American Foreign Policy.* Rev. ed. Ann Arbor: University of Michigan Press.

Holton, Richard. 1999. "Intention and Weakness of Will." *Journal of Philosophy* 96 (5): 241–62.

Hopf, Ted. 2010. "The Logic of Habit in International Relations." *European Journal of International Relations* 16 (4): 539–61.

Hurd, Ian. 2008. *After Anarchy: Legitimacy and Power in the UN Security Council.* Princeton, NJ: Princeton University Press.

Ikenberry, G. John. 2001. *After Victory: Institutions, Strategic Restraint, and the Rebuilding of Order after Major Wars.* Princeton, NJ: Princeton University Press.

Ingrao, Charles. 1994. "Paul Schroeder's Balance of Power: Stability or Anarchy?" *International History Review* 16 (4): 681–700.

Jackson, Patrick. 2004. "Forum Introduction: Is the State a Person? Why Should We Care?" *Review of International Studies* 30 (2): 255–58.

Jackson, Patrick, and Daniel Nexon. 1999. "Relations before States: Substance, Process, and the Study of World Politics." *European Journal of International Relations* 5 (3): 291–332.

Jaeger, Hans-Martin. 2010. "UN Reform, Biopolitics, and Global Governmentality." *International Theory* 2 (1): 50–86.

Jansen, Ludger. 2004. "Who Has Got Our Group-Intentions?" In *Experience and Analysis.* Papers of the 27th International Wittgenstein Symposium, edited by Johann C. Marek and Maria E. Reicher, 151–53.

Jelavich, Barbara. 1983. *History of the Balkans: Eighteenth and Nineteenth Centuries.* New York: Cambridge University Press.

————. 1991. *Russia's Balkan Entanglements, 1806–1914*. New York: Cambridge University Press.

Jelavich, Charles, and Barbara Jelavich. 1997 (1977). *The Establishment of the Balkan National States, 1804–1920*. Seattle: University of Washington Press.

Jepperson, Ronald. 2001. "The Development and Application of Sociological Neo-Institutionalism." Working Paper 2001/5, Robert Schuman Centre, European University Institute, Florence.

Jervis, Robert. 1983. "Security Regimes." In *International Regimes*, edited by Stephen Krasner, 173–94. Ithaca, NY: Cornell University Press.

————. 1986. "From Balance to Concert: A Study of International Security Cooperation." In *Cooperation under Anarchy*, edited by Kenneth Oye, 58–79. Princeton, NJ: Princeton University Press.

————. 1992. "A Political Science Perspective on the Balance of Power and the Concert." *American Historical Review* 97 (3): 716–24.

Johnston, Alistair Iain. 2001. "Treating International Institutions as Social Environments." *International Studies Quarterly* 45 (4): 487–515.

Johnstone, Ian. 2003. "Security Council Deliberations: The Power of the Better Argument." *European Journal of International Law* 14 (3): 437–80.

————. 2004. "US-UN Relations after Iraq: The End of the World (Order) as We Know It?" *European Journal of International Law* 15 (4): 813–38.

Kagan, Frederick. 1999. *The Military Reforms of Nicholas I: The Origins of the Modern Russian Army*. New York: St. Martin's Press.

Kagan, Korina. 1997/98. "The Myth of the European Concert: The Realist-Institutionalist Debate and Great Power Behavior in the Eastern Question, 1821–41." *Security Studies* 7 (2): 1–57.

Kaldor, Mary. 2003. "The Idea of Global Civil Society." *International Affairs* 79 (3): 583–93.

Kann, Robert. 1960. "Metternich: A Reappraisal of His Impact on International Relations." *Journal of Modern History* 32 (4): 333–39.

Kaul, Inge, Isabelle Grunberg, and Marc A. Stern. 1999. Introduction to *Global Public Goods: International Cooperation in the 21st Century*, edited by Inge Kaul, Isabelle Grunberg and Marc A. Stern, 1–13. New York: Oxford University Press.

Keene, Edward. 2002. *Beyond the Anarchical Society*. Cambridge: Cambridge University Press.

Keohane, Robert. 1984. *After Hegemony*. Princeton, NJ: Princeton University Press.

————. 2001. "Governance in a Partially Globalized World." *American Political Science Review* 95 (1): 1–13.

————. 2012. "Twenty Years of Institutional Liberalism." *International Relations* 26 (2): 125–38.

Kerner, Robert. 1937. "Russia's New Policy in the Near East after the Peace of

Adrianople; Including the Text of the Protocol of 16 September 1829." *Cambridge Historical Journal* 5 (3): 280–90.

King, David. 2008. *Vienna, 1814*. New York: Harmony Books.

Kinross, Patrick Balfour, Baron (Lord Kinross). 1977. *The Ottoman Centuries: The Rise and Fall of the Turkish Empire*. New York: Morrow.

Kissinger, Henry A. 1957. *A World Restored: Metternich, Castlereagh, and the Problems of Peace, 1812–22*. Boston: Houghton Mifflin.

Koremenos, Barbara, Charles Lipson, and Duncan Snidal. 2001. "The Rational Design of International Institutions." *International Organization* 55 (4): 761–99.

Kornprobst, Markus. 2008. *Irredentism in European Politics: Argumentation, Compromise, and Norms*. Cambridge: Cambridge University Press.

Kraehe, Enno E. 2002. "Section III: Introduction." In *"The Transformation of European Politics, 1763–1848": Episode or Model in Modern History?*, edited by Peter Kruger and Paul Schroeder, 161–64. New York: Palgrave.

Krasner, Stephen. 1999. *Sovereignty: Organized Hypocrisy*. Princeton, NJ: Princeton University Press.

Krasner, Stephen, ed. 1983. *International Regimes*. Ithaca, NY: Cornell University Press.

Kratochwil, Friedrich. 1989. *Rules, Norms, and Decisions: On the Conditions of Practical and Legal Reasoning in International Relations and Domestic Affairs*. Cambridge: Cambridge University Press.

Krebs, Ronald, and Patrick Jackson. 2007. "Twisting Tongues and Twisting Arms: The Power of Political Rhetoric." *European Journal of International Relations* 13 (1): 35–66.

Kupchan, Charles. 2010. *How Enemies Become Friends: The Sources of a Stable Peace*. Princeton, NJ: Princeton University Press.

———. 2012. *No One's World: The West, the Rising Rest, and the Coming Global Turn*. Oxford: Oxford University Press.

Kupchan, Charles, and Clifford Kupchan. 1991. "Concerts, Collective Security, and the Future of Europe." *International Security* 16 (1): 114–61.

———. 1995. "The Promise of Collective Security." *International Security* 20 (1): 52–61.

Lang, Anthony F., Jr., and John Williams, eds. 2005. *Hannah Arendt and International Relations: Readings across the Lines*. New York: Palgrave Macmillan.

Langhorne, Richard. 1981/82. "The Development of International Conferences, 1648–1830." *Studies in History and Politics* 2: 61–75.

———. 1990. "Establishing International Organizations: The Concert and the League." *Diplomacy and Statecraft* 1 (1): 1–18.

Larner, Wendy, and William Walters, eds. 2004. *Global Governmentality: Governing International Spaces*. New York: Routledge.

Levy, Jack. 2008. "Case Studies: Types, Designs, and Logics of Inference." *Conflict Management and Peace Science* 25: 1–18.

Lewis, Bernard. 1968. *The Emergence of Modern Turkey*. 2nd ed. Oxford: Oxford University Press.

Lindley, Daniel. 2003/4. "Avoiding Tragedy in Power Politics: The Concert of Europe, Transparency, and Crisis Management." *Security Studies* 13 (2): 195–229.

———. 2007. *Promoting Peace with Information*. Princeton, NJ: Princeton University Press.

Lipschutz, Ronnie. 1992. "Reconstructing World Politics: The Emergence of Global Civil Society." *Millennium* 21 (3): 389–420.

Lipson, Charles. 1994. "Is the Future of Collective Security like the Past?" In *Collective Security beyond the Cold War*, edited by George Downs, 105–31. Ann Arbor: University of Michigan Press.

Little, Richard. 1989. "Deconstructing the Balance of Power: Two Traditions of Thought." *Review of International Studies* 15 (special issue 2): 87–100.

———. 2007. *The Balance of Power in International Relations: Metaphors, Myths, and Models*. New York: Cambridge University Press.

Lord, Kristin M. 2006. *The Perils and Promise of Global Transparency: Why the Information Revolution May Not Lead to Security, Democracy, or Peace*. Albany: State University of New York Press.

Lossky, Andrew. 1970. "International Relations in Europe." In *The New Cambridge Modern History*. Vol. 6, *The Rise of Great Britain and Russia, 1688–1715/25*, edited by J. S. Bromley. Cambridge: Cambridge University Press.

Lynch, Marc. 1999. *State Interests and Public Spheres: The International Politics of Jordan's Identity*. New York: Columbia University Press.

MacGilvray, Eric. 2011. *The Invention of Market Freedom*. Cambridge: Cambridge University Press.

Magocsi, Paul. 1993. *Historical Atlas of Central Europe*. Seattle: University of Washington Press.

Malle, Bertram, and Joshua Knobe. 2001. "The Distinction between Desire and Intention: A Folk-Conceptual Analysis." In *Intentions and Intentionality: Foundations of Social Cognition*, edited by Bertram Malle, Louis Moses, and Dare Baldwin, 45–67. Cambridge, MA: MIT Press.

Mango, Cyril. 1973. "The Phanariots and the Byzantine Tradition." In *The Struggle for Greek Independence*, edited by Richard Clogg, 41–66. Hamden, CT: Archon Books.

Mangone, Gerard. 1954. *A Short History of International Organization*. New York: McGraw Hill.

March, James, and Johan Olson. 1998. "The Institutional Dynamics of International Political Orders." *International Organization* 52 (4): 943–69.

Marriott, J. A. R. 1940. *The Eastern Question: An Historical Study in European Diplomacy*. Oxford: Clarendon Press.

Mastnak, Tomaz. 1998. "Abbé de Saint-Pierre: European Union and the Turk." *History of Political Thought* 19 (4): 570–98.

Mattern, Janice Bially. 2005. *Ordering International Politics*. New York: Routledge.

Mattingly, Garrett. 1988. *Renaissance Diplomacy*. New York: Dover.

McKay, Derek, and H. M. Scott. 1983. *The Rise of the Great Powers, 1648–1815*. London: Longman.

Mearsheimer, John. 1994/95. "The False Promise of International Institutions." *International Security* 19 (3): 5–49.

Medlicott, W. N. 1956. *Bismarck, Gladstone, and the Concert of Europe*. London: University of London, Athlone Press.

Merlingen, Michael. 2003. "Governmentality: Toward a Foucauldian Framework for the Study of IGOs." *Cooperation and Conflict* 38 (4): 361–84.

Meyer, John, John Boli, and George Thomas. 1997. "World Society and the Nation-State." *American Journal of Sociology* 103: 144–81.

Miller, Seumas. 1995. "Intentions, Ends, and Joint Action." *Philosophical Papers* 24 (1): 51–66.

Mitchell, Ronald B. 1994. "Regime Design Matters." *International Organization* 48 (3): 425–58.

———. 1998. "Sources of Transparency: Information Systems in International Regimes." *International Studies Quarterly* 42 (1): 109–30.

Mitzen, Jennifer. 2005. "Reading Habermas in Anarchy: Multilateral Diplomacy and Global Public Spheres." *American Political Science Review* 99 (3): 401–17.

———. 2006. "Ontological Security in World Politics: State Identity and the Security Dilemma." *European Journal of International Relations* 12 (3): 341–70.

Moltke, Helmut von. 1854. *The Russians in Bulgaria and Rumelia in 1828 and 1829*. London: John Murray.

Moravcsik, Andrew. 1997. "Taking Preferences Seriously: A Liberal Theory of International Politics." *International Organization* 51 (4): 513–53.

———. 2004. "Is There a 'Democratic Deficit' in World Politics? A Framework for Analysis." *Government and Opposition* 39 (2): 336–63.

Morgenthau, Hans. 1948. *Politics among Nations: The Struggle for Power and Peace*. New York: Knopf.

Mueller, Dennis C. 2003. *Public Choice III*. Cambridge: Cambridge University Press.

Mueller, John. 1973. *War, Presidents, and Public Opinion*. New York: Wiley.

Müller, Harald. 2001. "International Relations as Communicative Action." In *Constructing International Relations: The Next Generation*, edited by Karin Fierke and Knud Erik Jørgensen, 160–78. Armonk, NY: M. E. Sharpe.

———. 2004. "Arguing, Bargaining, and All That: Communicative Action, Rationalist Theory and the Logic of Appropriateness in International Relations." *European Journal of International Relations* 10 (3): 395–435.

Nanz, Patrizia, and Jens Steffek. 2004. "Global Governance, Participation, and the Public Sphere." *Government and Opposition* 39 (2): 314–35.

Naurin, Daniel. 2003. "Does Publicity Purify Politics?" *Journal of Information Ethics* 12 (1): 21–33.

———. 2006. "Transparency, Publicity, Accountability." *Swiss Review of Political Science* 12 (3): 90–98.

Neumann, Iver, and Vincent Pouliot. 2011. "Untimely Russia: Hysteresis in Russian-Western Relations over the Past Millennium." *Security Studies* 20 (1): 105–37.

Neumann, Iver, and Jennifer Welsh. 1991. "The Other in European Self-Definition: An Addendum to the Literature on International Society." *Review of International Studies* 17: 327–48.

Nexon, Daniel. 2009. *The Struggle for Power in Early Modern Europe: Religious Conflict, Dynastic Empires, and International Change.* Princeton, NJ: Princeton University Press.

Nichols, Irby. 1961. "The Eastern Question and the Vienna Conference, September 1822." *Journal of Central European Affairs* 21 (1): 53–66.

Nicolson, Harold. 1946. *The Congress of Vienna, a Study in Allied Unity: 1812–1822.* New York: Harcourt Brace.

———. 1954. *The Evolution of Diplomatic Method.* New York: Macmillan.

Nye, Joseph S., Jr. 1987. "Nuclear Learning and US-Soviet Security Regimes." *International Organization* 41: 371–402.

———. 1999. "Redefining the National Interest." *Foreign Affairs* 78 (4): 22–35.

Ogg, David. 1970. "The Emergence of Great Britain as a World Power." In *The New Cambridge Modern History.* Vol. 6, *The Rise of Great Britain and Russia, 1688–1715/25,* edited by J. S. Bromley. Cambridge: Cambridge University Press.

Ortner, Sherry B. 2006. *Anthropology and Social Theory: Culture, Power and the Acting Subject.* Durham, NC: Duke University Press.

Osiander, Andreas. 1994. *The States System of Europe, 1640–1990.* Oxford: Clarendon Press.

———. 2001. "The Westphalian Myth." *International Organization* 55 (2): 251–88.

Ostrom, Elinor. 2000. "Collective Action and the Evolution of Social Norms." *Journal of Economic Perspectives* 14 (3): 137–58.

Owens, Patricia. 2007. *Between War and Politics: International Relations and the Thought of Hannah Arendt.* Oxford: Oxford University Press.

Oye, Kenneth, ed. 1986. *Cooperation under Anarchy.* Princeton, NJ: Princeton University Press.

Pape, Robert. 2005. "Soft Balancing against the United States." *International Security* 30 (1): 7–45.

Paris, Roland. 2006. "Bringing the Liberal Leviathan Back In: Classical vs. Contemporary Studies of the Liberal Peace." *International Studies Review* 8 (3): 425–40.

Payne, Rodger. 2001. "Persuasion, Frames, and Norm Construction." *European Journal of International Relations* 7 (1): 37–61.

Penn, Virginia. 1936. "Philhellenism in England." *Slavonic Review* 14: 363–70 and 647–58.

Peterson, Genevieve. 1945. "Political Equality at the Congress of Vienna." *Political Science Quarterly* 60 (4): 532–54.

Pettit, Philip. 2003. "Groups with Minds of Their Own." In *Socializing Metaphysics: The Nature of Social Reality*, edited by Frederick Schmitt, 167–93. Lanham, MD: Rowman and Littlefield.

Phillips, Alison. 1934a. "The Congresses, 1815–22." In *The Cambridge Modern History*. Vol. 10, *The Restoration*, edited by A. W. Ward, G. W. Prothero, and Stanley Leathes, 1–39. New York: Macmillan.

———. 1934b. "Greece and the Balkan Peninsula." In *The Cambridge Modern History*. Vol. 10, *The Restoration*, edited by A. W. Ward, G. W. Prothero, and Stanley Leathes, 169–204. New York: Macmillan.

Philpott, Daniel. 2001. "Usurping the Sovereignty of Sovereignty." *World Politics* 53 (2): 297–324.

Powell, Robert. 2006. "War as a Commitment Problem." *International Organization* 60: 169–204.

Ragsdale, Hugh. 2002. "Russian Foreign Policy, 1763–1815: Does It Exemplify Schroeder's Theses?" In *"The Transformation of European Politics, 1763–1848": Episode or Model in Modern History?*, edited by Peter Kruger and Paul Schroeder, 129–51. New York: Palgrave.

Reinerman, Alan J. 1974. "Metternich, Alexander I, and the Russian Challenge." *Journal of Modern History* 46: 262–76.

Rendall, Matthew. 2000. "Russia, the Concert of Europe, and Greece, 1821–29: A Test of Hypotheses about the Vienna System." *Security Studies* 9 (4): 52–90.

———. 2002. "Restraint or Self-Restraint of Russia: Nicholas I, the Treaty of Unkiar Skelessi, and the Vienna System, 1832–1841." *International History Review* 14 (1): 37–63.

———. 2006. "Defensive Realism and the Concert of Europe." *Review of International Studies* 32: 523–40.

———. 2007. "A Qualified Success for Collective Security: The Concert of Europe and the Belgian Crisis, 1831." *Diplomacy and Statecraft* 18: 271–95.

———. 2009. "Cosmopolitanism and Russian Near Eastern Policy, 1821–41: Debunking a Historical Canard." In *Das Europaische Machtekonzert: Friedens- und Sicherheitspolitik vom Wiener Kongress 1815 bis zum Krimkrieg 1853*, edited by Wolfram Pyta, 237–55. Vienna: Bohlau Verlag.

Reus-Smit, Christian. 1999. *The Moral Purpose of the State: Culture, Social Identity, and Institutional Rationality in International Relations*. Princeton, NJ: Princeton University Press.

———. 2002. "Imagining Society: Constructivism and the English School." *British Journal of Politics and International Relations* 4 (3): 487–509.

———. 2003. "Politics and International Legal Obligation." *European Journal of International Relations* 9 (4): 591–625.

Rich, Norman. 1985. *Why the Crimean War? A Cautionary Tale*. Hanover, NH: University Press of New England.

Richardson, Louise. 1999. "The Concert of Europe and Security Management in the Nineteenth Century." In *Imperfect Unions: Security Institutions over Time and Space*, edited by Helga Haftendorn, Robert Keohane, and Celeste Wallander, 48–79. Oxford: Oxford University Press.

Risse, Thomas. 2000. "'Let's Argue'! Communicative Action and World Politics." *International Organization* 54 (1): 1–39.

Risse, Thomas, Stephen Ropp, and Kathryn Sikkink, eds. 1999. *The Power of Human Rights: International Norms and Domestic Change.* Cambridge: Cambridge University Press.

Robinson, Piers. 1999. "The CNN Effect: Can the News Media Drive Foreign Policy?" *Review of International Studies* 25: 301–9.

Roelofsen, C. G. 1980. "The Negotiations about Nijmegen's Juridical Status during the Peace Congress." In *The Peace of Nijmegen, 1676–1678/79*, edited by J. A. H. Bots, 109–22. Amsterdam: Holland Universiteits Pers.

Rosenau, James. 1992. "Governance, Order, and Change in World Politics." In *Governance without Government*, edited by James Rosenau and Ernst-Otto Czempiel, 1–29. New York: Cambridge University Press.

———. 1995. "Governance in the Twenty-First Century." *Global Governance* 1 (1): 13–43.

Roth, Abraham. 2004. "Shared Agency and Contralateral Commitments." *Philosophical Review* 113 (3): 359–410.

Rothenberg, Gunther. 1989. "The French Revolution and Napoleonic Wars." In *The Origin and Prevention of Major Wars*, edited by Robert Rotberg and Theodore Rabb, 199–224. New York: Cambridge University Press.

Ruggie, John. 1982. "International Regimes, Transactions, and Change: Embedded Liberalism in the Postwar Economic Order." *International Organization* 36 (2): 379–415.

———. 1998. "What Makes the World Hang Together? Neo-Utilitarianism and the Social Constructivist Challenge." *International Organization* 52 (4): 855–86.

———. 2004. "Reconstituting the Global Public Domain—Issues, Actors, and Practices." *European Journal of International Relations* 10 (4): 499–531.

Saab, Ann P. 1977. *The Origins of the Crimean Alliance.* Charlottesville: University Press of Virginia.

Saab, Ann P., John M. Knapp, and Francoise de Bourqueney Knapp. 1986. "A Reassessment of French Foreign Policy during the Crimean War Based on the Papers of Adolphe de Bourqueney." *French Historical Studies* 14: 467–96.

Sacks, Benjamin. 1962. *Peace Plans of the Seventeenth and Eighteenth Centuries.* Sandoval, NM: Coronado Press.

Sanders, Lynn. 1997. "Against Deliberation." *Political Theory* 25 (3): 347–76.

Satow, Ernest. 1917. *A Guide to Diplomatic Practice.* Vol. 2. New York: Longmans, Green.

———. 1925. "*Pacta Sunt Servanda* or International Guarantee." *Cambridge Historical Journal* 1 (3): 295–318.

Sawyer, Jeffrey K. 1991. *Printed Poison: Pamphlet Propaganda, Faction Politics, and the Public Sphere.* Berkeley: University of California Press.

Sawyer, R. Keith. 2005. *Social Emergence: Societies as Complex Systems*. Cambridge: Cambridge University Press.

Schimmelfennig, Frank. 2001. "The Community Trap: Liberal Norms, Rhetorical Action, and Eastern Enlargement of the European Union." *International Organization* 55 (1): 47–80.

Schmid, Hans Bernhard. 2008. "Plural Action." *Philosophy of the Social Sciences* 38 (1): 25–54.

Scholte, Jan Aart. 2000. *Globalization: A Critical Introduction*. New York: Palgrave Macmillan.

Schroeder, Paul. 1962. *Metternich's Diplomacy at Its Zenith, 1820–23*. Austin: University of Texas Press.

———. 1972. *Austria, Great Britain, and the Crimean War: The Destruction of the European Concert*. Ithaca, NY: Cornell University Press.

———. 1993. "The Transformation of Political Thinking, 1787–1848." In *Coping with Complexity in the International System*, edited by Jack Snyder and Robert Jervis, 47–70. Boulder, CO: Westview Press.

———. 1994. *The Transformation of European Politics, 1763–1848*. Oxford: Oxford University Press.

Schutz, Alfred. 1951. "Choosing among Projects of Action." *Philosophy and Phenomenological Research* 12 (2): 161–84.

Schwartzberg, Steven. 1988a. "The Lion and the Phoenix—1: British Policy toward the 'Greek Question,' 1821–32." *Middle Eastern Studies* 24 (2): 139–77.

———. 1988b. "The Lion and the Phoenix—2." *Middle Eastern Studies* 24 (3): 287–311.

Schwegmann, Christoph. 2000. *The Contact Group and Its Impact on the European Institutional Structure*. Occasional Papers 16, Western European Union Institute for Security Studies.

Scott, H. M. 1990. "Introduction: The Problem of Enlightened Absolutism." In *Enlightened Absolutism: Reform and Reformers in Later Eighteenth Century Europe*, edited by H. M. Scott, 1–35. Ann Arbor: University of Michigan Press.

Searle, John. 1990. "Collective Intentions and Actions." In *Intentions in Communication*, edited by Philip Cohen, Jerry Morgan, and Martha Pollack, 401–15. Cambridge, MA: MIT Press.

———. 1995. *The Construction of Social Reality*. New York: Free Press.

Sending, Ole Jacob. 2002. "Constitution, Choice, and Change: Problems with the 'Logic of Appropriateness' and Its Use in IR Theory." *European Journal of International Relations* 8 (4): 443–70.

Setear, John. 2005. "Room for Law: Realism, Evolutionary Biology, and the Promise(s) of International Law." *Berkeley Journal of International Law* 23: 1–46.

Seton-Watson R. W. 1968 (1937). *Britain in Europe, 1789–1914: A Survey of Foreign Policy*. New York: Howard Fertig.

Sewell, William. 1996. "Historical Events as Transformations of Structures: Inventing Revolution at the Bastille." *Theory and Society* 25: 841–81.

Simpson, Gerry. 2004. *Great Powers and Outlaw States*. Cambridge: Cambridge University Press.

Sked, Alan. 1979. Introduction to *Europe's Balance of Power 1815–1848*, edited by Alan Sked, 1–13. London: Macmillan.

Slantchev, Branislav. 2005. "Territory and Commitment: The Concert of Europe as Self-Enforcing Equilibrium." *Security Studies* 14 (4): 565–606.

Slaughter, Anne-Marie. 2004. *A New World Order*. Princeton, NJ: Princeton University Press.

Smouts, Marie-Claude. 1998. "The Proper Use of Governance in International Relations." *International Social Science Journal* 155: 81–89.

Snidal, Duncan. 1997. "International Political Economy Approaches to International Institutions." In *Economic Analysis of International Law*, edited by Jagdeep Bandhari and Alan Sykes, 480–515. Cambridge: Cambridge University Press.

———. 2002. "Rational Choice and International Relations." In *Handbook of International Relations*, edited by Walter Carlsnaes, Thomas Risse, and Beth Simmons, 73–94. London: Sage.

Sofka, James. 1998. "Metternich's Theory of European Order: A Political Agenda for 'Perpetual Peace.'" *Review of Politics* 60 (1): 115–50.

Spruyt, Hendrik. 1994. *The Sovereign State and Its Competitors*. Princeton, NJ: Princeton University Press.

Stasavage, David. 2004. "Open-Door or Closed-Door? Transparency in Domestic and International Bargaining." *International Organization* 58 (3): 667–703.

Stavrianos, L. S. 2000. *The Balkans since 1453*. New York: New York University Press.

Steffek, Jens. 2003. "The Legitimation of International Governance: A Discourse Approach." *European Journal of International Relations* 9 (2): 249–75.

———. 2005. "Incomplete Agreements and the Limits of Persuasion in International Politics." *Journal of International Relations and Development* 8: 229–56.

———. 2008. "Public Accountability and the Public Sphere of Global Governance." RECON Online Working Paper 2008/03. www.reconproject.eu/project web/portalproject/RECONWorkingPapers.html.

Stein, Arthur. 1999. "The Limits of Strategic Choice: Constrained Rationality and Incomplete Explanation." In *Strategic Choice and International Relations*, edited by David Lake and Robert Powell, 197–228. Princeton, NJ: Princeton University Press.

Suganami, Hidemi. 1978. "A Note on the Origin of the Word 'International.'" *British Journal of International Studies* 4: 226–32.

Sugden, Robert. 1993. "Thinking as a Team: Towards an Explanation of Non-Selfish Behavior." *Social Philosophy and Policy* 10 (1): 69–89.

Sunstein, Cass R. 1995. "Incompletely Theorized Agreements." *Harvard Law Review* 108 (7): 1733.

Temperley, Harold. 1923. "The Foreign Policy of Canning, 1820–1827." In *The Cambridge History of British Foreign Policy 1783–1919*. Vol. 2, *1815–1866*, edited by A. W. Ward and G. P. Gooch, 51–118. New York: Macmillan.

———. 1966. *The Foreign Policy of Canning, 1822–1827: England, the Neo-Holy Alliance, and the New World*. 2nd ed. London: Frank Cass.

Temperley, Harold, and Lillian Penson, eds. 1938. *A Century of Diplomatic Blue Books, 1814–1914*. Cambridge: Cambridge University Press.

Teschke, Benno. 2002. "Theorizing the Westphalian System of States: International Relations from Absolutism to Capitalism." *European Journal of International Relations* 8 (1): 5–48.

Thompson, Alexander. 2009. *Channels of Power: The UN Security Council and U.S. Statecraft in Iraq*. Ithaca, NY: Cornell University Press.

Tilly, Charles. 1992. *Coercion, Capital, and European States, AD 990–1992*. Cambridge, MA: Blackwell.

Todorov, Alexander, and Anesu N. Mandisodza. 2004. "Public Opinion on Foreign Policy: The Multilateral Public That Perceives Itself as Unilateral." *Public Opinion Quarterly* 68 (3): 323–48.

Tollefson, Deborah. 2002. "Collective Intentionality and the Social Sciences." *Philosophy of the Social Sciences* 32 (1): 25–50.

———. 2004. "Collective Intentionality." Internet Encyclopedia of Philosophy. http://www.iep.utm.edu/c/coll-int.htm.

Tuomela, Raimo. 2005. "We-Intentions Revisited." *Philosophical Studies* 125: 327–69.

Ullmann-Margalit, Edna. 1978. "Invisible Hand Explanations." *Synthese* 39: 263–91.

Vagts, Alfred. 1948. "The Balance of Power: Growth of an Idea." *World Politics* 1(1): 82–101.

Vagts, Alfred, and Detlev Vagts. 1979. "The Balance of Power in International Law: A History of an Idea." *American Journal of International Law* 73: 555–80.

Velleman, J. David. 1997. "How to Share an Intention." *Philosophy and Phenomenological Research* 57 (1): 29–50.

Vinogradov, V. N. 1981. "George Canning, Russia, and the Emancipation of Greece." *Balkan Studies* 22: 3–33.

Ward, A. W., and G. P. Gooch, eds. 1922–23. *The Cambridge History of British Foreign Policy, 1783–1919*. Cambridge: Cambridge University Press.

Waters, Timothy. 2009. "'The Momentous Gravity of the State of Things Now Obtaining': Annoying Westphalian Objections to the Idea of Global Governance." *Indiana Journal of Global Legal Studies* 16 (1): 25–58.

Watson, Adam. 1987. "Hedley Bull, States Systems, and International Societies." *Review of International Studies* 13: 147–53.

Weber, Johannes. 2006. "Strassburg, 1605: The Origins of the Newspaper in Europe." *German History* 24 (3): 387–412.

Webster, Charles. 1925. *The Foreign Policy of Castlereagh, 1815–1822: Britain and the European Alliance*. London: G. Bell and Sons.

———. 1931. *The Foreign Policy of Castlereagh, 1812–1815: Britain and the Reconstruction of Europe*. London: G. Bell and Sons.

Webster, Charles. 1969. *The Congress of Vienna, 1814–1815*. New York: Barnes and Noble, Inc.

Webster, C. K., and H. W. V. Temperley. 1924. "British Policy in the Publication of Diplomatic Documents under Castlereagh and Canning." *Cambridge Historical Journal* 1 (2): 158–69.

Weintraub, Jeff. 1997. "The Theory and Politics of the Public/Private Distinction." In *Public and Private in Thought and Practice: Perspectives on a Grand Dichotomy*, edited by Jeff Weintraub and Krishan Kumar, 1–42. Chicago: University of Chicago Press.

Weldes, Jutta, and Mark Laffey. 1997. "Beyond Belief: Ideas and Symbolic Technologies in the Study of International Relations." *European Journal of International Relations* 3 (2): 193–237.

Wendt, Alexander. 1999. *Social Theory of International Politics*. Cambridge: Cambridge University Press.

———. 2001. "Driving with a Rear View Mirror: On the Rational Science of Institutional Design." *International Organization* 55 (4): 1019–49.

———. 2003. "Why a World State Is Inevitable." *European Journal of International Relations* 9 (4): 491–542.

———. 2004. "The State as Person in International Theory." *Review of International Studies* 30 (2): 289–316.

Wheeler, Nicholas J. 1992. "Pluralist or Solidarist Conceptions of International Society: Bull and Vincent on Humanitarian Intervention." *Millennium* 21 (3): 463–87.

Whiteneck, Daniel. 2001. "Long-Term Balancing and Short-Term Balancing: The Lessons of Coalition Behavior from 1792 to 1815." *Review of International Studies* 27: 151–68.

Wight, Colin. 2001. "The Continuity of Change, or a Change in Continuity?" *International Studies Review* 3 (1): 81–89.

Williams, John. 2005. "Arendt and International Space In-Between." In *Hannah Arendt and International Relations: Readings across the Lines*, edited by Anthony F. Lang Jr. and John Williams, 199–220. New York: Palgrave Macmillan.

Williams, Michael C. 2005. *The Realist Tradition and the Limits of International Relations*. Cambridge: Cambridge University Press.

Wolf, John B. 1951. *The Emergence of the Great Powers, 1685–1715*. New York: Harper.

Wolfe, Klaus Dieter. 1999. "The New Raison d'État as a Problem for Democracy in World Society." *European Journal of International Relations* 5 (3): 333–63.

Woodhouse, C. M. 1998 (1968). *Modern Greece: A Short History*. London: Faber and Faber.

Yack, Bernard. 2006. "Rhetoric and Public Reasoning: An Aristotelian Understanding of Political Deliberation." *Political Theory* 34 (4): 417–38.

Young, Oran. 1983. "Regime Dynamics: The Rise and Fall of International Regimes." In *International Regimes*, edited by Stephen Krasner, 93–113. Ithaca, NY: Cornell University Press.

Zerilli, Linda. 2012. "Value Pluralism and the Problem of Judgment: Farewell to Public Reason." *Political Theory* 40 (1): 6–32.

# Index

Italicized page numbers refer to figures.

Abdülmecid, 179, 180, 181–82, 189
Aberdeen, Earl of (George Hamilton-
  Gordon), 171, 172, 184, 185, 188–89, 190,
  190n54, 193, 207, 208
absolutism, 66
agency, 3n9; and collective intentionality,
  5, 6–7, 34, 37, 50; and follow-through,
  36; group agency, 3–4, 30–31, 223, 225;
  human agency, 4; and joint commitment, 40; location in the international
  system, 12–13, 30; and mainstream international relations scholarship, 212;
  and many hands approach, 16; and no
  hands approach, 15; and responsibility,
  4, 223; state agency, 4; without a unitary
  agent, 30
Aix-la-Chapelle (Aachen), 1818 meeting at,
  77, 93, 94n135, 106n12
Albania, 147, 198
Alexander I, 84, 85, 191; death of, 152; determined to act for Greece through Concert, 149; early view of Greek revolt as
  bilateral issue, 126; fear that revolution
  would lead to war, 125, 128, 137; and
  Final Coalition, 86; and Hanover strategy, 132, 133–36, 202; liberal education,
  99n156; placed commitment to Concert
  ahead of interests of his state, 136–37;
  proposal for formation of autonomous
  Greek principalities, 150; proposal for
  joint meeting to discuss Spanish revolution, 106–7; proposal of Holy Alliance,
  90–91; recognition of Europe's collective

interest in Greek revolt, 214; suspension
  of Saint Petersburg conference of 1824,
  150; "two power standard" for Russian
  army, 102n4; ultimatum to Ottoman
  sultan, 127; and Vienna Settlement, 96,
  99. *See also* Russia; Russia, and Eastern Question; Russia, and Greek revolt;
  Russo-Turkish Wars
Alexander II, 198n92
"Almond Lippmann consensus," 219
anarchy: and interstate violence and war, 11,
  30, 48; mechanics enabling cooperation
  in, 218; shift from religious hierarchy to
  secular anarchy, 66–73
Anderson, Sheldon, 22
antitrust law, distinction between rational adaptation and concerted action, 1,
  65–66
Arendt, Hannah, 5n11
argument, as unstable social practice, 48
Athens, 156, 170
Augsburg meetings, 77
Austerlitz, Battle of, 85
Austria: commitment to the Concert, 25;
  fear of French and Russian ambitions,
  27; and final Coalition, 86; and First
  Treaty of Paris, 88; French declaration
  of war on, 83; and Greek Question,
  129; and Holy Alliance, 91, 203; and
  Naples revolt, 110–12, 114–15, 116–19,
  121, 122; and Napoleonic Wars, 83, 85,
  86–87; neutrality pact with Prussia in
  1854, 197n85; opposed joint response to

Lightning Source UK Ltd.
Milton Keynes UK
UKOW05f1254280617
304231UK00001B/75/P

9 780226 060118